CREATIVE STRATEGY
AND TACTICS
IN ADVERTISING

GRID SERIES IN ADVERTISING AND JOURNALISM

Consulting Editors
Arnold M. Barban, University of Illinois
Donald W. Jugenheimer, University of Kansas

Bailen, Student Workbook to Accompany Basic Advertising
Barban, Jugenheimer, & Young, Advertising Media Sourcebook and Workbook
Burton, Advertising Copywriting, Fourth Edition
Burton and Ryan, Advertising Fundamentals, Third Edition
Burton and Sandhusen, Cases in Advertising
Dunn & Lorimor, International Advertising and Marketing
Ernst, The Creative Package, A Working Text for Advertising Copy and Layout
Fletcher & Bowers, Fundamentals of Advertising Research
Francois, Beginning Newswriting: A Programed Text
Francois, Introduction to Mass Communications and Mass Media
Jugenheimer & White, Basic Advertising
Jugenheimer & Turk, Advertising Media
Michman & Jugenheimer, Strategic Advertising Decisions
Patti & Murphy, Advertising Management: Cases and Concepts
Pickett, Voices of the Past: Key Documents in the History of American Journalism
Porchey & Carlson, Style: A Guide to Journalism Expression
Quera, Advertising Campaigns: Formulations and Tactics, Second Edition
Rotzoll, Haefner & Sandage, Advertising in Contemporary Society
Simon, Public Relations: Concepts and Practices, Second Edition
Simon, Public Relations Management: Cases and Simulations, Second Edition
Simon, Publicity and Public Relations Worktext, Fourth Edition
Smeyak, Broadcast News Writing
Tan, Mass Communication Theories and Research
Zeigler & Howard, Broadcast Advertising: A Comprehensive Working Textbook
Zeigler & Johnson, Creative Strategy and Tactics in Advertising

OTHER BOOKS IN THE GRID SERIES IN ADVERTISING AND JOURNALISM

Francois, Mass Media Law and Regulation, Second Edition

CREATIVE STRATEGY
AND TACTICS
IN ADVERTISING

A Managerial Approach to Copywriting and Production

Sherilyn K. Zeigler

Adjunct Professor, Department of Marketing,
University of Hawaii, Honolulu

J. Douglas Johnson

Senior Vice-President (ret.)
McCann-Erickson Worldwide, Inc.

Grid Publishing, Inc., Columbus, Ohio

© COPYRIGHT 1981, GRID PUBLISHING, INC.
   4666 Indianola Avenue
   Columbus OH 43214

Printed in the United States

1 2 3 4   4 3 2 1

Library of Congress Cataloging in Publication Data

Zeigler, Sherilyn K.
   Creative strategy and tactics in advertising.

   (Grid series in advertising and journalism)
   Includes bibliographical references and index.
   1. Advertising. I. Johnson, J. Douglas, joint author. II. Title.
HF5823.Z4   659.1   80-23899
ISBN   O-88244-229-5 (pbk.)

CONTENTS

Advertising Factors; Examining Advertising Factors—Perception, Communication; Measurement Techniques—Ranking vs. Rating - Rankings, Ratings; How to Begin; When to Do Copy Research—The Pretest, The Coincidental and Posttest; Where to Do Copy Research: Telephone Interviewing, Research Conducted Through the Mail, Laboratory Research; The Role of Research; Study Questions; Endnotes

The Local Scene—Local Advertiser, Local Advertising Agency, Local Media, First Local Self-Regulator—Types of Complaints, The Monitoring Process; Second Local Self-Regulator, City Regulator, County Regulator, State Regulator; The National Scene— National Advertiser, National Advertising Agency, National Media, National Self-Regulator, Federal Government Regulators; Study Questions

PREFACE

This book introduces a type of contemporary alchemy. For centuries, medieval chemists searched for a formula that would combine baser metals into gold. They failed repeatedly, and finally realized there was no magic process. Today, people in advertising search for a similar formula. Gold is still the ultimate goal, translated in business terms into net sales. But unlike tenth century chemists, modern practitioners frequently achieve spectacular results. True, no one claims to have found one surefire potion. But a deliberate, well-organized system of media and creative planning, applied to the baser metals of market and product information and objectives, can lead to consistent successes in the marketplace.

Drawing on their combined backgrounds in industry and education, your authors explain and illustrate what they believe to be the most productive procedure yet devised to create effective advertising. It requires a good deal of scientific input—and an ability to channel "artistic flashes" to meet practical demands—but it's also a highly challenging and richly satisfying creative pursuit for the talented and dedicated individual.

The highly detailed Marketing Plan and Tactical Check Chart, provided in the appendices of this book, permit an endless variety of "involvement opportunities" for students interested in applying what they've learned—and they offer instructors the chance to design both in-class and out-of-class projects involving brand-name products, services, and stores, in all major media, while keeping within the framework of chapter discussions.

The text is extremely flexible (chapters can be studied in several different sequences without losing continuity), and graphic exhibits represent both national and local advertisers in both print and broadcast media. Students will learn the proverbial "what to say and how to say it"—but also when, where, and, perhaps most importantly, *why* to say it.

They will understand the roles played by marketing and the behavioral sciences (advertising's two parent disciplines) in the creation of successful advertisements and commercials. And it is hoped they will develop a deep appreciation for the value of creative strategies, and for the importance of a systematic execution of creative ideas.

Sherilyn K. Zeigler
J. Douglas Johnson

February 1981

THE CREATIVE FUNCTION IN ADVERTISING

American businesses will spend well over $50 billion this year to advertise their products and services. They will communicate to prospective customers the qualities and benefits of their merchandise, and will do so in an infinite number of creative ways.

To create is to build something new—something previously unknown, untried, or unexpected. Most of the ingredients involved, however—the words, pictures, sounds, and movements that appear in today's advertisements—are the same ones which have been used countless times before.[1] Indeed, creativity has been variously defined as: "new combinations, arrangements, or designs . . . of existing concepts, elements, or data . . . which form, reveal, or result in . . . fresh insights, original viewpoints, or unique relationships."[2] And, in advertising, the consensus is that creativity must be goal-directed—oriented toward decision-making or problem-solving—if it is to be productive.[3]

For example, advertising may help improve manufacturer/dealer relations, or dispel negative impressions consumers have about a store or product. It can introduce a new company, explain comparative-product test results, or extend a brand's reputation to a long line of products from the same manufacturer.

Sometimes, advertising is used in business as an economical preseller, or "door-opener." For instance, a recently-run McGraw-Hill trade press advertisement asked: "Isn't it worth just 15¢ to start the sale before you start the sales call?" The copy pointed out that a business sales call now costs nearly $140, but a magazine advertisement can contact the same prospect, arouse his or her interest, and create product preference for as little as 15¢. A company's sales staff is then free to concentrate on its own specified job: making proposals and closing orders.

A study conducted by Business Marketing Services found that buyers are 15 times more likely to contact suppliers who advertise than those who don't, and 40 times more likely to contact suppliers who run dominant advertisements.[4] Another study revealed that advertising in industrial and trade magazines was considered the most important source of information in keeping buyers of machine tools informed about products and services; 37% of the industrial buyers surveyed selected it "most important."[5]

BACKGROUND FOR ADVERTISING CREATIVITY

Effective advertising creativity requires a systematic, logical accumulation of facts: about products (and services and stores), markets and consumers, media and audiences. It must be geared toward stimulating the acceptance or sale of a particular class or brand of product, a specific type of service, a given store or dealership, or, sometimes, an idea or cause. Hence, a sound marketing and behavioral science background precedes the development of most advertising campaigns. Before creative teams— writers, artists, and technical production specialists—can begin turning out advertisements, they must have the full product and consumer-buying picture: the who-what-when-where-why-and-how story that lies behind the sale of every successful product and service. So, research must supply a "scientific" input to advertising creativity before the "artistic" side can take over.[6]

But advertising is a business of imagination and ideas, too, because consumers respond in terms of their own self interest. They choose to buy or not to buy according to personal wants and needs; interesting, credible advertisements which speak directly to these predispositions are, thus, the ones which do the best job of communicating their selling messages. In fact, creative ideas have been called the most human factor in the advertising business.[7] They're often surprisingly simple and realistic, yet "sparkling" in their ability to zero in on a knotty problem, to pinpoint a delightful solution, and to captivate audiences in the process.[8]

Granted, no Einstein has yet developed any Theory of Advertising Creativity.[9] In fact, the creative element in advertising seems to defy any kind of mathematical treatment. TV commercials for two different laundry detergents may appear very similar in terms of product presentation and discussion; yet, one may do a far superior job in achieving the goals established for it—especially if they deal with company image. Results of a recently conducted experiment among supermarket shoppers supported the view that image-oriented advertising may have a substantial influence on con-sumers' perceptions of particular brands of products.[10]

Of course, every advertisement is part of a long-term investment in brand image—*for* one product and/or *against* another. But the more we know about an individual product and its marketing environment, specified consumers and their purchasing habits, and the media which carry sales information to prospective customers, the more effectively and efficiently we can proceed with message creation and development. In summary, we might say that while *imagination* is undisciplined, it supplies the building materials which *creativity* then shapes and molds into a full-fledged communication structure. Advertising creativity is disciplined to follow the rules of effective communication, guided in every case by a well-defined marketing purpose or strategy.

MARKETING AND ADVERTISING STRATEGIES

In the performance of advertising's creative function, questions may arise as to where "basic conceptualizing" ends and "mechanical production" begins. In this text, your authors have adopted a strategy-and-tactics approach derived from military terminology. *Strategy* refers to the broad, overall planning of an activity or operation—the means for attaining objectives—while *tactics* are the detailed maneuvers required to implement or execute the plan.

In advertising, a creative strategy is only one among many long-range plans involved in the entire marketing process. For instance, there are also product and pricing strategies, distribution and inventory-control strategies, anti-competitive and sales promotion strategies. Further, within advertising itself there are both creative and media strategies (which, ideally, should be developed along parallel courses, since they're interrelated). Certainly, no guidelines for messages can be laid until a decision is made as to physical form: for example, magazine graphics versus the sounds of radio. Or, within the medium of magazines, a large, new-package illustration, and a bold display of "discovery" headline type, might require a two-page spread rather than a single page to make its point. On the other hand, if a selling message requires active demonstration in order to get its meaning across, the use of television becomes mandatory.

Since this book is concerned most directly with advertising creativity, however, we'll focus on the *origination of concepts* and the *development of content* for messages. We'll spend a fair amount of time on *planning procedures*, and on the isolation of key pieces of information for the creative team—and then we'll examine the translation of this material into communicable (informative and persuasive) forms.

THE ROLE OF A CREATIVE STRATEGY

The basis for any advertisement or series of advertisements is a statement of creative strategy; and underlying it is a basic marketing problem which needs to be solved. Some planners use only a single statement to express a strategy—one which permits precise examination of communication potential. For example, check the following strategy for a TV commercial:

> Freshen-Up bubble gum is loaded with flavor and offers a unique oral experience, because each pillow-shaped piece is filled with a minty-tasting liquid that squirts into the mouth with the first bite and lasts as long as the gum is chewed.

Notice that nothing is said about televised action. The strategy doesn't mention that someone will be shown biting into the gum. Nor does it explain that an animated part of the commercial will show the shape of the gum and the minty-tasting liquid being poured in. Why? Because these are *executions* of the strategy: the actual *tactics*.

The strategy "dramatizes" the product and, ideally, articulates a point of difference between it and others in the same category. It "positions" the product—carving out a special "niche" for it among competing brands. And it encompasses the message that's going to be delivered to consumers.

A fair amount of supportive material surrounds every creative strategy, and some planners include it in the official statement. The strategy is then presented in a kind of outline form which contains basic background. Study the Taco Bell example in Figure 1-1.

FIGURE 1-1

Creative Strategy for Taco Bell

1. *Target Audience*: Primary: fast food customers aged—18 to 34
Secondary: fast food customers aged—12 to 17

2. *Basic Attributes*: Fresh ingredients (unlike some other fast food restaurants).
Servings prepared fresh to order.
Food is wholesome and delicious.
Food is different from ordinary fast food fare but made from common, accepted ingredients.
Variety of dishes available.

3. *Strategy Statement*: Taco Bell serves fresh, delicious, wholesome, food prepared fresh to your order, that provides a change from the usual fast food meals.

4. *Message Goals*:   To convince fast food customers to dine at Taco Bell because Taco Bell offers great tasting food, made from fresh ingredients, and prepared fresh to order.

    To suggest that dining at Taco Bell vs. ordinary fast food restaurants is a good idea.

    To position Taco Bell in the mainstream of American fast foods.

The *Target Audience* is included so everyone will remember to whom the advertising will be directed. *Basic Attributes* are listed because they're the elements used to construct the statement. And planners and approvers can review them. Has any product virtue been left out? If so, now's the time to put it in, because the creative group is bound to work within the structure of selected attributes. Then, the one-sentence *Strategy Statement* is a result of squeezing and pressing these qualities to extract their essence. Finally, a number of *Message Goals* are listed—the ones which ultimate advertisements and commercials can be expected to achieve.

Note carefully that: (1) the strategy is written so there's no question in anyone's mind as to what the creative team must communicate; (2) the statement is economically phrased, is straight to the point, and highlights a unique product difference which can be transformed into a consumer benefit; (3) the words explain what is to be stated or shown in the advertising, but not how the benefit is to be expressed; and (4) all of the message goals are feasible and can be tested (measured).[11]

THE VALUE OF A CREATIVE STRATEGY

When a writer, artist, and commercial producer are supplied with a creative strategy, they can work under the best of all possible conditions: (1) they know that the strategy, as part of an overall marketing plan, has been reviewed and approved by all of the client and agency executives responsible for promoting the product; (2) they have good reason to believe that the strategy will be effective, because it's based on thorough objective and subjective research; (3) they're spared the work of deciding what to communicate, and are allowed to concentrate on work they're trained to do—namely, selecting the tactics to be used in communicating the selling proposition; (4) they can conserve their energy, channel their efforts, and work on a single project at a time, instead of preparing a set of hit-or-miss explorations; and (5) they know their advertisements will be evaluated fairly on the basis of pre-established expectations, because measurable results are built into every marketing and creative plan.

William Bernbach, of the highly creative Doyle Dane Bernbach advertising agency, summarized this whole situation when he said that: "A good strategy gives a good creative man (or woman) something to be creative about." And when even "highly creative" messages fail in their communication tasks, it's often because the underlying strategy was at fault. That is, the original problem was not properly identified, or the strategic solution proposed was somehow off base.

CREATIVE TACTICS

Now we can look briefly at the creative tactics used to develop and produce advertisements. These are the responses to the question: "What techniques will get the job done most effectively?" One of the most primitive ways to get attention is simply to SHOUT, or to employ some kind of emotional outburst. There's a decisive difference, however, between making *advertising* appealing and making a *product* (much less a specific *brand* of product) inviting. Similarly, clever slogans may be highly *memorable*, but marketing objectives are to sell *products*, not advertisements.[12]

In addition, today's advertising messages must fight to get through a wall of "clutter" before reaching consumers: a mass of advertisements (many with conflicting sales stories), plus audience indifference, skepticism, and general fatigue. Advertising, of course, can't make a whole sale by itself, but deciding which part of the sale it should make is a critical selection process.

Should it, for example, strive to induce trial of a product, to intensify usage, to sustain brand preference, or to change a habit?[13] Does it aim to spread news or to remind? To enhance a value or to overcome inertia? To raise a question or to reassure?

Sometimes, advertising may be asked to promote new uses for a long-established product. Years after Arm & Hammer baking soda tapped the (then new) market for refrigerator-odor-absorbers, it went after yet another one: this time for carpet fresheners. But whatever their tasks, advertising messages are called upon to do them *unobtrusively*. Social psychologists use the "theory of attribution" to explain why people link observable events with presumed—but unseen—causes. If the reason for an advertisement's appearance is clearly "read" by consumers as: "the company's desire to make money," few purchases (or favorable attitudes) are apt to result. But if the message is perceived as a communication vehicle for actual product features and values, it is paving the way for sales (and goodwill).

Unfortunately, not all of the attributes in a creative strategy can be conveyed in every advertisement; and, for the sake of clear communication, some of the message goals or functions may also be left out. The length or size of individual advertisements limits what can be said or shown, as does the consumer's ability or willingness to absorb information. But advertising *campaigns* may feature a whole *library* of different messages, so different minor attributes can be highlighted in each execution. Then, after the consumer sees and hears a half dozen or so, the basic strategy has been implemented and comes across.

Now, Figure 1-2 shows the tactics used to execute the Taco Bell strategy presented previously.

FIGURE 1-2

Creative Tactics for Taco Bell

Medium:	Television
Length:	30 Seconds
Tonality:	Upbeat and spirited—to show the excitement of eating at Taco Bell and the enjoyment of the food.
Cast:	Teenaged couple, businessman, construction worker, little league team and coach. (All appear in separate commercials: "Car Trouble" "Soft Ball" and others.) All are typical customers.
Announcer:	To give slogan line emphasis
Setting(s):	a) Location: Inside Taco Bell restaurant where food is eaten; b) Location: Outside Taco Bell building where food is found; c) Studio: Table to show food.
Key Shots:	a) Extreme close-ups of food - to show freshness and ingredients, to create appetite appeal, and to identify a selection of available, trade-marked dishes. b) Close-ups of eaters—to show enjoyment of food.
Sound Effect(s):	Ringing of bell - to symbolize the company.
Musical Effect(s):	Beat for emphasis
Group:	Sings rhymed copy. Jingle attracts attention and helps make spot memorable.
Graphics:	a) Taco Bell logotype, for identification. b) Superimposed line in modern type style - "Now that's a *fresh* idea!" to communicate creative strategy.
Synopsis:	Burrito Supreme is shown in tight close up from changing angles. Teen couple are shown eating the Burrito inside a Taco Bell restaurant with arches in the background. Tight close up of a Taco. A man in a business suit is seen eating inside the restaurant.

Close up of an Enchirito being prepared. Hand puts on olives.

Construction worker with Enchirito in each hand - smiling and eager to eat. He is in restaurant.

Tight close up of Tostada.

Close up of little league coach and two team members taking Tostada off of counter in restaurant.

Wide shot of restaurant as coach and players find a table.

Wider shot of customers and employees in the restaurant. All cast members seen previously appear.

Exterior of restaurant showing familiar building exterior used for all Taco Bell construction . . . Mexican adobe style. Super "Taco Bell" logotype and "Now that's a *fresh* idea!" slogan on black below building.

The clang of a bell is used when the building appears, before announcer says the slogan.

The *Medium* is specified because characteristics vary across newspapers, magazines, radio, television, and other vehicles. *Length or Size* is vital information because it's the space or area available in which to present the message. In its own way, it may be considered "restrictive" (although we prefer to regard it as *challenging*!). The remaining items are purely descriptive, and are written in a "what-and-why" style. "What" expresses the technique to be used that will convey information to the consumer, and "why" explains the way some point in the creative strategy, or some advertising message function, will be communicated.

Many of these tactical points are the same in advertisements prepared for all media. Other points differ. Television may include descriptions of music, singers, particular camera effects or movements, dominant colors, and the use of a package. Radio may need special effects and music. Print can require a description of the illustration, use of a package, and detailed information about type specifications. Figure 1-3 gives you an idea of how the actual Taco Bell commercial we've discussed appeared on the air.

Of course, differing opinions on what it takes to make "great advertising" abound in today's business circles—as well as on college campuses and in casual conversation. Most experts agree, however, that successful advertisements are *not* copywriters' ego trips; on the contrary, advertising creativity is a very anonymous (and usually "team") effort, and the only participant who's allowed personal glory is the product or service being promoted.

It's nonsense to believe that consumers' minds are buzzing with advertising slogans or that audiences hop blithely from advertisement to advertisement, giggling at stale puns, marveling at gimmick-ridden claims, and then rushing out to buy. Rather, shoppers are sensibly interested in—and, yes, even eager for—proposals that fit their own personal lifestyles: promises which are relevant, credible, and sincere.

Granted, all advertising campaigns need a "big idea"—a creative flair, a special promise, or what we'll later call an "X-Y-Z appeal"—

FIGURE 1-3

"GREAT FOOD"
30-Second TV

When you're hungry

for a (musical beat)

Burrito Supreme® .

Really hungry for a Taco

you know what I mean.

Got a cravin' for an (musical beat)

Enchirito® or two,

want a Beefy Tostada ™ here's what you do

Just say hey! hey! What you say

we all go down to Taco Bell® today

and head for Taka Taka Taka Taka Taco Bell® . . .

taka taka taka taka Taco Bell®.
("Bong" SFX) Now that's a fresh idea!

around which to build. But, in the above example, no matter how "good" the Fresh Idea notion for Taco Bell might *feel* to a *copywriter*, it's only as valuable as its ability to meet potential customers' demands.

BRINGING STRATEGY AND TACTICS TOGETHER

Happily for the American economy, lively, memorable, effective advertisements don't have to involve well-known fast-food establishments or popular household products. Creative sparkle surrounds many corporate and service campaigns as well. The following abbreviated examples serve as illustrations:

(a) When International Telephone and Telegraph's marketing strategy called for an increase in consumer understanding of ITT's operations and contributions to society, and the shifting of anti-business sentiments, the advertising campaign slogan (tactics) became: "The best ideas are the ideas that help people." Informational, but dramatic, portrayals of such subjects as fiber optics, auto safety devices, and underseas power cables appeared in magazine advertisements and TV commercials.[14]

(b) E. F. Hutton's marketing strategy was to increase public awareness of the company, and to create favorable attitudes toward it. The goal was to promote the firm's experience, integrity, and reliability. So, the creative slogan, "When E. F. Hutton talks, people listen," was spoken over freeze-action (silent) TV scenes, and reproduced in magazine advertisements which described the brokerage service in detail.[15]

(c) *The New York Times* recently wanted to position a special pullout section called SportsMonday as #1 in coverage of weekend sports. The TV advertising campaign featured popular sports figures reading SportsMonday, and their pictures also appeared in newspaper advertisements. The slogan? "SportsMonday . . . for people who take their sports seriously."[16]

APPLICATIONS AT THE LOCAL LEVEL

Sometimes creative strategies are strongly influenced by the medium in which messages will appear. For example, local stores and recreation facilities may appeal to radio audiences through use of vivid word descriptions—personal, involving narratives—and appropriate mood music. And, they may speak to listeners' immediate gift-giving or entertainment needs. The commercial in

Figure 1-4 brings a flower shop to life by giving it a "Green Thumb" personality.

FIGURE 1-4

Radio Commercial for Flowers by Dee Dee

Knoxville, Tennessee	60 Seconds
February, 1980	Valentine's Spot

ANNCR: (AUTHORITATIVELY) Meet Buddy West . . . mild mannered, regular guy by night . . . by day, Buddy West becomes: (ECHOES) *The Green Thumb*!

MUSIC: FLIGHT OF THE BUMBLEBEE, UP AND UNDER

ANNCR: He and his faithful servant, Planto, labor daily in their hide-out, Flowers By Dee Dee, creating floral arrangements of all kinds: for weddings, banquets, birthdays, and (PAUSE . . . THEN, AS FORCEFULLY AS POSSIBLE) *Valentine's Day*. Dedicated to making your life a little more beautiful, the Green Thumb and Planto never tire of their primary task—creating delightful arrangements of fresh and dried flowers . . . dish gardens of green plants . . . terrariums . . . and more! For your special someone. And you can count on the Green Thumb and Planto to deliver those special arrangements *throughout Knoxville and—the world*! Any time . . . anywhere. When you need his services this Valentine's Day, call the Green Thumb's hotline: 584-0107 . . . or come by his hideout on Papermill Road. For creative—and unusual—floral displays . . . it's Flowers By Dee Dee, for *your* Valentine. Trust Buddy West, the Green Thumb . . . and pay him a visit today.

MUSIC: UP AND OUT

Compliments of WIMZ/FM, Knoxville, TN

Likewise, in Figure 1-5, a commercial for a new rock and roll club stimulates audience participation from the very first line. Some listeners, in fact, were driving along the exact stretch of highway mentioned in this message as the commercial came on their car radios.

FIGURE 1-5

Radio Commercial for Continental Club

Knoxville, Tennessee	60 Seconds
February, 1980	Teaser Spot

(NOTE: LET MUSIC FILL PAUSES TO SIMULATE DRIVING)

MUSIC: SPACY BEAT, UP AND UNDER

ANNCR: Take a mental trip with me . . . it's Saturday night . . . March 1st. You're driving. Driving south on Chapman Highway . . . you pass many stores . . . many houses . . . you crest the hill—and suddenly there are huge shopping centers on each side of the road. As you pass under the John Sevier Highway underpass, you think: "only one more mile" . . .

MUSIC: PICK UP TEMPO HERE

ANNCR: Minutes later you see the flashing yellow beacon . . . and you *know* you've arrived. At Knoxville's newest space to rock and roll, the Continental Club. And now that you're here, you know you're at the kind of club you've been waiting for . . . Knoxville's only pure rock club . . . the Continental Club. Coming to South Knoxville, this Saturday night. An experience you won't want to miss!

MUSIC: UP AND OUT

Compliments of WIMZ/FM, Knoxville, TN

THE CREATIVE INDIVIDUAL

Finally, before we examine the marketing and behavioral inputs to advertising creativity in detail, we should note some of the characteristics generally shared by successful advertising creative personnel. Of course, these traits aren't *required* of those bent on entering this field, but if they're part of your personal lifestyle and you're interested in becoming a copywriter, artist, or commercial producer, let's just say you may have a head start.

Creative people frequently have: (1) a nonconforming, or independent, spirit . . . or at least a leaning toward the unconventional; (2) a highly energetic, adventurous, innovative nature; (3) a strong imaginative, insightful capacity; (4) a wide variety of cultural and artistic interests; (5) a competitive willingness to take risks and to make (and learn from) mistakes; (6) a mind and personality that are open to new ideas and new experiences; and (7) a never-satisfied curiosity—about people, places, and events.[17]

They tend to be dissatisfied with the status quo, and adept at envisioning a "better way." They're remarkably sensitive to the wants and needs of consumers, and to the actions and reactions of customers. They have a great deal of empathy, too—that prized ability to know, to understand, and to communicate personally with mass media audiences, no matter how diverse their backgrounds. And finally, they exercise self-restraint: they know when and how to play a sales story up or to play it down. Products and messages possessing "inherent drama" are presented without fanfare, while those lacking it are creatively infused with just the "right amount" to give them top billing in the minds of shoppers.

Can advertising creativity be taught and learned? Of course—if we accept the notion that everyone has some measure of it before he or she ever enters the classroom. (Instructors simply help students *develop* what's "already there.") The more natural ability you have, the less you must apply yourself in order to "keep pace"; but creativity which is both intuitive *and* learned is the kind that ultimately (and repeatedly) succeeds.

STUDY QUESTIONS

1. What three goals can effective advertisements accomplish—other than persuading people to shop and buy?
2. What role does research play in effective advertising creativity?
3. Is advertising creativity the same as imagination? Explain.
4. What is the basic difference between creative strategy and creative tactics?
5. What lies behind—or at the heart of—every statement of creative strategy?
6. What four items are discussed in a creative strategy statement?
7. Of what value are creative strategies to copy, art, and production personnel?
8. What personal characteristics are shared by many employees in the field of advertising creativity?

ENDNOTES

1. See Alfred Politz, "Creativeness and Imagination," *Journal of Advertising*, Vol. 4, No. 3, 1975, p. 12.
2. Tom Dillon, "The Triumph of Creativity Over Communication," *Journal of Advertising*, Vol. 4, No. 3, 1975, p. 16.
3. See Leonard Reid and Herbert Rotfeld, "Toward an Associative Model of Advertising Creativity," *Journal of Advertising*, Vol. 5, No. 4, 1976, p. 25; and Draper Daniels, "The Second Meaning of the Word 'Creative' Should be First in the Hearts of Advertising People," *Journal of Advertising*, Vol. 3, No. 1, 1974, p. 31.
4. "Ads Have Direct Bearing on Sales, Study Says," *Industrial Marketing*, March, 1979, p. 34.
5. Charles H. Patti, "Communication Channels and Industrial Advertising: A Study of Information Sources in the Capital Equipment Industry," in Leonard W. Lanfranco, ed., *Making Advertising Relevant*, American Academy of Advertising, 1975 Proceedings, Columbia, South Carolina, p. 19.
6. William L. Hill, "Creativity is Not Sole Province of Creative Department," *Southern Advertising Markets*, August, 1978, p. 6.
7. Michael Gallney, "Creative Advertising is Achieved Through Hard Work," *Southern Advertising Markets*, August, 1978, p. 4.
8. Gordon E. White, "Creativity: The X Factor in Advertising Theory," *Journal of Advertising*, Vol. 1, No. 1, 1972, p. 31.
9. Tom Dillon, op. cit., p. 15.
10. Leonard N. Reid and Lauranne Buchanan, "A Shopping List Experiment of the Impact of Advertising on Brand Images," *Journal of Advertising*, Spring, 1979, p. 28.
11. See "What Advertising Strategy Is—And Is Not," *White Paper Number 1*, McCann-Erickson, New York, 1973, p. 3.

12. Politz, op. cit., pp. 12-14.
13. See Paul C. Harper, "What Advertising Can and Cannot Do," paper delivered to the 1976 Marketing Conference of The Conference Board, New York, and reprinted by the American Association of Advertising Agencies.
14. See J. Douglas Johnson, ed., *Campaign Report Newsletter*, September, 1979, American Association of Advertising Agencies, New York.
15. See J. Douglas Johnson, ed., *Campaign Report Newsletter*, January, 1980, American Association of Advertising Agencies, New York.
16. See J. Douglas Johnson, ed., *Campaign Report Newsletter*, September, 1978, American Association of Advertising Agencies, New York.
17. Gary A. Davis, "In Frumious Pursuit of the Creative Person," *Journal of Creative Behavior*, Vol. 9, No. 2, 1975, pp. 77-78.

2

THE MARKETING BACKGROUND

As noted in Chapter 1, the foundation for successful advertising creativity is a carefully constructed marketing plan. A complete 158-item outline for such a plan appears in Appendix I. It provides a structure for accumulating facts and making decisions, and within it lie the basic platform planks for almost every conceivable (past, present, and future) advertising campaign.

Why do such enlightened marketers as Procter & Gamble, General Foods, Colgate-Palmolive, Kraft, and Sears Roebuck (among numerous others) go through the tedious efforts required by this outline? Why not sit down, write an advertisement, draw a layout, and take a chance on inspired creativity to sell the product? Because the risks are too high to rely on whims. In today's unmerciful marketplace with its harsh competition and climbing media prices, every thought must score, each word must count, every illustration has to work, and every exposure to consumers must pull its own weight.

DEVELOPMENT OF A MARKETING PLAN

The marketing plan employs a completely deductive process, moving from the general to the specific, in the finest tradition of detective fiction; and, in many respects it's just as exciting and stimulating as any Sherlock Holmes investigation.

Marketing and advertising sleuths begin by gathering clues. They observe: (1) the resistant market of potential buyers; (2) the deadly competition; (3) the fast-paced, ever-changing industry; (4) the opinionated consumer; (5) the client's heroic product, and (6) the critical manufacturing process which dictates price and quality. Look specifically at items 1 through 57 in the Marketing Plan Outline. They're used to collect statements of fact. Read the headings and think for a moment what each might contain. This input prepares a platform for deductive reasoning and furthers the plot.

In the Arthur Conan Doyle classics, Mr. Holmes sits sullenly and puffs on his pipe, or moodily plays his violin, as he reviews clues and sorts them through in his mind. He assembles different patterns to draw conclusions. Marketing and advertising planners follow the same technique. Notice that items 58 through 76 in the Outline contain *problems* derived from the facts previously gathered, and suggest *opportunities* for solutions.

From these conclusions, then, a five- to ten-year marketing strategy evolves, and appears in items 77 through 100. This section of the document covers elements that will gauge the product's health and growth over time as the advertising runs its course.

Next, activities for the first year—marketing tactics—are detailed in items 101 through 131. This is the specific method that will be used to accomplish the plans outlined in the previous section: details, perhaps, about the launching of a new product, or the maintenance or improvement of an established product's position in the marketplace.

Finally, if the product is new, a "test market" project is planned and presented in items 132 through 137; and then, twenty different advertising and merchandising factors are examined and discussed in items 138 through 158—in hopes of making the test market experience as valuable as possible.

Obviously, a great amount of investigation is required before a complete marketing plan can be written. A large number of public, or syndicated, studies are available to advertisers and their agencies at little or no cost, and others must be funded by the companies themselves. But without the information called for in the Outline, educated decisions can't be made. Through this plan, potential growth opportunities stand out. Competitors' weaknesses are highlighted, and potential difficulties with the advertiser's product or planning are noted.

Granted, every item in the Outline can't always be covered, since input may be sparse or unavailable; but a statement should never be eliminated entirely because its conclusions might be critical. Also, some item "adaptation" may be needed in the case of selected advertisers. A few words may have to be changed so the phrasing "fits" better, but minor adjustments can make the plan applicable to a service, an idea, a cause, an independent firm, a retail outlet, or any other type of concern.

ADVERTISING'S ROLE IN THE MARKETING PLAN

You may be surprised to find so few entries in the Marketing Plan Outline about advertising. Does this mean that copywriters and art directors should ignore the remaining items? Far from it. In fact, the correct creative strategy may come from any statement that appears after any item in the plan. For instance, look at item 17: facts about PRICING, under "competitive information."

In a Panasonic marketing plan, this statement might contain a chart comparing prices and features of so-called hand-held, pocket, or personal dictating machines. Quality recorders made by IBM, Lanier, Norelco, Sanyo, and others sell for well above $100.

Then, in item 66: PRICING examined as a "problem and opportunity," it would be suggested that a machine priced at $100 or less would appeal to a wide market.

Now check item 79: PRICING in terms of "long range marketing strategy." Here, the market planners could state that the Panasonic Micro-cassette Recorder will be sold to the trade at $70, so a $100 retail price is practical.

Continuing, item 82 looks at *advertising's* "basic selling idea." Suppose the information here is that: "The Panasonic Micro-cassette Recorder will be positioned as a lower cost item than its competitors."

Then, item 83's "most effective benefits to be featured in copy" are: (a) capstan drive for precise tape speed; (b) a lockable pause control so the user can stop speaking a moment to think, without turning off the machine; (c) a rewind system that makes it easy to find material that's been recorded; and (d) the availability of a 60-minute tape.

Finally, for item 104—advertising *specifics*—the creative team decides on the headline: "Don't let the low price scare you" . . . copy which says: "It costs under $100 (Manufacturer's suggested retail price.) Yet, it has features costing twice as much" . . . and the layout which appears in Figure 2-1.

Get the idea? Let's try one more example. Begin this time with Marketing Outline item 50: facts about "product supply sources." In a marketing plan for Procter & Gamble's coffee division, a chart might appear listing sources of supply in the western hemisphere (See Figure 2-2).

Brazil, Colombia, and Mexico appear as leaders, and the statement goes on to note that these countries are ideal for cultivation because of their mountainous areas. There is also mention of the fact that the drinking quality of coffee relates to altitude: the higher the plants can be grown, the milder the taste.

Now, move on to item 39: product characteristics "liked and not liked by the consumer." Here there is a comment about the bitterness

FIGURE 2-1

Magazine Advertisement for Panasonic

FIGURE 2-2

Sources of Coffee Supply

WESTERN HEMISPHERE

Total Harvested Coffee Production

	Percentage Exportable	Thousands of Bags - 60 Kilos
BRAZIL	62.9	23,600
COLOMBIA	79.3	7,000
MEXICO	51.1	3,200
EL SALVADOR	93.3	2,400
GUATEMALA	87.2	2,000
COSTA RICA	88.0	1,330
PERU	77.2	1,030
VENEZUELA	29.3	920
NICARAGUA	85.8	600
DOMINICAN REP.	63.6	550
OTHER WESTERN HEMISPHERES	59.1	3,318

Exportable . . . 31,082,000 - 67.6%
Total   45,948,000

Source: Tea & Coffee Trade Journal, August 1976

of other brands. Forty-five percent of consumers studied played back the idea that beans grown at a higher altitude have a milder flavor.

So, for item 82's "creative positioning," the marketing planners identify the benefit of mild taste as the major brand advantage and state that: "The coffee has a delicious, mild taste because it is grown at a high altitude."

Item 104's "advertising specifics" include the creative team's decision on a headline: "Introducing Mountain Grown Folger's," supported in copy with the statement: "And mountain grown coffee is the richest, most aromatic kind of coffee." A slogan then repeats the idea with: "Taste how rich and delicious coffee can be. Mountain Grown Folger's."

Last, when item 106 calls for "actual ad message prototypes," the art director provides a symbol for the brand that turns the word "mountain" into a peak, and drawings illustrate how the symbol can be animated for television. The word first appears in a normal horizontal type setting, and then the center letters expand upward to form the top of the mountain. The layout in Figure 2-3 also appears. (Note: although this Folger's advertisement seems to present the brand for the first time, it has been marketed in the Middle West and West for years. The ad was used in an introductory campaign when Folger's expanded its market into the East.)

These two examples show briefly how facts thread their way through a marketing plan: (1) to become opportunities that are then (2) transformed into strategies, which in turn (3) require tactics to turn them into advertisements. Throughout the text, we'll be referring to items in the Marketing Plan Outline by number. Take a few moments now, before moving on, to read through them again. Don't try to memorize them, but become familiar with their positions and sequence.

MARKETING MANAGEMENT'S REVIEW OF ADVERTISING CREATIVITY

Assuming, now, that a complete marketing plan has been prepared for a given advertiser, the question arises: who is responsible for approving it? The organization chart in Figure 2-4 is typical of a marketing-oriented company that is in the consumer-goods business . . . and the "top" man or woman has the final say-so (be it a Board Meeting or an Advertising Campaign). It's important to understand the entire review process, however, so let's go through it level by level.

The *President and Chief Executive Officer* (CEO) titles usually go together—or, at least the duties do. On this person's desk is a sign which reads: "The buck stops here," because the CEO is responsible

FIGURE 2-3

Magazine Advertisement for Folger's Coffee

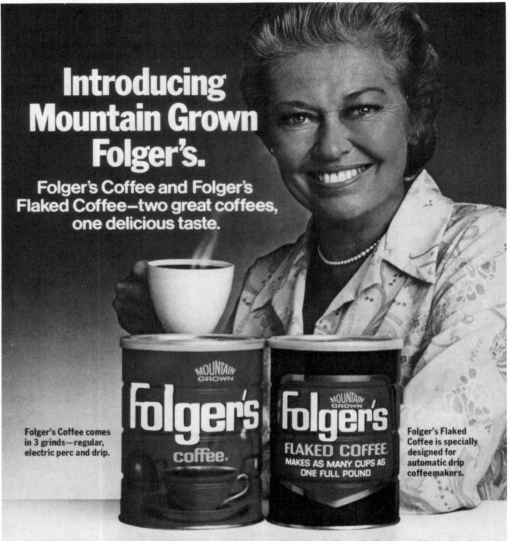

FIGURE 2-4

Company Organization Chart

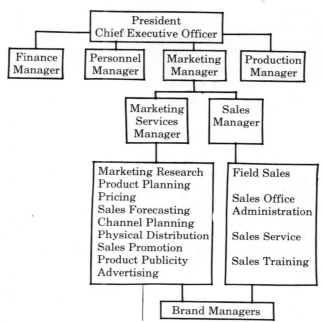

for every action a corporation takes. In smaller companies, the president's tasks may be handled by a general manager, the owner, or an executive committee. But whatever name is given to the highest rung of the ladder, this is where company decisions are made before any plan—advertising or otherwise—is activated.

Right below the CEO, the job which relates directly to advertising is the *Marketing Manager*. This executive (and his or her staff) is responsible for making recommendations, putting them into brief, understandable documents, and forwarding them to the CEO for consideration. Executives on two parallel rungs assist the Marketing Manager in developing plans and carrying them out.

The *Sales Manager* handles the field force, maintains records of orders at headquarters, answers complaints from wholesalers, retailers and customers, and trains salespeople. He or she may have some "say" about the advertising, but it is the primary responsibility of the *Marketing Services Manager*.

Look at the chart to see which "services" this executive manages. *Research* covers the gathering and analyzing of information about marketing operations including consumer attitudes and actions, sales activity and advertising effectiveness. *Product Planning* deals with brands or lines to be offered in the future and the markets to whom they'll be sold. *Pricing* develops information about product costs and company margins, while *Sales Forecasting* estimates probable movement (often seasonal) of the product through distribution channels to the consumer. *Channel Planning* considers various times and ways products can be offered to the consumer through different outlets.

Physical Distribution is concerned with (1) actually delivering a constant supply of the product to outlets by using transportation vehicles and warehousing, and then (2) relating them to inventories that will satisfy retailer and consumer demand. *Sales Promotion* plans and prepares display pieces for in-store use, publishes brochures and pamphlets for retailers and salespeople to distribute, and plans dealer contests and other activities.

Product Publicity develops releases and photographs about the brands and distributes them to the media as news or background. And finally, there is a department headed by an *Advertising Manager*. He or she makes the final selection of copy and art, decides on the media to be used, allocates total funds, budgets the money for each advertising project, and keeps the sales department informed about print insertion dates and commercial broadcast times. To get all of this work done, this manager (and staff) usually works with at least one *Advertising Agency*. Figure 2-5 outlines its major contributions.

FIGURE 2-5

The Job of an Advertising Agency

The American Association of Advertising Agencies defines the major work of the agency as "interpreting to the public or to that part of it which it is desired to reach, the advantage of a product or service." The Association lists the following requirements for the agency to do this job:

1. A study of the client's product or service in order to determine the advantages and disadvantages inherent in the product itself and in comparison with competition.

2. An analysis of the present and potential market for the product or service as to:
   (a) location,
   (b) volume of possible sales,
   (c) season,
   (d) trade and economic conditions, and
   (e) nature and amount of competition.

3. A knowledge of distribution and sales and their operations.

4. A knowledge of all the available media and means which can be used profitably to carry the interpretation of the product or the service to the consumer, the wholesaler, the dealer, the contractor or other factors. This knowledge covers:
   (a) character,
   (b) influence,
   (c) circulation—quantity, quality, location
   (d) physical requirements, and
   (e) costs.

5. *Formulation of a definite plan* and presentation of this plan to the client.

6. *Execution of the plan by*:
   (a) writing, designing, and illustrating advertisements or other appropriate forms of the message;
   (b) contracting for space, time, or other means of advertising;
   (c) incorporating the message in mechanical form and sending it with proper instruction for the fulfillment of the contract;
   (d) checking and verifying insertions, display, or other means used;
   (e) auditing, billing and paying for the service, space, and preparation.

7. Cooperation with the client's sales work, to insure the greatest effect from advertising[1]

The agency's creative department consists of advertising specialists, writers, art directors, musicians and broadcast commercial producers. The buck may *stop* with the Chief Executive Officer at the top of the ladder, but it *starts* here with the *Creative Team*. A writer and an art director are assigned to implement the advertising strategy agreed upon in the marketing plan. They add the tactics: developing the copy, layouts, storyboards, and tapes. Then, their prototypes go into the plan and move back up the ladder as examples of the recommended campaign. They travel rung by rung, obtaining approvals (and sometimes are returned for modifications) until they reach the CEO and, perhaps, the Board of Directors for final okay. The advertising program is then fully developed (based on prototypes), and produced, distributed to media, and circulated or broadcast to consumers.

Now, look at the bottom of the chart in Figure 2-5. In very large companies, there are so many products that each is placed under the supervision of a *Brand Manager*. These executives report directly to the Senior Marketing Manager and are responsible for making sure their respective brands remain healthy. They use marketing services to prepare their plans and rely on salespeople to move each brand into the marketplace.

Having met the cast of characters who review and approve advertising in a marketing-oriented, consumer-goods corporation, we can next consider several kinds of *objectives*. Only selected ones will be shown as goals for advertising messages, and it's vitally important that they be set apart from the others.

ESTABLISHING OBJECTIVES

Objectives are crucial parts of a company's various business plans. Different types play different, but equally important, roles and must be clarified.

PROFIT OBJECTIVES

A *profit objective*, established by a company's chief executive officer and the controller or financial officer, usually appears in the corporation's forward or annual plan. The figure predicts performance for the entire company and is written as follows:

To earn _____% on a $_____ capital investment during the year(s) _____.

Return-on-investment (ROI) is a frequently used criterion for earning success, but two other indicators are also considered: *return-on-sales* (ROS), and *return-on-assets* (ROA). In any case, the intention is to establish goals that anticipate an increase in dollar contributions to the firm's profit.

These figures can*not* be related directly to advertising, although promotion effectiveness does contribute to net sales. To say: "*Advertising* will provide the company with a five percent return-on-investment," is ludicrous because that's the function of *sales*, plus *operating economies*, plus *interest on capital*, plus *tax savings* and other items.

SALES OBJECTIVES

A *sales department objective* is a marketing goal which anticipates product movement. If the company is a single product manufacturer, only one brand will be considered, while a multi-product producer will compute the probable movement of every item in the line and total them for the sales department's goal. (To find these figures in the Marketing Plan Outline, check item 75.)

The numbers are established by the sales, marketing, or brand manager, and must be approved by the company's CEO. Either or both of two statements may be written:

(a) To achieve _____% of $_____ total industry sales during the year(s) _____; or
(b) To achieve a _____% share of _____ total units produced by the industry during the year(s) _____.

Again, it is irresponsible to promise: "*Advertising* will produce a seven percent increase in share of industry sales (or of units) for the brand," since that is the job of the entire *sales*, *marketing*, and *production* departments. The accomplishment is reinforced, in fact, by all elements in the marketing mix: product quality, price, sales promotion, distribution, public relations, spending, packaging, personal selling, and others. In retailing, even the weather on the day of a sale has an influence on results.

Where are industry sales and unit figures found? Some trade associations and magazines publish annual figures. For example, *The Wine Marketing Handbook* is published each year and contains world, national, and state production and consumption figures, media usage by company and brand, consumer preference data, and many other facts. Similar information is available in annual publications for appliances, automobiles, drugs, food, and other products.

The U.S. Government, and individual states and counties, survey practically everything that is taxed and publish frequent statistical tabulations. Corporations who subscribe to A. C. Nielsen surveys can receive annual and/or periodic reports on any product a firm requests. Units, packages, or tonnage is shown along with consumer dollar sales. Also included are the trend of the brand, competitive sales trends, package-size details, distribution trends, and regional information.

Gross figures for merchandise lines and services appear in the *Guide to Consumer Markets*, published each year by The Conference Board, Inc., 845 Third Avenue, New York. It also contains an abundance of information about population, income, expenditures, production, distribution, and prices.

The point is that someone is tracking almost every item manufactured and sold. These figures can be applied to the sales or marketing department objective in terms of all or a specified portion of industry dollar or unit sales.

ADVERTISING OBJECTIVES

The *advertising department objective* is established by a client's advertising or brand manager, accepted by the marketing or sales manager, and approved by the CEO. It can be expressed:

> To gain _____% in penetration (or awareness)
> of the selected message function: _____,
> among _____ in the established consumer
>   (NUMBER)
> target market during the year(s) _____.

Recall that the purpose of most advertising is to interest the public in a brand, a service, or an idea and prepare them to act—in short, to perform as the product's "persuasive voice." Advertising efforts are combined with those of personal selling, publicity, and sales promotion, and some companies make no attempt to differentiate the jobs and effects of these departments.

It's impossible to win any game, however, unless *rules* are specified and followed. So, we might well ask whether *any* factor in the marketing mix can accomplish its task if the people responsible do not know exactly what they are expected to do. In other words, is "to interest the public" a specific enough advertising objective? The answer is no.

Advertising performance must be measured against the percent gain anticipated in communicating a particular message. The audience to be affected is not the entire public, but a numbered group or segment of the population. The advertisements must also be given time to work. Basically, then, the four premises are:

How much . . . (PENETRATION)?
Of what . . . (MESSAGE)?
Among whom . . . (SEGMENT)?
In how long . . . (TIME)?

Now let's examine each one in detail.

Penetration

"Penetration" is a term for the percentage of the "right" people who got the gist of a message. How well did the idea sink in, and among how many of the selected audience? Consider the name *Smooth 'n' Close* for a shaving cream. It's brand new—nobody's ever heard of it. Thus, when the advertising is launched, awareness is zero; so planners project a 15 percent gain from scratch. Six months later, a survey shows that 20 percent of the target market has heard of Smooth 'n' Close. A year later, the penetration is up to 30 percent, and it's fair to say that advertising has made a major contribution.

Now the question: "Penetration of what?" The product name is the vital message . . . but there are other important ideas that could be projected. In fact, these alternatives are so important they're worthy of a separate section which follows. But first, here's a curve ball to make a point. Smooth 'n' Close registered an increase of 20 percent in six months, right? Everybody is elated. What they do not know at the moment is that some of the target segment associated the name *not* with shaving cream, but with a new, heavily advertised lawnmower called Trim 'n' Close. An easy mistake. If the specific message function, "to associate the brand name with the product category" had been tested, results would have read: 20 percent name identification, but 10 percent *misidentification*, or association with another product. Obviously, there is ample reason to test more than one message function.

Beware of one danger here, though. With a number of possible message functions available, a hungry advertiser or inexperienced copywriter may ask: "Shouldn't we use them *all* . . . for the strongest, most complete message possible?" The answer is: *one* major message, and (maybe) a few auxiliary sub-messages per advertisement . . . and, often, per *campaign* as well. The reason is not that a six-page magazine insert or a three-minute commercial is incapable of reciting the whole catechism about a product. The reason is that neither a reader nor a listener or viewer will cope with a laundry list. The public has more to do each day than read a hundred brochures or hear a hundred lectures about varied merchandise. No message will hold attention unless a person is actually shopping, comparing products, and ready to buy.

Message

Now we move to the "of what" blank after penetration—and find that it will be filled with one of many expressions that can be termed Message Goals or Functions. A number of them are shown in Figure 2-6, and will be referred to frequently in the text. Read through the

FIGURE 2-6

Advertising Message Goals or Functions

Among Potential Customers

To announce that the (new) brand exists;
To inform about a special benefit (or benefits) the brand offers;
To make potential customers recognize the brand name;
To make potential customers recognize the package;
To associate the brand name with the product category;
To associate the brand name with the product slogan;
To associate the brand name with a product symbol;
To associate the brand name with the manufacturer's name;
To encourage potential customers to try the product;
To explain how the brand can be used;
To tell where the brand can be obtained.

Among Present and Potential Customers

To give them an urgent reason to buy, such as: reduced price . . .a percent discount . . . an imminent scarcity . . . a bonus . . . a sales event . . . a trade-in . . . a sudden availability;
To tell them about an improvement in the brand;
To reply to claims competitors make that might take present customers away from the brand;
To correct false impressions about the brand among present and potential customers;
To inform about additional ways the brand can be used;

To improve company image;
To give factual reasons to buy or try the product;
To provide emotional motivations to buy or try the product.

Among Present Customers

To encourage them to buy larger sizes of the brand;
To encourage them to buy the brand at an other-than-traditional time of the year;
To encourage them to buy the brand more often;
To remind them to buy;
To encourage them to specify the brand with retailers.

list to see that each statement has a single purpose: to inform about the product and help create brand selection or preference. And, as noted previously, this is really what advertising is all about: to present and promote goods, services, and ideas, in order to influence positive attitudes, and, in many cases, purchasing action.

Segment

The "segment" or target market is the group of most probable purchasers. Do Smooth 'n' Close research people ask a sample of everyone in the United States (about 225 million) for product-name recall? If they try to—fire them! They should summarily drop about 25 million beardless boys under 15 years of age, and should probably eliminate 115 million women (although some do buy their men's shaving cream at the supermarket, and may even use it themselves). These actions would whittle the target market down to about 85 million male shavers; and, that number could be refined even more to include only dark-haired, stubble-bearded men who are heavy users and lather more liberally than their blond-haired contemporaries. These people have a specific reason to be interested, so the right message might get through to them.

Time

The selection of a number to fill the "time" blank relies on a number of factors. It seems only fair to give advertising "long enough" to reach the percentage goal for penetration. A 300-line ad in the paper, featuring 20 percent off on a little black dress at a women's ready-to-wear shop, may have only one day in which to work; advertisements that require immediate action must prove themselves immediately. There is no question about whether they pull or not: empty racks, shelves, or bins are proof positive. Usually, retailers rely on past experience, often rather vaguely recorded, to tell whether one, two, three, or more appearances of the same advertised offer will be most effective.

Evaluations of national campaigns are handled more scientifically, but there are still questions about how long they have to run before their impact can be judged. Influencing the time factor in advertising exposure are:

(a) consumers' inherent interest in the product;
(b) the nature of the message (its forcefulness, simplicity, and memorability);
(c) the speed and impact of media delivery;
(d) the budget committed;
(e) the frequency of publication or broadcast; and
(f) the competition.

Each of these warrants further attention.

Inherent Product Interest

Product classes, like people, have a certain amount of built-in magnetism. Syndicated research firms have gathered indications of the "charm quotient" for each category, and broken them down into interest levels for men and women. Figure 2-7 is a composite of several lists we have seen based on print advertisement reading. Product interest shifts around because of changes in life-style but some categories stay high on the list for each sex.

FIGURE 2-7

Interest Levels By Product Class

Women's Interests	Men's Interests
Food	Passenger cars
Women's clothing	Men's clothing
Women's health and beauty aids	Aircraft
Photographic equipment	Trucks and recreational vehicles
Household furnishings	Sporting goods
Clothing accessories	Men's toilet goods
Radio, TV and stereo equipment	Photographic equipment
Household supplies	Automotive accessories
Drugs and remedies	Radio, TV and stereo equipment
Men's clothing	Clothing accessories
Pet food and supplies	Cigarettes, pipe and tobacco
Men's clothing	Industrial and chemical products
Building and decorating	Travel and resorts
Children's clothing	Alcoholic beverages
Travel and resorts	Insurance and finance

Of course, products do move in and out of fashion. Think about jogging shoes ten years ago, and blue jeans or overalls ten years before that. The markets consisted mainly of athletes or farmers. In essence, people read, watch, or listen to advertisements about products that are relevant to them at the moment. Messages about a low-interest item must have more time to work, while those about a high-interest product penetrate faster.

Nature of the Message

If an ad page or commercial spot packs a special wallop, it can shrink required exposure to scanty months, and even overwhelm low product magnetism. And while a jolting, highly memorable message is not appropriate for some products, others can take a more bombastic treatment. You hear and see assertive commercials when the circus comes to town, when a funny car rally is a week away, or when the county fair is in progress. This is "event advertising" and it almost always comes on strong. Sears Red Tag sales do, too . . . and, occasionally, a unique—even explosive—product demonstration attracts immediate attention.

Media Delivery

Newspapers and Sunday supplements reach and have their effect on readers within 24 hours. Radio and TV commercials have even shorter lives; they are self-destroying even as the clock ticks, and there's no way to refer back to them. If a message is not repeated, and given numerous chances to communicate, the details in it will probably be lost. Magazines, on the other hand, have a slower speed of delivery. *Reader's Digest* may be picked up and read for a month or more. Professional journals are sometimes kept for years, as are *National Geographic* and *Gourmet*.

Each medium also has its own level of assertiveness. For example, one of the most intrusive forms of communication is a handbill passed from one individual to another on the street. There is a personal confrontation, eye-to-eye and hand-to-hand, and delivery (while it may be offensive) is inescapable and memorable. A sound truck, sky writing, and telephone solicitation are almost as impressive.

More basic vehicles also have relative forcefulness. Television is the strongest because it combines sight, color, motion, and sound. Radio usually follows, and then newspapers and magazines.

Budget

In theory, an unlimited pile of dollars behind an item would allow ample exposure to establish it with everybody. However, the blank check method could be wasteful. The point is to reach just the right people as economically as possible with just the proper pressure to tell them what you want them to know. A blank check is also unrealistic. Advertisers all seem to be conserving their money today, and tend to budget less than is actually needed.

Money buys media repetition or frequency. How much is needed? Carefully tabulated track records within product classes are usually the best guides. Marketing-oriented companies have such background information readily available.

Frequency

If a TV spot is broadcast every hour on the hour for a week, it should penetrate by sheer muscle. And when some campaigns are launched, it may seem to viewers that one commercial is on the air constantly. That, of course, is the advertiser's plan. The highest level we have ever heard about is 1,000 advertising impressions (by households) in Japan in one week. In the United States, a product introduction for beer or a soft drink, or a name-change campaign for a major consumer goods corporation, may run 500 impressions a week nationally. Political television spots consistently run 400 a week and even 100 per day in a local market "blitz" just before the polls open.

Why don't all advertisers shoot their budgets in a week or two? Obviously, because customers come into the market for products over a period of time that may last longer than weeks. Think how often your family buys a tube of toothpaste or a box of cereal or detergent. Research shows that more people are directly influenced to buy when messages are spread out over time.

Competition

It takes more time, budget, and frequency to get through to consumers when other advertisers in the same category are running heavy schedules. Viewers, listeners, and readers become overloaded and confused. In the days before Christmas, games are hard to separate, toys all begin to look the same, and home appliances blend into one loud whirr. Many names, benefits, and appearances become unidentifiable.

The media strategy for competitive seasonal pushes is written to anticipate high levels of frequency. In theory, this gives the creative team's efforts a chance to break through the jamming. A similar situation may occur in the test marketing of a new product when the manufacturer wants accurate read-outs on sales and penetration. Competitors try to confuse the scores by running local campaigns in test areas to take sales away from the newcomer. They make their message frequency more assertive so the new brand will not register clearly.

To the new manufacturer's creative team, of course, the challenge is to develop messages that have more impact than any of the oldtimers' efforts—and which can, in effect, offset their frequency.

Much of the remainder of this text will be devoted to examination of the "what" and "among whom" parts of advertising objectives. And because people are clearly more important than things, we'll start with a study of human behavior.

STUDY QUESTIONS

1. Explain and give an example of the deductive process inherent in a well-developed Marketing Plan.
2. Who is responsible for reviewing and approving: (a) a Marketing Plan (before it is ready for implementation by creative teams), and (b) suggested creative tactics?
3. Differentiate between a profit objective, a sales objective, and an advertising objective.
4. What four premises must be considered before advertising's creative performance can be measured?
5. What factors influence the "time" element in advertising exposure?

ENDNOTES

1. Frederic R. Gamble, "What Advertising Agencies Are—What They Do and How They Do It," American Association of Advertising Agencies, New York, 1963, pp. 6-7.
2. See also National Industrial Conference Board, Inc., *Studies in Business Policy*, No. 102, New York, 1962, pp. 10-12.

3

THE BEHAVIORAL
SCIENCE BACKGROUND

We've noted that successful advertising helps consumers make decisions (solve problems) in the marketplace. It does so primarily by providing information, because the decision-making activity requires answers to basic questions: which shampoo is the most gentle on heavily-damaged hair? Where is the best place to go for a quick, inexpensive fish dinner? How do the major auto manufacturers compare in terms of new car warranties?

Potential customers are complex individuals, however; they may consult many different information sources before they buy. And when it comes to explaining and predicting consumer actions and reactions, research has indicated that the strategies people use in seeking information may be more important than the specific knowledge gained.[1] Sometimes, a commercial or two may provide the bulk of the selling stimulus; at other times, advertising plays only a minor role behind personal selling and firsthand experience. Also, advertisements may serve different communication functions at different times along the selling continuum—from the consumer's first mind-contact with a product-idea, right through to the ultimate cash register purchase.

For instance, a brief evening TV spot may introduce a new family game, and after they see it, Bonnie and Bobby Miller start asking their parents to buy. A week later, Mr. and Mrs. Miller attend a friend's party, notice the advertised game on a table, and ask about it. Several more days pass, and a detailed magazine advertisement for the game catches Mother's attention, because it confirms what the friend said. Next comes personal contact with the game at a store . . . but Mom doesn't buy, since the price seems too high. She mentions it to Dad, however, and he suggests waiting for a sale.

Finally, a weekend newspaper advertisement says: "Come in today! Everything half price at Frank's Fun Store!" And the Millers buy the game.

A second family, the Taylors, may buy the same game the day after they saw the introductory commercial, without giving the matter another thought . . . and two other families might decide to reject the commercial entirely. In one case, the characters in the commercial remind them of some very unpleasant neighbors, and in the other, the musical jingle strikes them as distasteful. Product-buying decisions start with individual attitudes and beliefs, so a knowledge of consumers' lifestyles becomes an essential prerequisite to the development of advertising messages.

In fact, any marketing planner or advertising communicator can do a better job when he or she can visualize the specific buying market or receiving audience for whom the product, service, or message is designed. Today, several metropolitan newspapers even have "lifestyle sections" to cater to specialized interests. And, it's important to know something about those who *influence* buying decisions, too (See Marketing Outline item 24).

THE IMPORTANCE OF LIFESTYLE

But what is a "lifestyle" per se? As far as advertisers are concerned, it's primarily the manner in which certain consumer groups spend their time and money:[2] (a) indoor and outdoor time and money; (b) job and entertainment time and money; (c) eating and traveling time and money; (d) private and social time and money. And what determines the course which a person's lifestyle will follow? Economic theories of rationality, based on the assumption that all consumers try to "maximize utility," offer one answer.

Rational man supposedly lists alternative courses of action, ranks the consequences, and selects the best one. Frequently, however, shoppers neither take the time nor make the effort to achieve such listings and, hence, do not act according to calculated odds. Instead, as Katona points out, they respond to certain cues from the environment, see a well-known product or service in a new context, and arrive at a different way of ordering alternatives; changes in behavior then result.[3] In other words, we may abandon our habitual forms of behavior when we perceive that a new situation prevails, calling for a new reaction.

The basic norm of existence is reward—getting something for something. Early in the twentieth century, Pavlov fathered behavioral control when he learned how to make dogs salivate on command. Later, Harvard psychologist B. F. Skinner created modern behaviorism when he discovered he could get varied kinds of action from pigeons by rewarding and punishing them systematically. Today, communication theorists continually try to explain advertising effects from a behavioral viewpoint, since it has been clearly demonstrated that advertising succeeds only when it shows a consumer why it's in his or her own best interest to try a particular product or service.

MOTIVES

The motivation of human behavior has long been a central concept in psychology. Every human experience involves a motivating factor which ultimately produces some kind of response. The acceptance of a new idea, product, activity, or responsibility is contingent upon incentives—which, in turn, motivate and stimulate action.[4] A motive can't be directly observed; rather, it's something we infer in order to account for what is directly observed (that is, behavior). For our purposes, motives may be thought of as attitudes—representing what behavioral scientists would *like* to measure, not what they actually measure. Hence, motives, or attitudes, are *intervening variables*; they're affected by advertising (or educational or political or religious) messages and, in turn, affect resultant behavior.

ATTITUDES AND BELIEFS

Authorities disagree on exact meanings for attitudes. Still, we need some working definitions if we're going to discuss these important variables in terms of advertising effects. Newcomb defines an attitude as a predisposition to perform, perceive, think, and feel in relation to an object—a state of readiness to be motivated toward or against it.[5] For example, your attitude toward studying this book for a test may be negative (too much to read, too time-consuming, too many new concepts to master). On the other hand, your attitude toward succeeding in advertising may be very positive (exciting business, challenging work, good pay).

Groups of attitudes combine to form broader "belief systems." For instance, the woman who has a negative attitude toward a particular brand of powder make-up, because she feels the container is inferior, may have a belief system (or value system) concerning health and sanitation in the area of facial products.

Psychologist Dr. Milton Rokeach maintains that such belief systems are comprised of tens of thousands of beliefs arrayed along a continuum of importance. Numerous research studies have shown that the more important a belief or attitude is to a person, and the more firmly the attitude is held, the more it will resist change.[6] Deeply entrenched attitudes are difficult to alter even over long periods of time.

For many years, National Safety Council campaigns have tried to convince Americans that seat belts should be worn on every automobile trip—be it three blocks, or 3,000 miles. Decades of safe driving without seat belts, however, led millions to believe them unnecessary; hence, even when no car on the road will run until belts are fastened, it's probable that negative attitudes toward them will prevail.

Advertisers and their agencies are most often concerned with associating relatively unimportant beliefs (such as those involving the choice between two brands of physically similar products) with ones which are psychologically consequential (such as those concerning cleanliness or the credibility of a well-known personality). Attitudes regarding the need for detergent in a given community may be highly positive, while feelings for six locally available brands may be almost neutral. Local advertisements might then stress a specific brand's effect on hands, speed and ease of cleaning, ability to fight tough stains, economical advantages, package design, or one of a score of other claims—depending on the belief systems identified among members of various media audiences. The change in attitude sought by the advertiser (from "indifferent" to "selective") is minor, but it's one which can have major repercussions in terms of ultimate sales. Usually, companies aren't nearly as interested in how a consumer group perceives their brands *alone* as they are in how the brands are ranked competitively in the minds of prospective buyers.[7] (Check Marketing Outline items 39 through 42.)

Some messages, however, are designed to reinforce existing firmly-held attitudes. Consider, for example, political advertisements for an incumbent seeking re-election in a district which overwhelmingly supports him or her.

IMAGE

On a similar note, the term "image" has played an important role in the development of psychology, particularly in relation to perception, thinking, and memory. In advertising, it involves mental pictures of a product or firm which the consumer currently holds, or ones which the advertiser hopes to establish. Such images are not so much accurate representations as they are compositions of consumer attitudes and beliefs regarding the items or companies in question.

Image has become increasingly significant for the advertiser as more and more products and services have become objectively indistinguishable from one another. In advertising messages, product attributes which contribute to a favorable image should be retained and reinforced, and weaker attributes should be discarded.

MOTIVATION AND VALUE ORIENTATIONS

Now let's consider these attitudes and belief systems in terms of our broader concept of motivation. If we're going to design successful advertising messages, we must keep in mind that inner needs, or drives, as well as environmental incentives stimulate consumers to act. Motivation can be classified according to: (1) physiological origins, such as hunger, thirst, sex, or fatigue; (2) conscious elements, such as the awareness of a specific action-triggering event, or an intent to achieve some purpose or goal; and (3) social factors, such as gregariousness, the urge for recognition and approval, or the desire for adventure or security. It is this final category with which the creators of advertising messages are most directly concerned, because human beings have an innate capacity for acquiring motives by interacting with one another.

One approach to the study of motivation in advertising involves an examination of major American value orientations. A value may be considered a form of motive—a thing which interests people as members of society. It can be something people wish to possess, to become, to achieve, to enjoy, or in which they desire to participate or become involved. Common values in this country (those which are shared in varying degrees of intensity) help advertisers and their agencies understand why consumers act as they do. (See Marketing Outline item 64.) Examples include the following, derived from a recent study by Stanford University social psychologist, Alex Inkeles.

SELF-RELIANCE, ACTIVITY AND SUCCESS

Americans stress determination and an independent spirit, along with personal and occupational achievements, which are often equated with standards of excellence. In fact, in evaluating a candidate for a job or other activity, an employer or project director looks not so much at the person, as at his or her accomplishments. Work hard, says the traditional Protestant ethic, and rewards will follow. Those who are never successful are assumed to have some character defect.

Wealth is a symbol and measure of success, of intelligence, and of power; in most cases, however, it is valued more for its evidence of personal worth than for what it buys. Similarly, many things are "good" simply because they are "big." General Motors, long recognized as a giant in American industry, prompted a familiar slogan: "As G.M. goes, so goes the country." (In other words, what was good for the huge General Motors Corporation was good for America as a whole.) Even with the popularity of the small car, the value of the G.M. name prevails; and, recently, 747 and Concorde jets have come to symbolize the ultimate in air travel.

Then, too, in pioneer days, the United States had no leisure class, no aristocratic class, and no stigma on hand labor. Work was stressed as an end in itself. ("He who does not work shall not eat.") Further, the Puritan tradition gave religious approval to successful occupational activity; profitable work was a sign of grace. Today, America is still the land of haste, of strenuous competition, and of vigor and often agitation. Even in areas of cooking and eating, people keep "on the go;" so, frozen dinners and quick-fix meals do a thriving business.

The emphasis on long working hours and constant, dedicated pursuit of work-a-day goals, however, has diminished; labor unions, the decline of farming, and the rise of a leisure class have contributed to a new pursuit of recreational activity and "work" in support of avocations.

MORALITY AND TRUST

An ethical quality seems to underlie this country's total cultural orientation. Here again is evidence of the Puritan ethic—a resolution to carry out whatever purposes are undertaken and a commitment to integrity, fair dealings, and an orderly life. Cynics are negatively regarded for their loss of faith in the efficiency of the moral code.

Middle class parents may try to teach their children a moral system which is considerably more stringent than that practiced by adults, but today's offspring are quickly disillusioned. There is always a tendency to see things as right or wrong, in or out, black or white—rarely along a continuum as shades of gray. Because of the ethics people are *supposed* to have, and because of current social realities to which they're *expected* to conform, there is ritualism, lip service, and hypocrisy.

History offers evidence of numerous conflicts in these areas—particularly in racial and religious concerns. Is one race really born more or less intelligent, privileged, or capable than another? Is the literal Bible really true—or are theories of evolution just as plausible?

Persuasive messages urging fair play and justice for all may take many different forms, but appeals are designed to touch the moral heartstrings of the audience. Specific reasons why these claims are important need not be spelled out; it's assumed that message recipients will understand and act accordingly.

VOLUNTEERISM

America has a tradition of generosity to others—a kind of unbiased concern and spirit of kindliness. Be it national disaster or local misfortune, spontaneous aid appears, in the form of both physical necessities and personal compassion for those in distress. Granted, the love of one's neighbor often clashes with the pursuit of rugged individualism, but in these cases people seem to close their eyes to inequities which exist. (Consider, for example, that the country's millionaires number only in the tens of thousands, while millions are unemployed; also, ethnic groups and handicapped persons are frequent victims of discrimination.)

Still, Community Chest drives, service clubs, and public welfare organizations and efforts are extremely successful. There is a genuine tendency to identify with the underdog, to dislike the "fat cat," and to make the nation a haven for the downtrodden and the oppressed. Numerous advertisements stress the spirit of giving— and not only during gift-giving seasons.

EFFICIENCY AND PRACTICALITY

"Efficient" is a highly-praised word in a society which continually emphasizes adaptability, innovation, and expediency. Other nations have long recognized the streamlined efficiency (standardization, mass production) of American industrialism. Companies develop codes of good job behavior, stressing productive output and the most effective (and efficient) means of achieving desired ends.

Similarly, practicality has come to indicate pursuit of a highly approved lifestyle in American culture: the relentless, methodical striving for promotion or victory. The practical human being is a respected individual who enjoys solving problems because they're part of a short-range adjustment to life's situations. In most cases, concerns are for *today's* achievements or *tonight's* pleasures. Or, when future planning does enter the picture, the party involved does all it can to make the procedure as simple and short-lived as possible. A good example is a bank which uses advertisements to stress the ease of saving for a new home or college education.

OPTIMISM AND PROGRESS

The United States was the first country to emphasize change for change's sake. Our love of progress forces us to look with disdain at businesses and merchandise labeled out-of-date, backward, or stagnant. The present is better than the past, and the future will be greater still; nothing is impossible if we have faith in change, and we grow up believing that most changes are good ones. (See Figure 3-1.)

For example, we can justify the expenditure of billions upon billions of dollars to reach the moon (real progress), even though we receive no direct personal gain. And, a major corporation shares its progress with us through advertisements, hoping in return that we'll contribute to its continued success through purchase of its products.

MATERIAL COMFORTS AND (NATIONAL) PRIDE

Americans also place great value on a high level of material comfort, often demanding that their smallest whims be gratified. The focus is on receiving, and consumption has become a kind of idol. As new wants emerge and are satisfied, they're taken for granted; suddenly, they become "rights" to which we feel we have a moral claim. Indeed, America's high standard of living positions it as a nation of takers—and advertising indexes the trend. It emphasizes comfort along with an almost effortless satisfaction of desires. Advertisements proclaim: "Eat this . . . use that . . . take a vacation . . . be pampered . . ." (and receive a "reward" in the process).

The Leo Burnett advertising agency, in Chicago, once categorized rewards into four basic areas. Appeals in one classification may meet the motivational needs of one group of people, while those in another classification may be better suited to a different group. It should be emphasized, however, that reward categories cut across product lines; it is up to the creative team, in consultation with their partners in research, to decide where to position a product or service:

KIND OF REWARD	TYPE OF APPEAL
Rational	Gets clothes cleaner. Needs no mixing. Seals in flavor.
Sensory	Gets rid of headache pain fast. Smells fresh—tastes homemade. High-quality sound and a smooth, wood-grain finish.

FIGURE 3-1

"Progress" Advertisement from Lennox

41

Lenox enters a new age in dinnerware. Temper-ware.

Stronger than any ironstone, stoneware, or earthenware.

Informal dinnerware will never be the same again. Because with Temper-ware, Lenox enters a whole new age in dinnerware. An age where your dinnerware's inner beauty is as important as its outer appearance.

The Lenox Formula for Success.

Lenox wants your first set of Temper-ware to be the last set of informal dinnerware you'll ever need.

So years of testing and scientific research in our laboratories went into developing Temper-ware. Until we found that special formula. The perfect balance of materials that gives Temper-ware amazing strength.

It didn't happen overnight.

But the tests never stopped. Temper-ware is still constantly tested to see how it stands up to the traumas of daily use. During our breaking test, Temper-ware stands firm. And numerous Modulus of Rupture tests,* prove Temper-ware to be stronger than the strongest ironstone, stoneware, or earthenware.

So strong you can actually take Temper-ware cook and serve pieces from an icy freezer and put them in a hot oven, even a microwave oven, without defrosting.

And you can serve in them in style. Even run them through the dishwasher as often as you want.

The final test.

And just like Lenox fine china, Temper-ware is given the ultimate Lenox test. It's placed on the table. One look and you'll see that Temper-ware is worthy of the name Lenox.

The Temper-ware Warranty.

What's more, every piece of Temper-ware comes with a warranty against breaking, chipping, cracking, and crazing for up to two years of normal use.

Compared to other informal dinnerware, Temper-ware is anything but ordinary.

In fact, it's years ahead of the rest.

Temper-ware BY LENOX®

Send for our free color brochure. Lenox, Lawrenceville, N.J. 08648.
*Strength as measured by Modulus of Rupture test —
the most reliable test for material strength in the ceramic industry.

Ego-Satisfying	For the family with discriminating taste.
	For the skin with the velvet touch.
	Because you deserve extra comfort.
Social	Be confident in a crowd.
	The symbol of the successful executive.
	The gift that shows you care.

Today's advertisers know that a woman does not buy nail polish, per se, but rather, attractive nails. She takes a dress off the rack, but she buys glamour. She bakes a cake for food, but really wants approval from her family. She shops, not for items but for rewards that are sometimes so complex she isn't aware of them herself.

Turning from products to services, we find that Jack LaLanne's exercise salon illustrates results with in-use situations. Advertisements may show a pool or a room filled with machines where exercising is done as a background, but they feature a gathering of slim, healthy-looking people who have benefited from using the pool and equipment. Consumers are persuaded by the results more strongly than by the means. This approach is tactically effective because it views the service from a consumer point of view rather than from the supplier's position. LaLanne could mistakenly think he is in the business of providing consumers with a space filled with exercise machines. Fortunately, he realizes his business is fitness and beauty that results in self-respect and sexual attractiveness.

EQUALITY AND INDIVIDUALISM

Inequalities of wealth, power, and prestige abound in America. The issue of civil rights, from taxation to criminal courts, is still today one of inequality, and the concept of property rights versus social welfare underlies much political maneuvering. Yet, equality is a powerful motivating factor.

In the corporation, the army, the local club or other organization, people accept the necessity of authority—but, while stressing the importance and goodness of teamwork, many detest the special privileges given to officers and executives. We're all members of groups, no matter how fleeting and informal, or how organized and stable they may be. And in daily activities, we take positions, arrive at decisions, and carry out actions against a backdrop of other individuals who exert pressures on us to act in concert with the group.

Is the grass really greener in someone else's yard? It is if people *believe* that it is. Do some families spend their lives merely trying to keep up with the Joneses? Yes—if they place a high priority on "equality" as thus defined. The expectation of approval or disapproval (from family, friends, reference groups, business associates, or others) has long been considered a major incentive in persuasion. Further, this approval or disapproval doesn't actually have to be received for it to be effective; the *expectation* of it is sufficient. Some behavioral scientists refer to this phenomenon as the "bandwagon effect." The majority view in a given situation serves as a cue for the anticipated reward of social approval.[8]

Of course, there are times when individuality is a prized possession, but America's individualism is group individualism. The desire for social acceptance is, in large part, what helps to make a society. Advertising does its own "communication thing" by passing along set conversation pieces, cliches, and slang expressions, as well as standardized public opinion.

FREEDOM

Freedom is both expensive and extremely fragile. In a country enjoying above-subsistence living, men and women are presumably entitled to the freedom of economic choice: to buy a new house or to put the money in a bank or in stock; which political candidate to vote for; when to pursue that college degree or urge to travel. The very essence of all of these freedoms is that we may choose to do things other people might consider foolish; we're free, that is, to make mistakes as well as to avoid them.

To exercise true freedom of choice, people must know what their alternatives are; and one of the crucial functions of advertising is to bring various options to their attention. In this respect, advertising is vital to the preservation of freedom; it's not only the sole practical source of advocating economic choices, but also the major support of the only communication system that's not under control of the state.

While all of these value orientations may be common to most Americans, they're held in varying degrees of intensity. In addition, priorities given to selected ones may change over time. Attitudinal research must be an on-going activity if it is to be helpful to advertisers. Every day of their lives, people are subjected to numerous influences—at home, at school, at work, or at the grocery store or country club. They develop new opinions on a great variety of topics and establish new sets of values and behavioral tendencies. So, good copywriters are constantly observing people—learning what makes them tick. They realize that looking within the mind is important in understanding the behavior of audiences, but they also look within the larger mind of society.

MARKETS AND AUDIENCES

Thus far, only brief mention has been made of the difference between markets and audiences. This distinction should be clarified before proceeding further.

MARKETS

First, markets are *people*, not places. As Eugene Pomerance, then Vice President and Director of Research at Foote, Cone & Belding, in Chicago, once remarked: "No city ever bought a bar of soap." *People* purchase products and services—and those who, because of their demographic and psychographic characteristics, could conceivably buy and use a particular product or service (in order to fulfill a want or need) are said to comprise an advertiser's target market.

Social scientist Kenneth Boulding has noted that it is the behavior of commodities, and not the behavior of men, which is the prime focus of interest in economic studies. Advertising, however, as a form of communication and a selling tool, necessarily involves people—complete with all the idiosyncracies which products do not possess. Today's pragmatic businessman or woman knows advertising is an essential element in marketing products, and uses mass media messages either to supplement or to replace the face-to-face contacts made by sales personnel.

AUDIENCES

The people who read, view, or hear one of these messages at a given point in time comprise the audience for the particular medium involved. Hence, an audience may be regarded as a subset of a market—that portion of the market which is attending a specific medium when the advertising message appears. (See Marketing Outline item 86.) Conceivably, the target market for a new automobile might consist of thousands of different target audiences every day—each one reading an advertisement in a particular newspaper, or seeing or hearing a commercial on a selected station, in cities across the country. Every audience shares some demographic and psychographic characteristics with the market as a whole—but not all of them; for much as they might like to do so, advertisers cannot even *reach* all members of their markets simultaneously (let alone appeal to individual attitudes and belief systems).

How, then, do advertisers judge the success or failure of their creative output? A later chapter will discuss the measurement of advertising effectiveness, but a brief word is in order here. Admittedly, action is the easiest kind of result to observe and measure; by itself, however, it doesn't usually explain any underlying phenomena—nor does it allow for prediction of future actions. In other words, the relationship between attitudes and overt behavior has not been exactly determined.

As pointed out earlier, though, behavioral scientists know *something* intervenes between consumers' contact with a persuasive message in the mass media and their ultimate response (in either mind or marketplace); and it's this "something" that we've called attitudes, beliefs, values—or, collectively, motivation. It should be evident by now that neither an advertiser's market nor a medium's audience can be defined clearly or understood fully unless attitudinal dimensions have been studied.

Demographics Versus Psychographics

We've been referring to two different types of market and audience information; now, let's consider the characteristics separately. A knowledge of both is required before an advertising creative team begins working.

Demographics. Traditionally, demographics described a market or audience to the satisfaction of advertisers and their agencies. Age, sex, race, income, education, occupation, and place of residence—all quantitative measures—were used almost exclusively to explain shopping and media behavior. After World War II, however, it became obvious that demographic information was not sufficient. Television, radio, daily newspapers, and a number of magazines appealed to large masses of people, and many families were heavy users of all media. In addition, product appeals cut across demographic lines. So, marketing and advertising practitioners began to ask: what are the *psychological* differences between people who use a lot of our product and those who use a little? How do consumers perceive our brand's features as opposed to those of competing brands—and what do they see as relevant benefits? Are shoppers' satisfactions and dissatisfactions with certain products based on physical uses or emotional appeals?

Psychographics. Questions such as these prompted noted psychologists such as Ernest Dichter to examine interactions between people and products, and to discover important *qualitative* characteristics of markets and audiences which weren't restricted by demographic classifications. These qualities came to be called psychographics, and opened the door to a whole new era of research.

During the 1950's, "motivational research" had its heyday—and findings made then seem humorous today. For example, Freudian psychology was used to explain why women preferred an opaque (or "dressed") food wrap to a transparent (or "naked") one. Innate hostilities toward the world about them showed why men selected specific foods which were crisp enough to afford chewing resistance (and then "triumph") during a meal.

Hand-in-hand with this type of research went experiments in what was then called "subliminal" advertising. Fears were widespread that somehow advertising could penetrate subconscious minds and force people to act against their will. Later, such studies were revealed to be deliberate attempts to exploit people's gullibility, and were shown to have no scientific support.

That kind of motivational research gradually died out, although experiments in the use of subliminal communication have continued. Attitudinal research, however—the study of motives and beliefs to help explain and predict human behavior—is very much alive today. While advertising research, as a behavioral science discipline, is barely beyond its infancy stage, a number of valuable insights have been gained which advertising creative teams often find very useful.

THE LEARNING SITUATION

More than 25 years ago, Steuart Britt, then Vice President and Director of Research at Needham, Louis and Brorby, in Chicago (now Needham, Harper & Steers), used some of psychology's rules of learning in recommending advertising message strategies. All of them are remarkably appropriate in the 1980's, too, since studies continually show that marketing and communication "actions" follow some kind of learned response pattern.

UNDERSTANDING

Teachers and psychologists alike maintain that things which are understood when they are learned are often better retained than things memorized by rote. Mere repetition of facts, claims, or instructions is of no great value unless the reader, viewer, or listener has some meaning for the material in question. Given a basic understanding and perceived relevance to his or her own state of affairs, however, a person will learn more effectively if information exposure occurs over periods of time than if it comes all at once. Advertisements which *explain* product features, operations, or procedures (depending on what the basic sales proposition is), and which take care to apply their messages clearly and specifically to audience lifestyles, have a better chance of succeeding than those which do not. And often the sales story is presented in different ways at different times and across different media (See Figure 3-2).

FIGURE 3-2

"Explanation Advertisement" from Johnson & Johnson

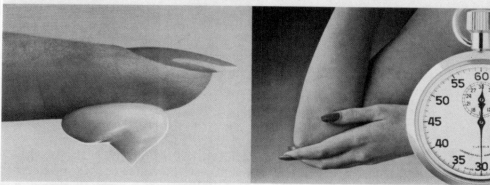

Four good reasons why *Johnson's* Baby Lotion is the best "grownup" body lotion you can buy.

Thicker and richer than other lotions.

Absorbs fast. Goes to work instantly.

Unique combination of 10 skin softeners.

Leaves you feeling beautifully soft all over.

When it comes to keeping skin soft, JOHNSON's Baby Lotion has everything you want in a body lotion and more. Its super-rich formula gives a new beauty to your skin and leaves it with a healthy, youthful glow. In short, JOHNSON's Baby Lotion is a terrific body lotion. We've told you four good reasons why. But don't take our word for it. Just give it a try.

It's a perfect lotion for grownup skin.

Johnson & Johnson

© J&J 1980

PARTICIPATION

When mechanical skills are involved, learning is enhanced if students can place themselves (mentally if not physically) in the role of the performer. If they can see the task completed as it would appear to them if they were doing the job themselves, their gain from a learning point of view will be maximal. How many children could learn to ride bicycles if their only instruction were from a printed page—or tape recording—removed from the bicycle itself? Again, learning is aided more by active participation than by passive reception. So, commercials invite audiences to "sing along," and print advertisements ask readers to answer riddles, fill in blanks, or put themselves into a particular picture.

IDENTIFICATION OF ERRORS

Assuming a basic learning situation is present, are there ways to improve the speed and efficiency with which people master new skills or grasp new ideas? Psychology offers several suggestions. First, demonstrating errors in performance can lead to increases in learning. Since beginners in any capacity are bound to make mistakes, a learning situation which takes them into account is very apt to reach wrongdoers on common ground.[9]

TWO-SIDED ARGUMENTS

In a related area, studies have involved messages presenting "both sides" of an issue (the pros and cons, positive and negative aspects, or "right" and "wrong" ways of assessing a situation). As in the case of demonstrating errors, research has shown that in most cases two-sided messages are more effective than one-sided messages in eliciting a desired response (especially when the audience is exposed to counterarguments, as they are daily and hourly in the case of advertising). Exceptions have been found in situations where message recipients were poorly educated and/or unfamiliar with the topic in question.[10]

FOCUS ON RESULTS

A knowledge of results leads to improved learning. Our earlier discussion of achievement and success as major American value orientations indicated that knowing "how well they are doing" can be a great aid to people pursuing a new learning experience. Then, when the road to accomplishment shows some material comfort (another value orientation) at its end, added educational gains can be expected. Nearly every advertising message, of course, features a "pot of gold" at the end of its sales story spectrum, so audiences can weigh the promised values against the work or effort demanded.

EXPLICIT CONCLUSIONS

Research in a similar vein has involved messages containing explicit conclusions as opposed to ones leaving conclusions implied. Again, it appears that the more specifically defined the path of action to a goal (conclusions explicitly drawn), the more likely that path will be followed. Regardless of the degree of audience commitment to the subject, attitude change is more favorably affected when messages state end results than when they merely imply what may be in store for those who respond.[11] The lesson for advertising creative teams is simply: don't play games with your audience. Don't leave them guessing as to what a product or service will do for them.

LACK OF INTERFERENCE

Any message is learned more easily if it does not interfere with previously acquired habits (or beliefs). Actions involving perceived threats to personal freedoms or progress, or those deemed impractical or inefficient cannot hope to be accepted—at least not readily. In advertising, the maxim is: start where your audience is. Identify existing attitudes, and show consumers how their own interests coincide with promises of product performance or with the goals or philosophy of a store or service organization. Research has also shown that material which supports a person's own point of view is better *retained* than is material containing conflicting views.[12]

NEED FOR REPETITION

Finally, despite all efforts to the contrary, people's rate of forgetting tends to be very rapid once learning has occurred. Although studies have shown varying percentages of recall following message exposure, consensus is that an initial recall rate of about 60% drops quickly, and then levels off near 30% after four weeks.[13] In any persuasive situation, therefore, repetition seems mandatory—but what kind of repetition? A study involving news stories presented one day in newspapers and on radio and television found that the items presented most frequently were the ones which showed the greatest audience recall, regardless of the medium concerned.[14]

Repetition of claims within a given message, however, also increases retention, and repetition *with variation* enhances both retention and interest.[15] Research sponsored by the American Association of Advertising Agencies stressed the importance of "continually refreshing the creative work, lest some of it pass into limbo."[16]

A popular research topic for more than 50 years has been the subject of primacy versus recency—the early or late placement of key material in a message or series of messages. Although factors such as audience interest in the content, and familiarity with topics presented, may have an effect on the debate, one solid conclusion can be drawn from the large number of studies undertaken in this area: placing important information at the beginning or the end of a message is superior to burying it somewhere in the middle.[17] Advertisements which repeat the vital sales proposition at the beginning and end would appear, therefore, to have it made (although there's no reason why we shouldn't opt for an "in the middle" position, too).

SOCIAL PSYCHOLOGY AND CREATIVE STRATEGY

Turning even more specifically now to advertising messages, we find that terms such as "attention," "interest," and "persuasion" come up frequently in discussion of creative strategies; but only rarely is any attempt made to study these concepts as social-psychological variables. Since a number of experiments have been conducted on their behalf, however, it seems appropriate to examine them here.

ATTENTION CUES

As early as 1929, communication research studied "vividness" devices used as attention cues in oral messages. The most effective ones included pauses, and the speaker's use of "now get this" before an important statement.[18] Similar findings were made in 1945.[19] Apparently, listeners regarded these two devices as indicators that something unusual or otherwise noteworthy was about to be said. Today, radio commercials may use musical "stingers" and other sound effects, as well as vocal patterns and verbal suggestions that an important item is coming. Of course, it's always up to individual listeners to decide whether or not they'll heed such cues, depending on their particular frames of mind or motivational states at that specific moment.

More recently, headlines were found to be attention-grabbers (and stage-setters) for newspaper readers, as were lead stories in radio newscasts.[20] Other devices in radio and TV, affecting both recall and credibility as well as attention, are vocal inflection, diction, and gestures. The more interesting the inflection, the clearer the diction, and the more dramatic the gestures, the higher the rate of recall and the more believable the message.[21]

In the print media, artists claim that certain colors are more arresting than others. Consider, for example, red, with which we associate stoplights, fire, and impending difficulty or danger, all of which call for immediate attention and response. On the other hand, green speaks of going—or growing—and indicates a cool, fresh, and springlike quality.

INTEREST-HOLDING FACTORS

A newspaper study found an overwhelming interest value in visual forms such as cartoons and photographs. Fifty-one percent of the total readership was determined by the presence of pictorial material—in support of the old Chinese proverb that one picture is worth 10,000 words.[22] Present-day critics claim that "it all depends" (on a host of other factors), but few will quarrel with the ability of pictures to place readers and viewers "at the scene," thereby emphasizing—even dramatizing—a value or reward.

Given some form of illustration, we can also examine its details. In an experiment in the 1960's, respondents asked to choose between pairs of pictures rated "irregular" designs more interesting than regular ones.[23] Complex patterns (nonsymmetrical ones) were better liked than simple ones, probably because they were more unusual.[24] On the other hand, messages which are well-organized and fluently presented have more interest appeal than those which are not.[25]

Several television studies have discovered that video elements often generate higher recall than do audio elements, especially in the case of complicated messages.[26] *Maximum* recall can be obtained, however, when audio and visual elements complement each other (that is, say and show the same thing simultaneously).[27] Given the choice, in a very visual and fast-moving world, it may be that people would rather look than listen. (And maybe, in a society that is continually emphasizing leisure, they find "looking" a little easier!)

Human interest or "spectacular" messages are usually more intriguing to audiences than are public affairs items, and familiar events tend to draw more interest than do strange ones.[28] Social psychologists insist that men and women are social animals; as such, they naturally enjoy looking at, listening to, or hearing or reading about other people—in situations where their human characteristics are especially prominent. The closer to home the situation, the better; or, each of us, as individuals, might simply say: "The people I like best are—like me."

PERSUASIVE ELEMENTS

Now we come to the real heart of most advertisements (and many other communication messages as well): their persuasive thrust. A number of elements and techniques have proven themselves effective in convincing message recipients to act; the following are a few of the most prominent.

Source Credibility

One of the most controversial elements in advertising message strategies is the "source behind the claims." Studies by Hovland and Weiss, and Kelman and Hovland, a number of years ago, resulted in identification of the so-called "sleeper effect"—the tendency among recipients of a message to dissociate the source (speaker) from the content, after a three-to-four-week period. Hence, the advantage of obtaining a highly credible source (for example, the president of the American Medical Association talking about the importance of a well-balanced diet) diminishes over time.[29]

Respect for authority is learned at an early age and more or less accepted throughout a lifetime. The value of including an expert source in an advertising message, however, is debatable. Recalling the importance of repetition in advertising, we might well ask: if messages are repeated within the above-noted three-to-four-week period, what happens to the effect of the source? Are his or her persuasive powers maintained? There is no definitive answer.

In attempting to apply the sleeper effect to advertising, one study dealt with messages which were initially *rejected* by respondents because of their content or style. Over time, as respondents received repeated exposure to these ads, they were found less and less likely to dissociate the message from the unfavorable environment.[30] Future research might suggest what would happen in the case of entirely *favorable* circumstances . . . or in situations where attitudes toward the advertising environment changed over time.

Still, many advertisers let source credibility go to bat for them regularly in their campaigns. For instance, when a company is well known in its trade category, its signature may play a vital role in introductory advertisements for a new product. (See Marketing Outline item 48.) For instance, if women know and respect Clairol as an expert manufacturer of hair care products, an advertisement for a new Clairol conditioning treatment will probably command a large amount of credibility. Likewise, when Kellogg's talks about cereals, in an institutional advertisement, consumers know an authority is speaking. The company name alone may communicate as valuable an image as a series of messages featuring different Kellogg's products.

Emotional Versus Rational Appeals

Another persuasive element is the emotional appeal, which is often contrasted with the rational one. Frequently, in advertising, the distinction is drawn between an emotional and a "reason-why" approach to persuasion; such classifications are, however, misleading. Both rational and emotional presentations can (and usually do) offer reasons why message recipients should respond in some prescribed manner. Both can be persuasive and at times it's difficult to separate one from the other, since "emotional" is a term which takes on different meanings at different times.[31]

In today's advertisements, emotional appeals are emphasized more than rational ones, so it would seem that emotional tactics are believed to be more effective in eliciting action. Research-wise, however, summaries of numerous studies show no superiority of one type of presentation over the other. Also, the measurement of emotional and rational appeals isn't often separated from the measurement of attention, comprehension, and overall message acceptance.[32]

Fear Appeals

Finally, consider persuasive techniques which involve fears or threats. A classic study in this area, made by Janis and Feshback, dealt with strong, moderate, and mild fear presentations regarding dental hygiene. The strong appeals resulted in the most emotional tension on the part of the audience, while the mild ones led to the greatest amount of conformity to suggestions given in the messages.[33] Apparently, when fear is strongly aroused but not fully relieved by reassurances in a persuasive situation, people tend to ignore or minimize the importance of the threats.

Once again, though, personal belief systems and value orientations must be considered a key criterion in any decision regarding fear or threat appeals. Aggressively aroused individuals are more often influenced by a punitively-oriented message than are their non-aggressive neighbors.[34] Also, as was true in the case of emotional appeals, there is a serious lack of workable definitions in the field of anxiety-producing stimuli.[35] Hence, message strategists will do well to pretest ideas in this area.

In a related category, think for a moment about some "necessary evil" products. These are items which consumers wish they did not have to buy but *need* in order to solve unfortunate, unhappy, irritating, fact-of-life problems. They add no pleasure or joy. They offer no self-indulgence. They are of low interest and create low enthusiasm. One example is a bandage—used only in the case of misfortune. The patient may be in pain and tears. The problem is shock and a cut or abrasion . . . and the solution can be a Band Aid, although there's no real enjoyment in using it.

Likewise, people rarely get excited about selecting toilet tissue, diapers, sanitary protection products, headache or cold remedies, mouth wash, deodorants, oven cleaner or laundry and dishwashing soap. One advertising strategy for positioning a "necessary evil" product involves showing the item as a *lessener* of evils. The message assures consumers that the discomfort, heartbreak, misery, pain, or bother of a problem is effectively eased or relieved by the advertised brand. (See Outline item 51.)

Sometimes, advertisements actually show a relieved, eased, satisfied customer—the positive approach (See Figure 3-3). Alternative approaches are (1) a negative treatment (featuring a problem, or type of "suffering"), and (2) a combination pain-plus-relief situation. In the first case, a child in bed with a cold or flu might be sorrowfully wishing he could join his friends outside, while the maker of a leading children's medication *joined* him in his hopes for a speedy recovery. In the second instance, skin that's rough and chapped might be shown "welcoming" the soothing emollients in a well-known hand-and-body lotion.

THE PERSONALITY FACTOR

Since the function of advertising is to influence consumers to take some action desired by the advertiser, creative teams must know as much as possible about the motives and beliefs which direct that action. They must be aware of the processes involved in developing, reinforcing, and changing attitudes; predispositions will affect not only a person's interest in a given message, but also his or her willingness to respond in the manner suggested.

Creative strategies designed to reach a leader (or innovator) in today's society might bore, confuse, or repel a crowd-follower. The

FIGURE 3-3

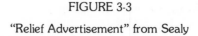

"Relief Advertisement" from Sealy

REPRODUCED WITH PERMISSION FROM SEALY, INC.

venturesome, ambitious individual doesn't always react the same way the timid, withdrawn person does—and, yet, both may buy the same products and partake of the same services every day. Price-shoppers, highly influenced by economic appeals, may not respond at all to news of expensive product developments, while a brand-loyal customer could find such information very welcome.

HALO EFFECT

If a woman has a high regard for a particular dress designer, she may find all of his outfits (and advertisements) appealing; conversely, if a man dislikes a certain shirt manufacturer, he probably will avoid contact with the entire line—and with the advertising messages as well. In this case, behavioral scientists would say the "halo effect" was operating. When a company as a whole is perceived favorably or unfavorably, everything related to it is often regarded the same way. In other words, the company image follows it around like a halo—and rubs off on its products and communication efforts.

SELECTIVITY

Behavioral research has consistently revealed that people operate *selectively* in terms of mass media messages: their exposure to, and perception and retention of programs, articles, advertisements, and the like is deliberate and willful. Once it was believed that audiences read, viewed, and listened to media fare only when it was in line with their predispositions. Later studies showed that some communications were chosen for other reasons (to "escape from reality," for instance)—but the *selective processes* remained very much in evidence.

Advertising research must identify this selective activity in mass media audiences who are also members of an advertiser's market. First, since value orientations and learning processes don't become operative until a consumer is *exposed* to an advertising message, media strategy demands careful planning.

Once exposure has occurred, however, the process of selective perception begins. Regardless of a message's content, its recipients are free to evaluate, interpret, and even distort at will—and they do so according to their own backgrounds, interests, beliefs, and biases. Ambiguous, or otherwise unclear material stands less than a fighting chance of being perceived exactly as the copywriter intended. Even concise, factual reporting can be misconstrued, but, in most cases, the more specific a message is, the less it will be distorted.

Selective retention takes place after a message has been read, viewed, or heard. Again, each member of the receiving audience elects (consciously or unconsciously) to remember all, part, or none of the communication, and, once again, the extent and accuracy of retention depends to a large extent on the message's value to individual lifestyles.

THE INFLUENCE OF ADVERTISING

Motivation is a sensitive area for most people; few of us ever admit to being influenced by advertising. Yet, in our cupboards and medicine chests are rows of nationally advertised products. "But," we may exclaim when questioned, "those products come from big, rich companies who can simply afford to advertise." (Is it even necessary to point out that these companies *became* big and rich partially through effective advertising?)

If advertising is, as Vance Packard and others have claimed, a "hidden persuader," it's certainly only one of many in today's society. Wants are created by a host of influences—governments, churches, schools, and social groups, to name but a few. People are free to choose from among alternatives in each case, as they seek personal satisfactions and comforts; but there's no evidence to prove that the *stimulation* of wants (beyond the physical needs of food, clothing, and shelter) runs counter to the pursuit of human welfare and happiness.

For example, a new car buyer wants more than just transportation. Motivations behind the choice of make and model may include comfort, style, safety, and status. But even after the purchase is made, the buyer may pay careful attention to advertisements for the selected automobile. Having made an important buying decision, the purchaser looks for proof that he or she has made the "right" choice. In behavioral terms, Leon Festinger calls this phenomenon "dissonance reduction." To the copywriter, it's merely another appeal (reassurance) which advertisements may incorporate.

Still, doubts and fears persist. Can advertising creep, like fog, on little cat feet, into someone's mind and create a new desire or demand for a product or service? That question closely parallels the old chicken-and-egg problem of "which came first" (in this case, the product or the desire for it). It is a thesis of this book that advertising can *stimulate* demand for needs and wants which already exist.[36] It has no magical, mystical power to create something from nothing. One of the jobs of the copywriter, working with a research team, is to identify and understand existing wants and needs, and then find ways of implementing them.

STUDY QUESTIONS

1. Explain and give an example of two different consumer "lifestyles."
2. Why are motives and attitudes regarded as "intervening" variables?
3. Name and discuss some major American value orientations and explain how they are utilized in advertising.
4. What's the difference between a market and an audience?
5. Why are demographics and psychographics *both* important to advertising creative teams?
6. Name and discuss some psychological rules of learning and explain how they can be utilized in advertising.
7. What findings from social-psychological research studies are useful to today's copywriters, artists, and commercial producers in terms of advertising *attention, interest,* and *persuasion*?
8. What is the "halo effect"?
9. What three *selective processes* do consumers display in their contact with mass media messages?

ENDNOTES

1. See Lewis Donohew, Leonard Lipton, and Roger Haney, "Analysis of Information-Seeking Strategies," *Journalism Quarterly*, Spring, 1978, pp. 25-31.
2. "Roundtable - Lifestyle," *Media Decisions*, January, 1978, pp. 60-61.
3. George Katona, *The Power Consumer*, McGraw-Hill, New York, 1960, p. 140.
4. See Kenneth E. Boulding, *The Image*, University of Michigan Press, Ann Arbor, 1956, p. 11.
5. Theodore M. Newcomb, *Social Psychology*, Holt, Rinehart and Winston, New York, 1950, pp. 31, 118-119.
6. Wilbur Schramm, ed., *The Science of Human Communication*, Basic Books, Inc., New York, 1963, p. 76.
7. Robert E. Smith, and Robert F. Lusch, "How Advertising Can Position a Product," *Journal of Advertising Research*, February, 1976, p. 38.
8. See Joseph T. Klapper, *The Effects of Mass Communication*, Free Press, Glencoe, 1960, pp. 125-126.
9. Steuart Henderson Britt, "How Advertising Can Use Psychology's Rules of Learning," *Printer's Ink*, September 23, 1955, pp. 74-80.
10. See G. C. Chu, "Prior Familiarity, Perceived Bias, and One-Sided vs. Two-Sided Communications,"*Journal of Experimental Social Psychology*, III, 1967, pp. 243-254; Carl I. Hovland, Irving L. Janis, and Harold H. Kelley, *Communication and Persuasion*, Yale University Press, New Haven, 1953, p. 245; Wilbur Schramm, ed., *The Process and Effects of Mass Communication*, University of Illinois Press, Urbana, 1955; and Wilbur Schramm, ed., *The Science of Human Communication*, Basic Books, Inc., New York, 1963, p. 76.
11. Stewart L. Tubbs, "Explicit Versus Implicit Conclusions and Audience Commitment," *Speech Monographs*, March, 1968, pp. 14-19.
12. Wilbur Schramm, op. cit., p. 68.
13. See Carl I. Hovland, Irving L. Janis, and Harold H. Kelley, op. cit., p. 245.
14. Alan Booth, "The Recall of News Items," *Public Opinion Quarterly*, winter, 1970-71, pp. 604-610.
15. Carl I. Hovland, Irving L. Janis, and Harold H. Kelley, op. cit., p. 247.
16. W. M. Weilbacher, "What Happens to Advertisements When They Grow Up," *Public Opinion Quarterly*, summer, 1970, p. 222.
17. Carl I. Hovland, Irving L. Janis, and Harold H. Kelley, op. cit., p. 245.
18. Arthur Jersild, "Primacy, Recency, Frequency, and Vividness," *Journal of Experimental Psychology*, XII, 1929, pp. 58-70.
19. Ray Ehrensberger, "An Experimental Study of the Relative Effectiveness of Certain Forms of Emphasis in Public Speaking," *Speech Monographs*, XII, 1945, pp. 94-111.
20. See Percy H. Tannenbaum, "The Effect of Headlines on the Interpretation of News Stories," *Journalism Quarterly*, XXX, 1953, pp. 189-197; and Percy H. Tannenbaum, and Jean S. Kerrick, "Effect of Newscast Item Leads Upon Listener Interpretation," *Journalism Quarterly*, XXXI, 1954, pp. 33-37.
21. See David W. Addington, "The Effect of Vocal Variations on Ratings of Source Credibility," *Speech Monographs*, August, 1971, pp. 242-247; and Percy H. Tannenbaum, and Jean S. Kerrick, op. cit., pp. 33-37.
22. Charles E. Swanson, "What They Read in 130 Daily Newspapers," *Journalism Quarterly*, XXXII, 1955, pp. 411-421.
23. D. E. Berlyne, "Complexity and Incongruity Variables as Determinants of Exploratory Choice and Evaluative Ratings," *Canadian Journal of Psychology*, No. 17, 1963, pp. 274-290.
24. D. E. Berlyne, "Curiosity and Exploration," *Science,* July 1, 1966, pp. 25-33.
25. James C. McCroskey, and R. Samuel Mehrley, "The Effects of Disorganization and Nonfluency on Attitude Change and Source Credibility," *Speech Monographs*, March, 1969, pp. 13-21.
26. See Robert P. Sandowski, "Immediate Recall of TV Commercial Elements - Revisited," *Journalism Quarterly*, summer, 1972, pp. 227-287; and Wilbur Schramm, ed., *The Process and Effects of Mass Communication*, University of Illinois Press, Urbana, 1955.
27. Thomas Fredrick Baldwin, "Redundancy in Simultaneously Presented Audio-

Visual Message Elements as a Determinant of Recall," unpublished Ph.D. dissertation, Michigan State University, 1966.

28. Thomas W. Harrell, Donald E. Brown, and Wilbur Schramm, "Memory in Radio News Listening," *Journal of Applied Psychology*, XXXIII, 1949, pp. 265-274.
29. Arthur R. Cohen, Attitude Change and Social Influence, Basic Books, Inc., New York, 1964, pp. 32-33.
30. Martin Weinberger, "Does the Sleeper Effect Apply to Advertising," *Journal of Marketing*, October, 1961, p. 66.
31. Ivan L. Preston, and Lawrence Bowen, "Perceiving Advertisements As Emotional, Rational, and Irrational," *Journalism Quarterly*, spring, 1971, pp. 73-84.
32. Arthur R. Cohen, op. cit., pp. 37-41.
33. See Daniel Katz, ed., *Public Opinion and Propaganda*, Holt, Rinehart and Winston, New York, 1954.
34. Arthur R. Cohen, op. cit., pp. 37-41.
35. G. R. Miller, "Studies on the Use of Fear Appeals: A Summary and Analysis," *Central States Speech Journal*, XIV, 1963, pp. 117-125.
36. See R. L. Moore, and G. P. Hoschis, "Teenagers' Reactions to Advertising," *Journal of Advertising*, Fall, 1978, pp. 24-30.

4

THE COMMUNICATION PROCESS

Armed with a background in marketing and the behavioral sciences, we can now turn to advertising's communication potential. It draws constantly, we find, from both of these "parent" disciplines, since advertising's ultimate goal is almost always to *help* marketing sell products and services—*by* communicating. The late Fairfax Cone, Chairman of the Board of Foote, Cone & Belding, once noted that "advertising is what you do when you can't go see somebody in person." Speaking in media terms, if a salesman can't communicate with a prospective customer face-to-face, he uses one or more of the communication media: frequently TV, radio, newspapers, and magazines—or, sometimes, direct mail, outdoor posters, and transit media.

Modern society places a growing reliance on the mass media for news about an ever increasing number of people and events in the world at large, and for information concerning products, stores, and services available to meet the wants and needs which arise in a complex socio-economic environment. As newspapers, magazines, and broadcast stations in the United States have increased in number from hundreds to thousands, and advertising messages presented daily from millions to billions, their impact on personal lives and on culture and the economy as a whole has become the subject of much serious discussion and study.

Before turning to *mass* media channels and messages, however, we must first consider communication itself—the theoretical term as well as the societal byword which has become a sort of catchall for both achievements and problems. For example, satellites have advanced the field of "international communication"—and, in some cases, understanding, cooperation, and peace. On the other hand, negotiation failures (between nations, between labor and management factions within an industry, or between parents and offspring) are often blamed on a "breakdown in communications." Progressive companies install sophisticated "communication systems," and some universities have departments and schools of communication—or communications. But exactly what *is* communication (and when should it be used in plural form)?

NATURE OF COMMUNICATION

Research indicates that Americans spend approximately 70% of their active hours in verbal communication. We listen, speak, read, and write (in that order of emphasis) for more than ten hours per day.[1] But then, communication *is* the carrier of our social process; it makes interaction possible, and permits the collection, accumulation, and exchange of knowledge. Without it, we would have no news of current events, no interpretation of issues or means of reaching consensus on important decisions, and no education or method of transmitting cultural heritages from one generation to another. In fact, communication is as fundamental to human existence as eating and breathing; and, it's a dynamic process, continually employing the results of one message (feedback) in the production of the next. Such messages (actual communications) are, however, only one link in a sometimes intricate chain of communication activities.

A COMMUNICATION MODEL

As a social process, communication naturally includes more than one person. Then, too, since it involves a sharing of information and ideas, it requires both a channel (through which communications can flow) and a method of placing the material at hand into the channel and removing it therefrom. Of course, since parts of the communication process occur within people's minds, we can't observe or investigate them directly; still, it's important to be aware of each individual element. So, behavioral scientists have built communication models, just as a child builds a model airplane, while an architect draws a blueprint, and a window dresser works with mannequins. Models call attention to the dimensions of items being studied and aid in predicting relationships. Only with this power of foresight do we have any measure of communication control.[2]

Figure 4-1 is one model of the communication process—whose purpose, ultimately, is to affect human behavior.

FIGURE 4-1

Model of The Communication Process[3]

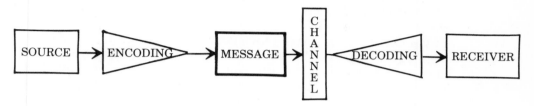

We may dispense with four very familiar elements in this model rather quickly:

The *source* is the message conceiver or originator: the student, the political candidate, the photographer, or the advertising copywriter;

The *message* is the source's creation: a letter requesting money from home, a campaign speech, a home movie, or a full page advertisement;

The *channel* is the transportation system, or the manner in which the message is delivered: the postal service, a public address system, an 8 mm projector, or a weekly magazine;

The *receiver* is the person or persons representing the destination of the message: the parent who reads the letter, the convention delegation which hears the speech, the neighbor or relative who watches the movie, or the reader who sees the ad.

ENCODING

Now let's look more closely at the activity called *encoding*. Traditionally, philosophers have differentiated human beings from lower animals by their powers of reasoning; but we're also unique in our ability to communicate through codes—in effect, to create a symbolic world. Coding activity ranges from letters and designs on road signs, to advertisements and commercials made up of words, pictures, sounds, and movements. A musical score is the composer's way of encoding a rock song or operatic aria, while a series of Brailled dots on special paper communicates through texture (touch) to the blind. By creating, improving, and multiplying these technical processes, mankind continues to free communication from the limitations of time and space.

In the process of encoding, a writer must translate his or her thoughts into a limited number of signs and symbols—thereby omitting some elements, distorting others, and ultimately transforming the whole message into something quite different from what it was originally (that is, ideas and images tucked away in a human mind). Yet, these restrictions are a small price to pay for the portability of our modern verbal and visual languages.

More specifically, *signs* are usually regarded as letters, words, and phrases—or gestures and facial expressions—which are utilized according to certain rules. In writing, there are rules of grammar and syntax; or, in terms of culture, we have the handshake (a sign of greeting), and the wink (a sign of mischief or frivolity).

Symbols, too, are items which represent other things. H_2O is a chemical (verbal) symbol which stands for water, while a red light on a street corner is a traffic (visual) symbol which says stop. But these examples are what Erich Fromm would call "conventional" symbols—those generally accepted and understood throughout modern society.

Two other types of symbols account for the problems people have in communicating clearly. "Accidental" symbols are personal ones—words, sounds, pictures, or combinations thereof, which represent something specific to one person (or, perhaps, to a small number of people) because of past experiences, specific behavior patterns, or individual characteristics. A jar of pure, sweet honey may represent a pleasant taste sensation or a company specializing in natural products; but to a camper recovering from bee stings, the significance may be quite different. Similarly, while most of us find a bag of garbage (or even the thought of it) somewhat repulsive, soil experts might regard it as a genuine organic plus. Finally, though the sound of a doorbell may, for many people, signal the presence of an unknown visitor, those familiar with a long series of TV commercials have been known to chorus: "Avon Calling!" whenever the situation arises.

"Universal" symbols are those rooted in the experiences of mankind as a human race: fire symbolizes power, energy, and warmth, while tear-streaked faces are symbols of sadness, fear, loneliness, or release, and the act of kneeling or bowing represents servitude or supplication.[4] Here, too, however, reactions may be highly divergent and, hence, cause a message encoder all kinds of difficulties. For instance, how do *you* view a brand new, full-sized Cadillac: (a) as a symbol of wealth and power; (b) as a gas-guzzler; (c) as an attempt at snob appeal; (d) as an example of engineering excellence and beauty; or (e) as an air-pollutant? (And now . . . see if you can think of someone who views it in each of the other ways.)

Religious and holiday symbols, romantic and sex symbols, and symbols of youth, adventure, sportsmanship, and health, are all used every day to encode messages for audiences of one or of millions. They're used in poetry and in advertising; at school, at home, at work, and at leisure; on paper and on tape and film.

DECODING

As the reverse of encoding, decoding is done by the message receiver instead of the source. Decoders translate from the encoded messages they see or hear (or perceive through one or more of their other senses) back to the original ideas and images which the source attempted to communicate. As should be clear already, the extent of knowledge and experience held in common by sources and receivers, and their mutual expectations, behavioral roles, and beliefs determine in large measure how similar the encoding and decoding processes are; and, obviously, no message can trigger a desired response unless and until it's correctly interpreted.

Realistically, however, we can't ever expect to communicate perfectly, because there are no perfect symbols. A "real thing" is just—and only—that specific thing; all symbols can do is represent it. Also, no communication channel is absolutely free of what Shannon and Weaver refer to as mechanical and semantic "noise." *Mechanical* noise is an engineering problem interfering with the accuracy of communication-symbol transmission. (For example, faulty equipment or an electrical storm might disturb the fidelity of radio or TV reception.) *Semantic* noise concerns the precision with which transmitted symbols convey intended meanings; problems here are those of misunderstandings.[5]

Clairol hair coloring gambled with public reaction years ago by asking: "Does she or doesn't she?" in a nationally-run advertising campaign. But while a number of agency personnel worried that the implication might be offensive, American consumers were quick to perceive that the message wasn't just a verbal one. In fact, much of the success of this campaign was attributed to the mother-and-small-daughter illustration which accompanied the question-headline. Later came the "Flick your Bic" campaign for Bic butane lighters. A visual lighter-flicking scene here, however, prevented the line from crossing any immoral boundaries. And, pictures of hairstyles "saved the day" for Prell shampoo's advertising which opened with a young woman's lament: "I was flat . . . till I went fluffy."

All three of these campaigns ran in both print and broadcast media . . . with no problems in audience interpretation. Obviously, however, both perceived and intended meanings are a vital part of the communication process. Like ideas, they're often quite elusive . . . and worthy of further discussion.

Levels of Meaning

As noted earlier, audience predispositions exert a great deal of influence on buying actions. In addition, they affect the meanings consumers have for words and messages. Behavioral scientist David Berlo maintains that all meanings are actually found within people, and not within words and pictures (or signs and symbols); further, he identifies three different levels on which meanings exist and are used.

First, relationships between words and physical objects form meanings at the *denotative* level. For example, the meaning a writer has for the five-letter combination, T-A-B-L-E, is equivalent to the four-legged object on which his or her typewriter rests. The table itself has no meaning, but *people* have meanings in mind when they point to, draw, or describe that object. Despite individual opinions of the quality of the table (or of its usefulness or style), the "meaning" which adults have for the physical object itself is basically the same one they had as children. At the denotative level, meanings are acquired through educational training and personal observation.

Second, relationships between two or more sets of non-word signs form meanings at the *structural* level. A child progressing through school learns to give meanings to arithmetic signs (+, -, ×, ÷, =), and later to algebraic equations (if $Y + 3 = 7$, then $Y = 4$). Letters, numbers, and signs indicating arithmetic operations performed have no meaning in and of themselves, but, over time, we come to associate them with meanings (mental ones this time), despite the lack of physical referents.

Third, relationships between signs, objects, and *people*, form meanings at the *connotative* level. Here, learning becomes much more personal, although the influence of peer groups and society at large is clearly evidenced. A picture is "beautiful" to you because you say it is—and there are no rules that prove you right or wrong. Here, you're making a judgment—expressing an opinion—and the only property involved is one of belief. You're free to change your attitude toward the picture at any time—while the physical table remains a table, and as long as $Y + 3 = 7$, Y will continue to equal 4. Collectively, the majority of intelligent people in the world will agree with basic meanings for T-A-B-L-E and $Y = 4$; but no one need ever agree with your particular concept of beauty. Yet, its meaning is still as clear and real to you as any physical object or algebraic equation will ever be.[6]

The communication process increases in complexity as it shifts from a denotative, to a structural, to a connotative level. Since agreement among people on specific meanings is more difficult to achieve when no physical referent is involved, or when reality exists only in terms of an individual (beauty is in the eye of the beholder), it's most difficult in the connotative area to communicate effectively. A popular expression, often found on posters or bulletin boards in college dormitories, capsulizes the problem:

"I know that you believe you understand what you think I said, but I am not sure you realize that what you heard is not what I meant."

An Example of Meaning

How many times do *you* say one thing and mean another? You tell a friend, perhaps, that you will try to make it to a party, but you know very well you're not going to attend. In Lewis Carroll's *Alice in Wonderland*, Humpty Dumpty said scornfully at one point: "When I use a word, it means just what I choose it to mean . . ."

"The question is," said Alice, "whether you can make words mean so many different things."

"The question is," said Humpty Dumpty, "which is to be master, that's all."

Now let's see how Humpty Dumpty's logic applies to each of the three levels of meaning. Recall that at the *denotative* level, we're concerned with the relationship between a sign and an object—in the physical domain. The following sentence illustrates this relationship:

"The well is full of water."

The meaning most Americans share for the term "well," as used here, is not generally disputed—although many would agree there are different types of wells (wishing and otherwise).

In the *structural* area, however, consider the following uses of the same term:

(1) "Well, *you* brought the package . . ."
(2) "*Well*? You brought the package?"
(3) "Well! You *brought* the package!"

The three intended meanings in this case may be quite different, and they are set apart solely through use of punctuation. In the first instance, the speaker might be suggesting that *as long as* the visitor brought the package, he or she should go ahead and open it. In the second example, the speaker seems to indicate that there may be *trouble* if the visitor *didn't* bring the package, and in the third situation, it's a 'wonders-never-cease' kind of remark: *despite everything*, the visitor still brought the package.

The meaning of the word "well" doesn't change—because words, by themselves, have no meaning. It's still the same letters, w-e-l-l, appearing in the same order; but the meaning *people give* to the word can change: between denotative and structural levels, and within the structural level, as formal signs (in this case, punctuation marks) are rearranged.

Finally, we're back to the *connotative* area, where reality exists in the social sense. A relationship is drawn between a sign (word), an object, and a person (or people):

"I'm happy to report that Grandma is well."

Each receiver of this brief message may have a slightly different meaning for the word "well": fully recovered from an illness or injury . . . getting along (with living) as well as can be expected for her age . . . mentally or emotionally stable (or back to normal following a disturbance of some sort).

The point is, there is no one physical "wellness" involved here, as there was in the denotative situation above, nor a structural concern with the placement and manipulation of signs. Connotative meanings for the word "well" may change from time to time and from circumstance to circumstance. Most advertising messages operate on the connotative level of meaning, especially when they emphasize emotional appeals.

FEEDBACK

The final part of the communication process is feedback—often taken as a measure of message effects. These are reactions, sent from the receiver back to the source: a word of appreciation or sympathy, applause or laughter, boredom or restlessness. Since communication isn't a static process, an alert and sensitive source will respond to the feedback with a message reflecting the information gained therefrom: the word of sympathy is acknowledged . . . the laughter is rewarded with another humorous anecdote . . . or the home-movie projector is turned off and the activity changed to a more interesting one.

All of these examples occur in *interpersonal* communication: in situations where sources and receivers can see and hear each other. But since advertising employs the mass media to reach audiences, it will behoove us to consider a few key differences between interpersonal and mass communication.

INTERPERSONAL COMMUNICATION

Interpersonal situations generally involve relatively small, homogeneous, and captive audiences seen by (or otherwise known to) the source. Message transfer is sometimes slow (as is true when a letter travels across the country, or a seminar or workshop extends over several days), and the message itself is frequently rather unorganized (spontaneous, sometimes rambling, and not particularly restricted by time or space).

In addition, these communications may be relatively private (in a classroom, for instance), and, in many cases, involve all five human senses. Finally, feedback is easily obtained—often instantaneous—and there's usually an opportunity for recipients to refer back to any part of the message deemed unclear or in need of elaboration.

MASS COMMUNICATION

Mass communication is a very different phenomenon. Audiences are large, heterogeneous, anonymous bodies which are easily and frequently distracted during receipt of a message. Transmission may be rapid (especially in the case of broadcast media), and messages tend to be highly organized and severely restricted in terms of time or space. The communications are clearly "public," and can involve only a limited number of senses. Feedback is difficult to obtain, and almost always delayed; and, of course, all radio and TV messages are transient, permitting no later referral at the will of receivers.

While the above may be considered disadvantages from a communication point of view, however, the advantages of mass media systems far outweigh them; in fact, America's second TV generation is now growing up, all but unable to comprehend a life without media involvement. And while advertisers utilize virtually *every* non-personal means for transmitting messages, the mass media pretty well carry the advertising business.

THE ADVERTISING PROCESS

Recall that advertising is commercial communication whose function is to inform and persuade so as to affect consumer behavior in the manner intended by the advertiser. Journalism students are familiar with news-writing's 5 W's—who, what, when, where, and why—and the advertising process involves 5 W's also, though they are somewhat different in nature (See Figure 4-2).

(a) WHO is the advertiser—for example, Duncan Hines . . . its agency, Compton Advertising . . . or an individual copywriter;

(b) WHAT is the message itself—the advertisement or commercial—for Double-Fudge Brownie Mix, complete with words, and pictures;

(c) WHICH CHANNEL is magazines, or newspapers, television, radio, or other media . . . and we include here the "when and how often" elements: the January issue of *Redbook Magazine* . . . or 500 Sunday newspapers, every Wednesday during prime-time TV, or radio drive-time, Monday through Friday mornings for six months;

(d) WHO is the reader, viewer, or listener who is both a member of the advertiser's target market (a potential Duncan Hines customer or, at least, an influential), and, obviously, a member of the audience for the particular medium involved; and

(e) WHAT EFFECT is a communication effect—results measured in terms of awareness, interest, information gain, persuasion, credibility, or any other form of communication. Ideally, of course, this effect will be translated later into sales for Duncan Hines and, ultimately, into dollars—and corporate profits.

These, then, are the elements of the communication process as seen from an advertising point of view. Now let's consider them in more detail.

FIGURE 4-2

Model of The Advertising Process[7]

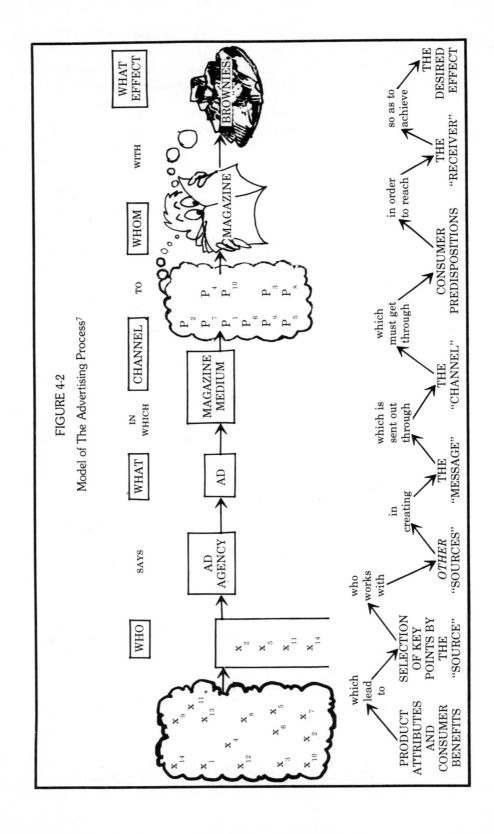

Drawing from research on product attributes and consumer benefits, suppose a copywriter decides to feature the consistency of Duncan Hines brownies in a magazine advertisement. Working with other members of the agency's creative team, and with client approval, the writer comes up with a basic theme (a "magic moisture" idea), decides on copy appeals (a flavor packet, delicious taste, and a "cling-together" picture), and selects a layout plan (half page in size, with a split headline and illustration, short, descriptive copy, and the package as logo). Now, the media team selects a specific magazine issue, and the completed advertisement appears, as in Figure 4-3.

Some readers will glance briefly at it, some will note the headlines and recognize the package, and others will read every word— depending on time and degrees of interest. Then, reactions will form in accordance with predispositions: (1) an "I'll keep that product in mind" response; (2) a "Wonder if the kids would like brownies tonight" response; (3) a "Too bad I'm on a diet" response; or (4) a "Wow! That's what I'll buy for the party!" response.

Between a reader's perusal of the advertisement and the acceptance of its appeals and promises may lie, among other things, a number of personal attitudes, an awareness of family wants and needs, and a perception of product and company image. The more a copywriter knows about the audience before he or she begins working, the more successful the communication will be; then, following exposure to the message, effects can be measured in terms of awareness of claims, acceptance of these claims (or the belief that they're true), an expressed intent to purchase (or at least to consider purchasing), or some other communication variable. But how do we decide which one? That is, how do we know when one specific advertising message is successful?

COMMUNICATION SUCCESSES AND FAILURES

In today's technologically sophisticated society, we've noted that the rapid transfer of messages from sender to receiver over great distances is no problem. New high-speed printing presses roll off millions of newspapers daily, while thousands of broadcast stations send instantaneous signals from coast to coast and, with the help of satellites, around the world as well.

However, as previous discussion has indicated, communication success depends not only on message *transfer*, but also on the message's ability to elicit the *same meaning* in the receiver's mind as that intended by the sender. Returning to an interpersonal situation, suppose Linda writes:

FIGURE 4-3

Advertisement for Duncan Hines

Dear Larry:
I'm sorry it has to end this way, but it'll be best for both of us.

Linda

Thinks Linda: I can't stand dating him when I *know* he's got another girl friend. I'd rather take my chances finding someone else, and this letter will show him I'm looking for a one-girl guy.

When Larry receives the letter, however, his reaction is as follows: I guess Linda's found a new love! And she's dropping me because I won't let her play the field!

A failure in message transfer? Not at all . . . but a breakdown in communication, yes. Linda, the message sender, had one meaning in mind, while Larry, the receiver had quite another. The purpose of Linda's communication was to affect Larry in a specific, prescribed manner. In short, she set out to *affect with intent*: to inform, and to persuade. That, in fact, is the purpose of all communication.[8]

Whether we're concerned with a pep rally, a classroom lecture, a Sunday sermon, or a TV commercial, the goal involved is production of some kind of reaction and response. In particular, an advertising message has as its purpose the eliciting of a specific mental and/or physical response from specific groups of people: the favorable mind's-eye positioning of a product; the active solicitation of additional product information; the resolution to purchase. Since the meaning of a message is in the receiver, however, copywriters must realize that the response they seek may be quite different from the one selected (and made) by the consumer.

For instance, an advertisement for sun tan oil might be designed to convince readers that it doesn't just tan *certain* skin types, but *all* of them (See Figure 4-4). If it accomplishes this persuasive task, it's deemed successful. But if it merely reminds a reader that she needs a new swimsuit, the communication process has broken down. Why? Because *unless the meaning intended by the copywriter is the same as that received by the desired reader, the message is unsuccessful as a communication vehicle.*[9] In other words, the effectiveness of an advertisement depends entirely on the communication objective it was designed to achieve.

By now you can begin to see that successful advertising communication does not come easily. There's never an exact, one-to-one relationship between a mental (or emotional) image and physical reality. Copywriters, however, are faced with the monumental task of "narrowing the gap" between the two as much as possible, because in advertising, the measure of successful *creativity* is the same as it is for communication. If a creative team, through its campaign messages, can create the intended response in members of the intended audience, they have achieved a communication (advertising) success; if not, they have a communication (advertising) breakdown. Now we can return to our discussion of signs and symbols, this time putting them in an advertising context.

FIGURE 4-4
Advertisement for Coppertone

SIGN PROBLEMS IN ADVERTISING

Recall that words are signs—triggering varied responses on the part of readers, listeners, or viewers. Suppose both Jan and Jill hear a radio commercial which claims that a new clock has an easy-to-read face, quiet ticking, and a pleasant-sounding alarm. Jan, whose eyesight is poor, and whose sleep at night is upset by every noise she hears, gets excited about the clock, and Jill agrees to pick one up on her way home from work.

But, calamity! While Jill has no trouble reading the hands of the new clock, Jan's eyes can barely make them out; and, while Jill goes to sleep five minutes after she gets into bed, Jan finds the ticking so annoying she hides the clock under her pillow. In the morning, the pleasant-sounding alarm rings rudely in her ear, and Jan is ready to sue the company for false advertising.

An extreme case? Perhaps—but it points out a serious communication problem. Jan's poor eyesight and highly nervous condition don't make her an ideal candidate for *any* alarm clock. Yet, she feels cheated because, to *her*, the radio commercial communicated something she wanted to hear; the meanings of the words "easy-to-read" and "quiet" in her mind were totally different from those in Jill's mind. A communication breakdown occurred—through no fault of the copywriter—but it might have been avoided if the commercial had been a little more specific in its claims. That is, the signs weren't clear to Jan; they didn't give her sufficient product details.

But was the commercial misleading? Certainly not in the legal sense, and not in the minds of most listeners. Still, the wise copywriter is aware of communication problems which *might* occur—*before* they occur. Intended message recipients may *look* at one thing, yet *see* another. They may *hear* a complete message, but *listen* to only part of it (which, when taken out of context, provides a product picture far different from the one presented by the total commercial).

SYMBOL PROBLEMS IN ADVERTISING

Pictures, as symbols, can motivate people to think or act along certain prescribed lines, depending on the impressions formed. Consider the real estate firm in New York seeking to interest local inhabitants in buying a piece of land in the Hawaiian islands. Advertisements appear in appropriate magazines—complete with beautiful photographs and glowing accounts of living in a tropical paradise. An out-of-work reader, who has never been out of the state of New York, immediately starts dreaming of exotic pleasures. A picture of a sandy beach communicates the idea of an easy life with easy-to-find jobs, and plenty of time for sunning, while hula girls in grass skirts perform to the tune of a slack-key guitar.   Of course, as anyone who has been to Hawaii knows, the cost of living in the islands is extremely high, and the unemployment situation just as real as it is on the mainland. To the well-seasoned traveler, this same message would communicate another story—even though the picture-symbols are the same.

Time Symbols

Other communication symbols used in advertising are a little less obvious. For instance, *time* communicates. In fact, Edward Hall, author of *The Silent Language*, claims it can speak more plainly than words—by "shouting the truth" loudly and clearly where words might lie. Because it's manipulated less consciously than is the spoken language, it's subject to less distortion.[10]

Let's look at a specific example. Between 1:00 and 3:00 *a.m.* on a given day, a telephone ring, the sound of a doorbell, or a rap at the window may communicate one of the following events: (1) serious news (an accident, an injury, or death); (2) danger (an intruder, a warning of fire, or a weather disaster); (3) an unfortunate prank.

Between 1:00 and 3:00 *p.m.*, however, these sounds rarely portend any such message, since the afternoon times do not, as a rule, convey the urgency that the early morning times do.

In advertising, time's "communication value" is frequently employed, as shown in Figure 4-5. In this example, the sales message centers around "waking up" time, and the copywriter's intent is that readers will identify with this communication element and then act accordingly.

By showing up for work an hour late, an employee communicates unfavorably with the boss. Likewise, a clerk who keeps customers waiting while he or she chats with another clerk communicates a negative impression personally, and often on the store's behalf as well. Advertising copywriters, on the other hand, capitalize on time's *positive* factors in developing powerful reasons why consumers should buy. And, while words may aid the communication process here, they certainly don't do the job alone.

Space Symbols

Space also communicates. To demonstrate this phenomenon for yourself, Mr. Hall suggests moving "too close" to an acquaintance who has just asked you a question. In most instances, you'll find that

FIGURE 4-5
Advertisement for General Electric

FOR PEOPLE WHO SLEEP TOGETHER BUT DON'T WANT TO WAKE UP TOGETHER. THE GE 'HIS 'N HERS' CLOCK RADIO.

Two people need two alarms. If he wants to set his at 6AM to go jogging, fine. She can set hers for later.

That's what this great General Electric Electronic Digital Clock Radio is all about. You can set it for two different wake-up times. And it will wake each of you at these times every day, until it's reset or turned off. It wakes you to music. Or to a gentle tone alarm. Today's technology provides other great features. Like an easy-to-read time and alarm display that can be adjusted forward or backward. An earphone jack for private listening. A control to adjust the brightness of the time display for your comfort.

It even displays the month and date at the push of a button. And because it's electronic, it's accurate and quiet.

The GE 'His 'N Hers' Clock Radio. With two separate wake-up times.

Model 7-4685

THE NEW GE 'HIS 'N HERS' ELECTRONIC DIGITAL CLOCK RADIO

GENERAL 〔GE〕 ELECTRIC

he immediately backs up to a more comfortable position. Or, try striking up a conversation with someone standing a distance away from you—and watch her move closer, even though she can hear you perfectly well from her original position.[11]

Copywriters utilize the value of space communication in at least two different ways. First, they take advantage of the social nature of human beings, and employ elements such as a "crowded condition" or, perhaps, a "romantic atmosphere" (either of which communicates a message by itself, without the addition of words or product). Any of several advertising messages capitalizing on the "stay close" situation may then tie in neatly: (1) a breath freshener or denture cleaner; (2) a bath soap or deodorant; or (3) a shampoo or brand of perfume or cologne.

On the other hand, copywriters may, in cooperation with artists, let space tell its own story through layout design. A lot of "white space" around key elements generally connotes a prestigious product, store, or image—even though one of the copy appeals is price. For example, look at Figure 4-6: an advertisement for one of 16 Parks Belk Company stores in the southeastern United States. The annual suit sale at this moderate-sized fashion department store is billed as a "classy" affair—but the company makes no secret of the fact that it competes head-on with stores such as Sears Roebuck and J. C. Penney.

A very "busy" advertisement (with almost *no* unfilled space) often bespeaks a discount store, or the sale of items whose main differentiating feature is low cost (as opposed to "high quality construction"). Figure 4-7, however, is another advertisement from Parks Belk—demonstrating that most *any* store having a massive clearance sale may choose to run a "boxes" layout filled with enticing discounts. The unusual reverse type (white-over-black) does set this particular advertisement apart from the more common sale notices run by some stores as often as once a week.

COMMUNICATION AND PROBLEM-SOLVING

Throughout history, men and women have sought solutions to major problems of national security and defense, and to minor problems of what outfits to wear or which movies to see. In most cases, problem-solving involves decision-making—choosing between alternatives (job offers, vacation spots, menu selections); and, to aid them in selecting the best options, consumers usually turn to some form of communication. Once they have mastered the "languages" of signs and symbols, they watch and listen, read and talk, and sometimes write—for information which will help make up their minds on an almost infinite number of matters. The daily

FIGURE 4-6
Sale Advertisement with Classy Image

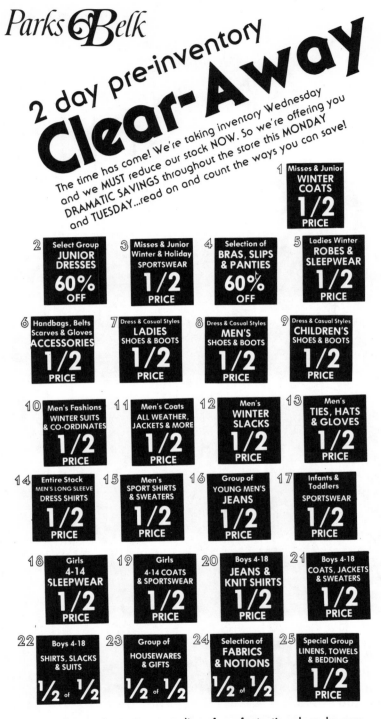

weather forecast aids selection of daily attire, and TV commercials, plus printed brochures or articles, may help identify an ideal travel package or entertaining theatrical performance.

Chapter 3 indicated that people generally prefer taking the line of least resistance in seeking solutions—the method which gives them the greatest reward (benefit) for the least effort (cost). Wilbur Schramm has expressed this attitude through what he calls the "fraction of selection." *Choice*, he says, is determined by the *expectation of reward*, divided by the *effort required*:

$$\text{CHOICE} = \frac{\text{EXPECTATION OF REWARD}[12]}{\text{EFFORT REQUIRED}}$$

Now, recall from grade-school arithmetic that we can enhance the value of a fraction by: (a) increasing the numerator, or (b) decreasing the denominator. Sometimes, advertising copywriters concentrate on the former (stressing rewards): feel refreshed, look attractive, save money; and sometimes they emphasize the latter (minimal effort): ready in 10 minutes, works while you sleep, protects while it cleans. Once in a while, they even do *both*, as evidenced by the TV commercial presented in Figure 4-8. Note that product characteristics promise the user time-saving, money-saving benefits, *and* less work: because a single towel does the job of two. But whichever approach is taken, communication is still just a means to an end. The copywriter writes to inform and persuade, and the reader reads to find a problem-solver which gives "the most for the least." (Note again the importance of product *positioning* through advertising: Marketing Outline item 68.)

In summary, because of the number of products and services available today, an individual obviously can't try them all personally; so, advertising communication steps in, with ads and commercials which explain and demonstrate specific brands and their capabilities (See Marketing Outline item 46). Of course, the consumer may rather ask a neighbor for advice (or check the shine on a friend's car and then ask which brand *he* uses)—but, chances are these people acquired at least part of their knowledge through advertising (either directly or indirectly). The point is, people *seek* information regarding products they buy, so they don't have to gamble with unknown quantities.

But, you may ask, aren't there *also* so many *advertisements* floating around that a person can't possibly see or hear them all? Certainly. And that's where the careful selection of communication signs and symbols becomes crucial. Once the media have done their jobs (zeroing in on *Sports Illustrated* readers or "As the World Turns" soap opera fans), the messages must stop those readers and viewers from turning the page when a specific ad appears, or from leaving the room during a key commercial.

FIGURE 4-8
TV Commercial Stressing Product Rewards and Minimal Effort

Introducing

Bounty

New Half - Sheet Performance Story

(SILENT)

MILLE: Rosie, here comes Isabelle Henson...and nobody can spill like she can.

(SFX: TEARS SHEET)
ROSIE: I'm ready.
MILLIE: Half a Bounty?

ROSIE: Bounty's extra-absorbent, Millie, so Bounty does more of what a towel's for.

Morning Izzie.
ISABELLE: Good morning.
Ooops!
(SFX: CUP SPILLS)

ROSIE: Here Izzie.
ISABELLE: Half a sheet?

It got the whole spill

Quick, too.
MILLIE: Wow! Bounty is extra-absorbent.

ROSIE: It absorbs quicker, and more, then any other leading 2-ply towel.

MILLIE: Any other?
ROSIE: Just watch.

Bounty against the next best brand. MILLIE: Bounty's drinking up the whole spill! Bounty got it all!

ROSIE: Other towels just can't absorb that much liquid. MILLIE: You're right!

ROSIE: And even wet, Bounty's the quicker picker-upper.

ISABELLE: Remarkable. But is it strong?

ROSIE: Strong enough to lift these potatoes, even wet.
ISABELLE: Rosie, Bounty's for me.

ROSIE: Right on, Izzie. Bounty's extra-absorbent. (SFX: TEARS SHEET) So Bounty does more of what a towel's for.

© THE PROCTER & GAMBLE COMPANY. REPRINTED WITH PERMISSION

COMMUNICATION'S UNINTENDED RECEIVERS

As we come to know the people with whom we communicate personally, we find it increasingly easy to attach meanings to their actions, as well as to their words. For example, consider Barbara, a new secretary who, as she arrives for her first day on the job, overhears Nancy, the woman she is replacing, say: "I've just got to get away. After all, enough is enough."

Now, given no previous knowledge of or contact with Nancy, Barbara might wonder just what she meant by that comment. Was the work load too difficult? Or was it her boss who annoyed her? Perhaps she's looking for a different line of work . . . ?

On the other hand, Nancy's friends knew exactly how to "read" her lines: bitterly-cold weather, coupled with long, crowded bus and train rides to and from work each day, had left Nancy a nervous wreck. She may have enjoyed her work immensely, but was headed for warmer climate and a housing arrangement nearer her office.

True, it could be argued that Barbara was not supposed to be part of that communication process—that she merely overheard a conversation which was not intended for her. And that situation occurs in advertising, too, because media selection is still far from perfect. A number of people may see, hear, or read an advertising message even though they're not members of that advertiser's target market and have no interest in trying the item or service advertised.

Fortunately, research has shown that advertisements designed to help increase sales on an immediate basis may serve a secondary purpose as well. Company image may be communicated to an audience which doesn't respond at all to the specific product featured; and, since predispositions are made up of large groups of experiences and impressions accumulated over time, a seemingly irrelevant message may have a positive effect on a purchase made even months later. Also, many companies today are diversifying—adding new products to their lines. A favorable company image established earlier (before a new product is introduced) may be retained by those who later become potential customers.

Finally, remember the importance of reference groups in influencing buying decisions. When product (or brand) *non*-users come in contact with users, another phenomenon may occur. Word-of-mouth advertising (interpersonal communication—carrying company image with it) may go into effect, and follow through to purchasing behavior.

COMMUNICATION AS SCIENCE AND ART

This chapter has examined communication from scientific and artistic points of view; both are useful in understanding the complexities of the communication process. In dealing with the former, however, it's important to remember that communication begins and ends with *people*. When behavioral scientists get too wrapped up in theoretical concepts, the personal side of the activity is apt to get left behind. Consider a final example.

One of the simplest human communication acts involves person A transmitting a message to person B, about an object C. Newcomb has found this basic model of interpersonal communication useful in predicting reactions to a set of circumstances. First, if A (Andy) likes B (Bob), and says something favorable to him about C (Cars), Bob's perception of Cars should be favorable also. Figure 4-9 diagrams the

FIGURE 4-9

Balance Theory
3 Positive Relationships

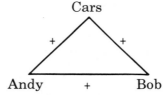

situation. But if Andy's message about Cars is negative, Bob's regard for Cars should be negative also, as long as Bob and Andy are friends. (See Figure 4-10.) If Andy and Bob were enemies, however,

FIGURE 4-10

Balance Theory
2 Negative and 1 Positive
Relationship

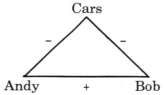

they would *not* be expected to share the same attitude toward the subject under discussion, and Figure 4-11 illustrates this possibility.

FIGURE 4-11

Balance Theory
2 Negative and 1 Positive
Relationship

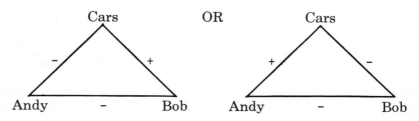

Behavioral scientists group explanations of these occurrences under "balance theories," and maintain that the three-point systems continually strive for "balance" or equilibrium. Further, they achieve this state when they contain an *even number of minus signs* (indicating unfavorable, or negative, relationships). Hence, since there are *zero* minus signs in Figure *4-9*, and *two* in Figures *4-10* and *4-11*, all of these systems are balanced.[13]

Granted, this operation looks simple on paper, and it's not difficult to understand that positive communications about a topic or object on the part of two people may draw them together. (Andy and Bob may, in fact, meet at an auto show, exchange favorable impressions of a particular car, and decide to become friends.) When strong human emotions become involved, however, theories sometimes go out the window. Watch what happens, for instance, when *CARS*, in Figure 4-12 . . . becomes *CAROL* in Exhibit 4-13! *Theoretically*, the situation in Figure *4-13* "can't exist" because it's outside a state of equilibrium (containing an *odd* number of minus signs). Real people, however, aren't obligated to follow prescribed models of behavior.

FIGURE 4-12	FIGURE 4-13
Balance Theory	Balance Theory's Breakdown
3 Positive Relationships	2 Positive and 1 Negative Relationship

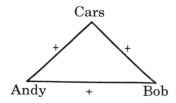

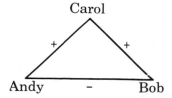

Scientific research in advertising can be extremely helpful to copywriters, of course; but the knack of combining words, pictures, sounds, and sometimes motion in that magical way that produces response is still an art.

Studies have shown that human beings "learn" in approximately the following ways:

83% through sight
10% through hearing
4% through smell
2% through touch
1% through taste

Notice the tremendous importance of the visual channel (reading and viewing . . . words and pictures . . . signs and symbols). Unfortunately, however, there are also studies which indicate that human beings have severe memory problems. In fact, on the average, we're apt to remember only:

> 10% of what we read;
> 20% of what we hear;
> 30% of what we see;
> 50% of what we hear *and* see;
> 70% of what we say;
>
> and 90% of what we say if we *do* it at the same time.[14]

Quite obviously, today's advertising messages have their work cut out for them. Successful communication strategies and tactics in advertising demand a high degree of expertise, and shouldn't ever be taken lightly.

STUDY QUESTIONS

1. Why do we refer to communication as a *dynamic* process?
2. List and describe the six elements in the communication model.
3. List and describe the three levels of meaning.
4. Name three basic differences between interpersonal and mass communication.
5. List and describe the five elements of the advertising process.
6. Under what one circumstance can we say a message is *effective* (or "successful") as a communication vehicle?
7. Discuss some communication symbols in advertisements and commercials—other than words and pictures.
8. Is there any value to advertisers if a person outside of their target markets comes in contact with their messages? Explain.
9. How important is the *visual* sense in terms of human learning?

ENDNOTES

1. David K. Berlo, *The Process of Communication*, Holt, Rinehart and Winston, New York, 1960, p. 1.
2. James H. Campbell, and Hal W. Hepler, eds., *Dimensions in Communication: Readings*, Second Edition, Wadsworth Publishing Company, Belmont, California, 1970, p. 9.
3. Freely adapted from Wilbur Schramm, "How Communication Works," in Wilbur Schramm, ed., *The Process and Effects of Mass Communication*, University of Illinois Press, Urbana, 1955, p. 4.
4. See Erich Fromm, *The Forgotten Language*, Holt, Rinehart and Winston, New York, 1951, pp. 13-18.
5. See Stuart Chase, *Power of Words*, Harcourt, Brace and Company, New York, 1954, p. 18.
6. David K. Berlo, op. cit., pp. 175, 193-213, 277.
7. Freely adapted from Bruce H. Westley, and Malcolm S. MacLean, Jr., "A Conceptual Model for Communications Research," *Journalism Quarterly*, Winter, 1957, pp. 31-38.

8. David K. Berlo, op. cit., p. 12.
9. *Ibid.*, p. 188.
10. Edward T. Hall, *The Silent Language*, Fawcett World Library, New York, 1959, p. 15.
11. *Ibid.*, p. 160.
12. Wilbur Schramm, op. cit., p. 19.
13. Theodore M. Newcomb, "An Approach to the Study of Communicative Acts," *Psychological Review*, November, 1953, pp. 393-404.
14. Matthew P. Murgio, *Communication Graphics*, Van Nostrand Reinhold Company, New York, 1969, p. 15.

5

THE STRATEGY OF IDEAS

With advertising firmly situated as a communication force and a marketing tool, we can now examine creative idea strategy in two parts: first, the verbal area (all forms of "copy," including headlines, body copy, slogans, and picture captions), and second, the non-verbal area (graphic effects, including all types of designs and color combinations). Since later chapters will be devoted exclusively to radio and television, we'll concern ourselves at present with the print media.

Advertising begins and ends with people. As a communication force, it travels from source to receiver and back again through feedback; as a marketing tool, it's involved with people's wants and needs—and, ultimately, with their satisfactions or complaints. An advertisement, however, as just one part of the advertising process, must begin and end with ideas; and, as noted earlier, when the process is successful, the ideas picked up by media audiences are approximately the same as those expressed by the respective copywriters.

IDEA DEVELOPMENT

Intangible, yet potentially powerful elements called ideas are sometimes referred to as thoughts, notions, whims, fancies—even inspirations. Almost everyone agrees, however, that they're *elusive* characters—images in a mental or emotional sphere which (except, perhaps, in the case of extrasensory perception) must be translated into a more physical form for purposes of communication.

Before we examine the transfer from mind to paper, however, we need to consider where these images come from: how do we really get ideas? One answer might be: in *crazy* ways! They pop into our heads while we're eating a pizza, taking a shower, watching a ballgame, or listening to music. Or, we dream them up while we're doodling—or dusting—or driving—or dancing! As human beings, we're *all* "creative" in that we're able to think—to imagine—to wonder "what if . . . ?" And in our thinking, when we associate familiar factors (people, objects, issues, and events) with one another, we can "create" unique relationships. They may be humorous, exciting, daring, even frightening—but they represent a different way of looking at something already known, understood, or accepted.

The headline in Figure 5-1 gives a creative twist to a common word, and thereby helps create a personality for the advertised product.

FIGURE 5-1

Advertisement with Headline Twist

COMPLIMENTS OF LAWRY'S FOODS, INC.

THE CREATIVE PROCESS

So far, it all sounds like a simple procedure. If imagination is an innate human quality, and if, as psychologists, philosophers, and religious leaders assure us, we are all unique individuals, creative ideas should be easily tapped. Unfortunately, however, as a spontaneous, inner-directed process, creativity is very unpredictable. It may or may not appear on command, and it escapes most attempts at manipulation and control.[1] As a matter of fact, by trying to *analyze* creativity, we almost deny the spirit of the act itself. Still, for learning purposes, we need to examine some findings of experts in this area, most all of whom agree that it takes time, hard work, and organized thinking to generate ideas which meet specified requirements and are, thus, useful in advertising.

THE REQUIREMENTS

As previously noted, when creative efforts are called for, there must be agreement on what the exact communication problem is. For instance, if the task is to set kitchen cleanser A apart from competitor B, the creative wheels can't start rolling until we know whether we're looking for: (1) a new way to say 'removes stubborn stains from your sink' (the basic cleaning message), or (2) a way to say something new about the cleanser itself (focusing, perhaps, on additional uses, specific chemical make-up, or recent laboratory tests involving the product). Obviously, these two communication tasks are quite different, and before we start "creating," we must first define clearly the question-situation with which we're faced.

Second, if we're going to associate and combine existing elements into novel relationships, we need a head full of basic ingredients. Granted, the more experiences we've taken in through our five senses, the more material we have to draw from; but, in most cases, we're forced to gather new product and consumer information as well. Specific, relevant data is acquired through reading and asking questions, through listening and observing, and through digging— doing personal research and experimentation.

Third, we must sift through our findings, let elements interact, and then sort them into logical, meaningful categories. In effect, we grind everything up, and then mix and match the pieces (mentally, or on paper if we choose). Alex Osborn compiled an excellent list of "thought-prodders"—questions for copywriters faced with the need to tell a "new story" about a product.[2] Notice how they tie in with Marketing Outline items 49-51:

(a) Can the product be put to different uses; are there new ways to use it as it is, or would there be other uses if it were modified?

(b) Can the product (or basic sales message) be adapted; what else is similar to it—or what other ideas does it suggest? (See, for example, Figure 5-2.)

(c) Can it be modified . . . with a new twist, or a change of color, motion, sound, odor, form, or shape? (See, for example, Figure 5-3.)

(d) Can it be magnified; can something be added to it: more time, a greater frequency, an extra value, a "plus" ingredient? Can it be made higher, longer, or thicker . . . or can it be duplicated, multiplied, or exaggerated to prove a point?

(e) Can it be minified; can something be subtracted or omitted, so it's condensed, smaller, lower, shorter, lighter, more streamlined, split up, or understated . . . or can it appear in miniature?

(f) Can something be substituted: another ingredient, material, process, power, place, or approach?

(g) Can something be rearranged: components, patterns, layout, sequence, pace, or schedule?

(h) Can things be combined or blended: units, purposes, appeals, or ideas . . . or can they appear in assortment or as an ensemble? (See, for example, Figure 5-4.)

(i) Can something be reversed, so it appears backwards, opposite, or upside down?

Fourth, it's time to lay the whole project aside and sleep on it, so our subconscious minds can tackle it head-on. Fifth comes illumination—the "Flash! I've got it!" phase we've been waiting for. Suddenly, the egg hatches, all the pieces fall into place, and we fall madly in love with our new idea. But a vitally important sixth step requires backing off a few paces and taking a second look at our young creation. Before it can be executed in a full-fledged plan of action, it must be reexamined in the harsh light of reality. Usually, in assessing its utility, we'll find the idea needs some polishing and refining, and often it must also be tested for practical application.[3]

A scientific procedure for the "art" of producing ideas? *Yes* . . . and that's just one of the paradoxes facing advertising's creative problem-solvers. Clyde Bedell put it very well when he noted that in advertising: "art and science must meet in method."[4] True, differing circumstances will demand differing amounts of time and effort at each level, but most successful creative ideas do pass through these six stages.

THE RESULTS

It should be clear by now that advertising's creative people are doers as well as thinkers. They're involved with life in all of its forms. They study products, consumers, and competitors from the inside out, upside down, and backwards. And they're never satisfied

FIGURE 5-2

Advertisement with New Idea Suggestion

FIGURE 5-3

Advertisement with Product Modification Idea

COMPLIMENTS OF M & M/MARS, INC.

FIGURE 5-4

Advertisement with Assorted Ideas

until they find those "winning" combinations of words, pictures, and ideas which audiences see, much later, as advertisements. Then, ideally, prospective customers interpret the ideas presented in the manner intended by the creative teams, so purchasing action, or some other behavioral activity, results.

CODING IDEAS WITH WORDS

Now we're ready to see how ideas can be transformed from the mind to the printed page, remembering that, at best, the process is incomplete. Any "code" is merely a representation of the thing it stands for—a sort of shorthand for the (often complex) message it helps communicate. One such code consists of letters put together to form "words": fascinating little devices imbued (some writers maintain) with magic, magnetism, and mystique. But no analogy your authors have come across is more delightful than the one presented by J. Donald Adams. Words, he claims, are very much like money:

> . . . they're a medium of exchange, sometimes inflated and frequently devalued; they're alternately put into circulation and withdrawn therefrom; they're coined, borrowed, hoarded, and lavishly spent; they accumulate interest, blur with age, and are all too often accepted merely at face value.[5]

Chapter 4 made it clear, however, that meanings are in people, not in words. Let's review this contention with a couple of examples. First, consider some modern connotations of the word "sophisticated": knowledgeable, refined, or professionally proficient. In fourteenth-century Middle English, however, the term "sophisticated" was introduced as "an adulteration of the truth," and in the fifteenth century, it was used to mean "a fallacious argument." By the sixteenth century, the word referred to "corruption or perversion of a statement," and in the seventeenth century, it was "primitive simplicity." Finally, eighteenth century users of "sophisticated" meant "made artificial," while *originally* the word was used to describe characteristics of Sophists, a school of Greek philosophers in the fifth century B.C.

Words pack power, and unless they're used with discretion, they can seriously mislead and confuse. A second example stays contemporary, but illustrates an equally complex phenomenon. Suppose an automobile manufacturer advertises that "Lightning Strikes Our New Car Twice," and pictures a double-bolt of lightning which "brands" the new car with "HIGH PERFORMANCE" and "LOW PRICE." The meaning of "strike" here, of course, is figurative, not literal . . . but because it *could* be either, we can argue that the identical term is sometimes used to convey two different meanings. But why stop there? How about the meaning behind "strike" up the band? Or:

. . . strike out a word . . .	. . . strike terror in an opponent . .
. . . strike down a foe . . .	. . . bowl a strike . . .
. . . strike a bargain . . .	. . . strike a match . . .
. . . strike it rich . . .	. . . strike home a point . . .
. . . strike below the belt . . .	. . . strike against a company . . .
. . . strike a balance . . .	. . . strike three and out.

Actually, modern society has more than a hundred meanings for "strike."[6]

Obviously, advertising copywriters must choose words carefully—not only for meanings they convey by themselves, but also for their communication value in context. In addition, the *number* of words selected for a given message should be the minimum necessary to express an intended meaning; when superfluous words are employed, they often obscure meanings (and tire audiences).

USING WORDS TO ACHIEVE EFFECT

Sometimes, words are specifically created to make writing more vivid and memorable. Edgar Allen Poe's "tintinnabulation" of bells is a favorite example of letters put together to form the sound of the object in question (a technique known as onomatopoeia). A veteran copywriter and author uses the term "echoism" to refer to a similar effect; examples of echoistic verbs are: blare, crack, crumple, hiss, hush, roar, sleep, and twinkle.[7] All are simple communication vehicles, but ones which are often more effective in advertising messages than are long strings of descriptive adjectives used to achieve the same ends.

Other devices writers find useful are similes and metaphors—both of which involve application of terms or phrases to things which aren't literally applicable (in order to suggest a resemblance). Generally, the difference between the two lies in the presence of the word "like" or "as" in the case of similes and its absence in the case of metaphors. Examples are: "Feel Like a Million Bucks" (for Buc Wheats cereal), and the "Sunshine Look and Taste" (for French's mustard).

In addition, names of products (and stores and services) often employ symbolism, and thereby lend themselves to a wide range of creative treatments. For instance, a "Dagwood" sandwich automatically suggests a large assortment of ingredients—plus a king-sized appetite. A "Rocky Road" sundae includes the nuts and other crumbly toppings needed to approximate our mind's-eye picture of its namesake. Automobile companies have long since jumped on the bandwagon here, and advertising copy frequently plays up images of the Mustang, Cougar, and Rabbit. Finally, even if a new store had done no preliminary advertising, consumers wouldn't have much trouble figuring out the type of merchandise carried by the "Stork's Cradle."

FREE CREATIVITY

The creative writer—poet, novelist, playwright—takes well-known words and phrases and develops a fresh, often brilliant manner of presentation. Thus, a perennial plant, a familiar season, and a bird's home became the classic: "Tree that may in summer wear a nest of robins in her hair," in the hands of Joyce Kilmer. And, while anyone who so desires might write about ambition and power, there's only one *Macbeth*.

In both these cases, the creator's purpose was self-expression. Similarly, a student who is assigned a creative-writing project lets his or her imagination run free. The purpose is to achieve a self-satisfying verbal portrayal of images and impressions. If the end product provides insight and enjoyment for others, so much the better—but even if reactions are negative, the work is no less creative.

Advertising copywriters write with a different purpose in mind—to achieve the objectives of a particular client: to convince people that one product is stronger than another; to inform them of an improved service; to enhance the credibility of a store's claims (or, perhaps, dispel negative attitudes toward the store). Note that these are not the "entertainment" objectives which may be held by comedy or dramatic writers. Still, few persons involved in advertising creativity believe that advertisements cannot or should not entertain.

The problem is one of creative channeling. The question becomes not, "How can we best entertain?" but, rather, "Is entertainment the best way to communicate our sales message?" In other words, can we successfully explain a product's benefits through entertainment, or can we more easily and effectively persuade people to try the product if we stick to a factual demonstration?

In any case, copywriters must put selling wheels under each creative idea so it can travel the marketing communication circuit successfully. And in terms of message strategy, we might note that the more carefully the tracks are laid, the more smoothly the message carriers (the ultimate advertisements) will roll.

THE "EXPOSURE" TRACK

First, and rather obviously, advertising messages must be available to potential audiences if exposure is to occur. (See Marketing Outline item 87.) Some copy decisions, therefore, must revolve around media feasibility. If a conceptualized advertisement is impractical with regard to production time, cost, or other resource limitations, it does little good for creative personnel to dream about it. For instance, a highly detailed two-page spread or fancy fold-out insertion in one of the nation's leading magazines may be considered ideal for presentation of a sales message, but it might also call for funds well beyond the advertiser's budget.

Similarly, a writer's brainstorm for a twenty-five-word headline in 18-point type might exceed space availabilities in the newspaper in which the advertisement must appear. In short, creative teams must channel their production demands around the resources at hand (remembering that more, not less, creative talent is often needed to develop an effective campaign around tight budget and facilities constraints).

Second, if an advertisement is directed to the wrong readers, even the most original, clever, dynamic copy is composed for naught. It matters little that ten million small and short people think an advertisement for a "big and tall" shop is cute, dramatic, or even captivating, if their big and tall counterparts are offended by it.

On the other hand, when an analgesic advertisement promises prompt relief to headache sufferers and sincerely interests them in buying the product, any displeasure expressed by *non*sufferers with reference to the advertisement is of little concern to the client.

In both cases, as Chapter 3 pointed out, audience selection refers to the choice of both appropriate demographics and relevant psychographics for the advertisement in question. Few would argue that different copy appeals are needed to sell shoes to sixteen-year-old girls living in a wealthy Eastern suburb, on the one hand, and to sixty-year-old farmers' wives living on the Kansas plains, on the other. In each instance, copy might include slogans, humorous appeals, or questions-and-answers with supporting evidence—but creative ideas must be channeled to reach each audience in its own language (through words and expressions meaningful to them—appropriate to their own ways of thinking).

The creative slant for decongestants changes as the market shifts from hay fever sufferers in a heavy pollen season, to persons bothered by nagging winter colds. While creative genius is called for in both situations, it must be channeled in each one to suit characteristics of the intended audience.

Finally, a choice example of audience identification in advertising was used by a bank in East Africa. The problem lay in communicating the idea of saving money and earning interest—to a populace just learning what money really *was* (and without the slightest notion of what was meant by "interest"). The solution was the following line, translated literally from the Swahili: "Put money in bank. Come back in a year . . . and money have babies!"

THE "ATTENTION-GAINING" TRACK

Suppose an agency's creative team has planned an advertisement for the appropriate audience, and in a way that's feasible in terms of resources. Now if the message fails to attract attention, and prospective customers don't bother to read it, the advertiser again fails to benefit.

There are many ways to achieve this attention-getting function, and future chapters will consider them in detail. Suffice it to say at this point that simply "having an idea" is not enough; the manner in which that idea is expressed can make a big difference in the stopping power of an advertising message, and in its exposure to intended receivers.

Headlines, for example, must give readers some reason for halting (at least temporarily) their progress through a newspaper or magazine; the whole headline idea should lead so directly and logically to other elements of the advertisement (illustrations, body copy, and signature/logo) that readers are actively encouraged to follow. Journalists often speak of "news value"—and relate it to personal impact, conflict, rare events, and public figures. They hasten to admit, however, that there is no foolproof way to determine exactly which events have the greatest value for readers. Similarly, in advertising, there is no set rule for predicting the attention value of specific words or expressions; the strategies discussed in this chapter, however, will be useful when we consider specific message tactics.

THE "INVOLVEMENT" TRACK

Interesting copy is friendly copy—inviting copy. Just as customers don't buy from rude or offensive salesmen, they won't contend with discourteous or insulting advertisements. Enthusiasm, on the other hand, actually beckons readers to participate. Notice the difference between the following sets of copy for Perry's Pizza:

COPY #1
You must buy Perry's frozen pizzas today. They can be cooked in the oven in ten minutes. You should not call a delivery service . . . and you have no right to spend extra money eating out when Perry's is available for less. There are six different ingredient-combinations, and that's enough to please even you. There are also three sizes so you can buy whichever one you want and eat as much as you want . . . and also let your date have some. Perry's frozen pizzas are sold at almost all supermarkets, and smart people will buy some right now. Don't even think about other brands . . . because there's nothing else to consider.

COPY #2
Hey, gang—how 'bout having a fresh, pipin' hot pizza right at home? No, don't call a delivery service . . . and save your extra cash, too. Just pop a Perry's frozen pizza in your oven! Choose from six varieties—and in ten short minutes, you'll have delicious, tangy pizza. Nibble on a small cheese . . . share a pepperoni regular with that special pizza-lovin' date . . . or eat hearty with anchovies, onions, mushrooms, *the works*—and king-size! So fresh, so tempting, so *good* you can almost smell

that aroma right through the box. Pick up a Perry's at your supermarket . . . for pizza-lovin' flavor at a pizza lover's price.

Fortunately, you aren't likely to encounter an actual advertisement written as poorly as #1 above, but it does underscore an important point. Once a headline has done its job (with or without visual support), a large part of an advertisement's success may depend on the presentation of invigorating body copy. Interesting, involving messages are developed through: (a) support of claims (for the sake of credibility), (b) repetition of claims (for the sake of memorability), and (c) relevance of claims to audience wants and needs (so the ultimate result is consumer action). Veteran copywriter William Bernbach once wisely advised that neither dullness nor irrelevant brilliance will sell.[8]

Numerous psychological studies also offer tips for copywriters on how to involve audiences with a message:[9]

(1) *Novelty*

In today's complex society, news breeds interest: fresh, intriguing, surprising things about people, places, and events . . . and news about products (and their features and uses), and services. From novelty devices, through fads and fashions, to the latest model cars—the desire to be up-to-date keeps pace with people's never-ending search for the "good life."

(2) *Familiarity*

On the opposite side, familiarity also stimulates interest. Research shows that something known inspires more confidence than something unknown.[10] Presentation of problems, needs, or desires familiar to an audience does a lot to involve them with an advertisement (as they discover how their *own* problems, needs, or desires can be met and solved). Of course, examples must use popular terminology so consumers comprehend readily—and the more specific (precise) the language, the more easily readers can identify with it.

The *minimum* effect of this principle can be seen if we apply our discussion of body copy back to headlines. Sometimes, readers take just enough time to catch a glimpse of an advertisement before turning the page. If the headline (a) names the product, service, or store in question, (b) identifies a well-known situation or event easily and memorably associated with that product, service, or store, or (c) leads so clearly to the illustration (which itself identifies the advertiser) that readers make the association, its existing image can still work in its favor long after audiences have tuned out. Even a little spark of interest can pay large dividends in terms of communication value.

(3) *Conflict*

Conflict seems to brew its own intrigue, challenging readers to play along with a character struggling to overcome odds, or to choose sides in a contest. Sometimes copywriters find they can use "battle language," too, if it helps establish the appropriate mood.

(4) *Suspense*

An air of mystery surrounding an advertisement is hard to ignore. A puzzle, by its very nature, begs to be solved—a riddle to be answered. Copywriters must just be careful not to make the solution so long and involved that readers wind up quitting halfway through.

(5) *Humor*

All the world may love a clown, but effective, humorous advertising copy is extremely difficult to write. Somehow, jokes are much more interesting than products, and while relevant humor *can* help sell, advertisements which do nothing more than provide laughs have failed as marketing communication vehicles. One successful radio commercial which used humor as a tactic appears in Figure 5-5.

FIGURE 5-5

Radio Commercial Using Humor

Client: Hopaco Stationers   Products: Office Supplies
Length: 60 Seconds   Station: KGMB

MUSIC:	LIGHT BKGD MUSIC UNDER THROUGHOUT
HERBERT:	I've been thinking, Felicia . . . I'd like to spruce up the office.
FELICIA:	For the "willowy one" from the typing pool, I suppose . . . ?
HERBERT:	Now whatever—
FELICIA:	Yes, Herbert, *whatever* you want for your office . . . *Hopaco* has it.
HERBERT:	Everything . . . at one place?
FELICIA:	Uh-huh . . . and you save on office machines, typewriters, files, and all paper products . . . plus clocks, furniture . . . *everything.*
HERBERT:	Wow!
FELICIA:	Except, perhaps . . . a secretary who takes dictation!
HERBERT:	Felicia, Miss Sweets is very good at doing just what I ask of her.
FELICIA:	I'm sure she is, darling.
HERBERT:	Yes, and she gives—I mean, she *adds* . . . I mean—
FELICIA:	Adding machines and paper clips . . . desk sets and decorator items—Hopaco has it all . . . including a beautiful new calculator. Which reminds me, Darling—
HERBERT:	Yes?
FELICIA:	Did Miss Sweets *also* work late last night?

HERBERT: We were checking her ribbons.

FELICIA: I'll bet!

HERBERT: Typewriter ribbons, Felicia . . . her typewriter ribbons . . .

FELICIA: Get them, too—everything for your office . . . at Hopaco.

HERBERT: At Hopaco!

Courtesy of K59 Radio, Honolulu

Of course, there are many other techniques for establishing reader involvement. In fact, aspiring copywriters would do well at this point to begin developing their own lists. As a rule, though, interesting copy includes *variety* in sentence construction and length, choice of words, and even combinations of letters. Such copy is usually livelier and more enjoyable to read than a constant barrage of highly similar and commonplace phrases. Also, the *personal* approach (often called the "you" attitude) is a must; copy which chats with readers is much more likely to score points than is copy which pompously instructs or preaches. Trite expressions (cliches used simply because copywriters are too lazy to think for themselves), generalities (which could apply equally well to dozens of competing products), and dull, formal speeches do not belong in advertisements for today's audiences.

THE "PERSUASIVE" TRACK

Economists often claim to be in favor of advertisements which inform, but opposed to those which persuade. Since meanings are in people, however, many familiar advertising claims can easily be construed as both informational and persuasive. For instance, the line "easy to use" might be regarded merely as "product description" (information), and read: "easy to *use*." Or, it could be considered as a real "urge to buy" (persuasion), and read: "*easy* to use!"

Examining this matter in another context, we might note efforts on the part of news media to keep editorial content separate from advertising, and fact separate from opinion. Traditionally, the promotion of lotteries has not been permitted on radio and TV. Recently, however, a number of states have adopted lotteries as fund-raising devices, and the announcement of winners' names is considered newsworthy information.

One school of thought sees this name-announcement as purely informational in content. If, however, a listener or viewer hears that a best friend (or, for that matter, a worst enemy) has just become a millionaire, might he or she not be persuaded (and very forcefully so) to buy a lottery ticket (or a dozen—or a hundred) immediately: to "keep pace" with the friend, or to "show up" the enemy?

Granted, inexpensive and non-technical products tend to be advertised with a great deal of "basic persuasion." When consumers are already familiar with the merchandise involved, copywriters often find they can create desire for a specific brand without a lot of verifiable data. (Examples include certain food products, cosmetics and toiletries, wine and tobacco.)

"Basic information," on the other hand, is needed in advertisements for products which require (1) advocacy of a point of view (institutional advertising), (2) mechanical operation (office equipment), or (3) special ordering/purchasing arrangements (insurance, books, records). In these cases, specific, verifiable facts are involved.[11]

It's important to stress, however, that both of the above strategies should incorporate a merchandise story *and* a consumer message. Sheer "product copy" for an appliance might wind up something like this:

> The Apco appliance has 14 moving parts, is available in three colors, and can be used in every room of the house at low, medium, and high speeds. It weighs seven pounds, has a plastic safety shield around the plug, and costs $10.95. Get one today.

In effect, this copy says: "Apco has this and this and this and this . . . so buy it." But consumer reaction is likely to be: *why*? What *about* all those features? What do they all do *for me*?

A sheer "benefit pitch," however, might lead to the following copy:

> The Apco appliance is the easiest to use, most artistic, dependable, and versatile appliance available in its field. It's the lightest, safest product of its kind, as well as the least expensive. Get one today.

Begging for a moment the question of claim legality (the use of superlative terms here might lead to legal complications), the copy is so boastful and exaggerated that a probable consumer reaction would be: I don't believe it! Where's the *proof*?

If a piece of copy is to do a persuasive job (converting audiences from mild interest to genuine conviction), it must show them both how and why they'll be better off with this product than without it. For example: "The Apco appliance is easy to use *because* it has 14 moving parts . . . attractive *because* it comes in three colors . . . safe *because* its plug is shielded."

Why must verbal strategy include the tying of consumer values to product features? Certainly not because consumers are too "dense" to figure out the relationships for themselves. In fact, if the copy is simple, clear, and specific (as it should be), readers should be able to draw conclusions easily. The point is, an audience will neither take the time nor make the effort to supply missing links in the chain of understanding—to prove to themselves that benefit B follows naturally from selling point A. If you read that the plug on a new appliance came equipped with a plastic shield, would you stop dead in your tracks to exclaim: "Hey! A new plastic shield! That's a safety device not found on other plugs . . . which means no more danger of electric shock . . . and, therefore, my kids can play safely on the floor and I won't have to worry!" Of course not . . . so the copy-writer does it for you.

In addition, given that consumers often pay only passing attention to an advertisement, and have relatively short memories, research evidence indicates that *one* major sales theme is usually plenty for one message. Minor selling points and benefits might also be included ("available in two convenient sizes," or "new green decorator boxes"), but powerful motivating elements such as time- and work-saving devices, health and cosmetic appeals, and safety and prestige factors had best be handled one at a time. If a single product or service has a number of these values, copywriters have enough material for a series of different message themes, in the same or different media. Just as they cannot gear a given message to an entire market (but must concentrate, rather, on specific audiences), neither do they include all possible selling claims and features in one advertisement.

THE "ADVERTISER IMAGE" TRACK

If advertising copy is to convince consumers to do business with one particular company, it must be channeled with respect to advertiser image. Hallmark greeting cards carry with them an aura of quality and good taste. Their well-known slogan, "When you care enough to send the very best," sets them apart from other cards. Suppose, however, that one day Hallmark created a card which sold for a penny. Would ads for such a card ever brag: "It's the cheapest card you can buy!" Certainly not—even though the claim was perfectly true. Hallmark would simply not stand for association with "cheapness." (Note, however, that there *are* ways to promote an inexpensive card: (a) to children, "Look what Hallmark gives you for your pennies," or, perhaps (b) to grandparents, "Remember when a penny was precious? It still is—at Hallmark.")

Anyone familiar with the "Aloha Spirit" in Hawaii (the attitude of fellowship, kindness, and love) will appreciate a second illustration here. While the word "aloha" represents a variety of meanings, one of the most widely accepted is "good-bye." One Hawaiian advertiser once asked copywriters to work "aloha" into a company theme line—using the words "GOOD *BUY*." Fortunately, the adver-tisements never ran, and a disastrous blow to company and advertising images was averted.

These examples underscore our earlier discussion of "digging for facts." Before copy teams can begin working, they must have background material on the product or service being advertised: descriptions of physical make-up (size, shape, weight, texture, color), packaging, and branding; details regarding usage, servicing, pricing, and availability; reports on past advertising successes and failures; and results of studies on consumer attitudes and buying behavior.

THE "CREDIBILITY" TRACK

Occasionally, a copywriter's claim—say, for a household cleaning agent—may appear to be mere "product puffery." Homemakers need only try the product once, however, before discovering the exaggeration, and ensuing copy for the same item, though highly "creative" in nature, will fall by the wayside. On the other hand, advertising which is accurate to the last detail is of little value if it's not believable.

For example, even if a medication is someday discovered for an instant cure of the common cold, advertising creative strategy will have to center around some very carefully-laid persuasive tracks; otherwise, consumers' deep-rooted skepticisms regarding cold remedies may prevent acceptance of the message. Actually, we have a kind of "truth battle" here, summarized by the following:

The Copywriter's _____

The truth isn't any good unless people believe you . . .
And they can't believe you if they don't know what you're saying . . .
And they can't know what you're saying if they don't listen to you . . .
And they won't listen to you if you're not interesting . . .
And you won't be interesting unless you say things originally and imaginatively . . .
And originality and imagination won't help unless you tell the truth![12]

The question is, would you place the word "dilemma" or the word "challenge" in the title of this piece? (Your answer may tell a lot about your future as a copywriter!)

While legal implications are discussed in Chapter 12, we're reminded here that *literal* truth or falsity isn't much of an issue in advertising today. The rise of consumerism and resulting government regulations have left us pretty well assured that advertisers claiming specific product ingredients and physically verifiable capabilities can, in fact, prove their contentions. What we're concerned with today is truth *as perceived by the consumer* ("credibility"). Without it, advertisements haven't got a chance for successful communication. William Blake's famous warning still rings true: "A truth that's told with bad intent . . . beats all the lies you can invent."

THE "ACTION" TRACK

American consumers have become conditioned to much of the advertising around them, and appear oblivious to most of it. Successful copywriters must recognize the difficulty of breaking through tough shells of indifference, and make certain that advertisements spell out precisely what the audience is expected to do: to visit (physically) a new restaurant, or to associate (mentally) a manufacturer's name with high-quality merchandise.

Assuming that the basic reward promised does indeed hit home with an audience, creative teams stress such action aids as: (1) convenient and ample availability; (2) simple payment terms; (3) immediate pick-up or delivery; and (4) special bonuses for buying *now*. Continued use of the consumer's own language, too, helps make a call to action both clear and inviting.

The importance of making it easy to comply with an advertiser's wishes should be obvious. The consuming public is, in certain respects at least, essentially lazy. Few of us really want to work any harder than absolutely necessary to get what we want: be it money and material possessions, leisure time, or that somehow always elusive thing called happiness. Even though advertising messages promise many sought-after benefits, however, some "work" is involved in getting them. Then, to make matters worse, these advertisements are often "interruptions" in the midst of a good magazine story or newspaper article. Hence, it's vital that copywriters develop ways to *ease* consumers into a sale—by understanding and developing the kinds of appeals which rank high in their value systems.

Finally, slogans are often employed as valuable, memorable devices which may continue inducing action long after the advertisements in which they appear have been forgotten. Three key questions for copywriters here are: (1) is the slogan catchy (because unless it grabs attention, it can't do its job); (2) is it short and simple (because it must be remembered . . . and set clearly apart from competitors' slogans); and (3) is it relevant to the basic selling theme . . . and in keeping with the other "creative channeling" efforts?

THE ULTIMATE STRATEGY: SALES MESSAGES, NOT "ADS"

Strange as it may sound, despite all the suggestions in this chapter for verbally effective advertisements, the best messages are those which are the least obvious. One of the copywriter's greatest challenges is to put the *product or service* in the spotlight, while the advertisement is all but overlooked (as an advertising message).

The story has been told of a room with a large picture window overlooking a beautiful garden. The room is vacant except for three mirrors on the wall opposite the window. A visitor and his guide enter the room and stop at the first mirror—which is dirty, scratched, and in generally poor repair. The guide points to this mirror and asks: "What do you see?" And the visitor says: "I see an ugly mirror."

Moving to the second mirror, an immaculate and ornate object with an elaborate, jeweled frame, the guide asks: "Now what do you see?" And the visitor replies: "I see a beautiful mirror."

The third mirror is clean and neat, but perfectly plain. "And what do you see now?" the guide asks. "I see," says the visitor, "a beautiful garden outside a picture window."[13]

The third mirror was the only one which really did its job. It reflected accurately the scene set before it—without intruding or calling attention to itself as a mirror. Similarly, advertising copy is a means to an end—never an end in itself. When it merely calls attention to *itself* (because "the cartoon character is cute" . . . "the picture is intriguing" . . . or "the punch line is funny"), the product and sales message are often lost.

This chapter has shown that just as advertising is a marketing tool, helping to sell goods and services, so ideas are creative tools, helping to formulate sales stories. Now it's time to examine creative tactics in detail—to explore the how-and-why-to-do-it process that can result in prosperity for both companies and consumers. We'll begin with the print media—newspapers and magazines—and then turn to radio and TV.

STUDY QUESTIONS

1. Identify and discuss the six stages through which most successful creative ideas pass before they are implemented in advertisements.
2. What are some of the *problems* facing copywriters in the choice of words to express an advertising idea?
3. What are some of the *opportunities* facing copywriters in the choice of words to express an advertising idea?

4. Discuss the communication "tracks" along which successful advertising messages travel.
5. What are some methods that psychological studies have suggested for *involving* audiences with advertising messages?
6. Explain why effective advertisements are really those which are *overlooked*.

ENDNOTES

1. Herbert Gutman, "The Biological Roots of Creativity," in Ross L. Mooney, and Taher Razik, eds., *Explorations in Creativity*, Harper & Row, New York, 1967, p. 3.
2. John E. Arnold, "Useful Creative Techniques," in Sidney J. Parnes, and Harold F. Harding, eds., *A Source Book for Creative Thinking*, Charles Scribner's Sons, New York, 1962, p. 254.
3. See Hanley Norins, *The Compleat Copywriter*, McGraw-Hill, New York, 1966, p. 89; Irving A. Taylor, "The Nature of the Creative Process," in Paul Smith, ed., *Creativity*, Hastings House, New York, 1959, pp. 62-66; and James Webb Young, *A Technique for Producing Ideas*, Crain Communications, Inc., Chicago, 1960, pp. 25-41.
4. Clyde Bedell, *How to Write Advertising That Sells*, second edition, McGraw-Hill, New York, 1952, p. 95.
5. J. Donald Adams, *The Magic and Mystery of Words*, Holt, Rinehart and Winston, New York, 1963, p. 3.
6. Matthew P. Murgio, *Communication Graphics*, Van Nostrand Reinhold Company, New York, 1969, Introduction.
7. Clyde Bedell, op. cit., pp. 35-36.
8. William Bernbach, "The Four Disciplines of Creativity," *Advertising Age*, July 5, 1971, p. 22.
9. See Jon Eisenson, J. Jeffery Aver, and John V. Irwin, "The Psychology of Communication," in Lee Richardson, ed., *Dimensions of Communication*, Appleton-Century-Crofts, New York, 1969, pp. 73-74.
10. See Alfred Politz, "The Dilemma of Creative Advertising," *Journal of Marketing*, October, 1960.
11. F. T. Marquez, "Advertising Content: Persuasion, Information, or Intimidation?" *Journalism Quarterly*, Autumn, 1977, pp. 685-690.
12. William Bernbach, op. cit., p. 22.
13. Alfred Politz, op. cit.

CREATIVE TACTICS FOR PRINT MEDIA: COPYWRITING AND VISUAL PLANNING

While every advertisement must perform as a total (single) motivator of audience response, for learning purposes we'll examine a number of creative elements individually in the next four chapters. In Appendix II, you'll find them listed in a Tactical Check Chart; and, there are spaces left for you to fill in your own elements and ideas, since we can't possibly cover all of them in one book. It's critically important, however, that you understand the reasons why certain options should or should not be selected in specific instances; so the Check Chart *isn't* a substitute for sound thinking and creative judgment. It *is* a valuable inventory of topics which can jog your memory (and, perhaps, spark your imagination) before you begin a creative assignment.

It may also be helpful in analyzing the effectiveness of completed advertisements—yours and your competitors'. Finally, when you're asked to justify the tactics you used in an advertisement, the Check Chart can remind you of alternatives you *didn't* select. Each time you look at it, though, remember that every creative idea *must* be in harmony with Marketing Plan objectives (campaign strategy). John Keil, Creative Director of the Dancer-Fitzgerald-Sample agency, calls this rule one of advertising's "simplest, but most often overlooked."[1]

We'll look first at printed advertisements and then proceed to radio and TV commercials. And we'll consider newspapers and magazines *together*—pointing out their physical similarities and differences as we examine their common communication goals: informing and persuading; stimulating and reinforcing; creating images and changing attitudes. Granted, the *media goals* of these two types of publications are often diverse, but the advertising *messages* they carry today serve the same "salesmanship in print" function ascribed to them by veteran advertising writer John Kennedy more than 50 years ago.

Keeping the above in mind, the first copy element to consider in a printed advertisement is the headline.

FUNCTIONS OF HEADLINES

Research shows consistently that an average of five times as many people read headlines as read the body copy; hence, 80 percent of an advertisement's dollars may be riding on its headline.[2] And, in Chapter 3, we noted that people's exposure to mass media content is selective; they don't read in a haphazard fashion, but rather, in a deliberate, motivated manner, according to their wants and needs of the moment. One of the major jobs of a headline, therefore, is to zero in on its intended audience—to cue specified readers that the message at hand is important enough to warrant the effort it takes to read it.

Consider women's shampoos and the consumer demand for thick, full-feeling hair. Now, think of three different women—Patty, Charlene, and Barbara—all young, active, well acquainted with hair problems, and in the market for shampoo. (See Marketing Outline item 80.) Suppose Patty is a meticulous shopper who insists on "proof" before she buys. She expects advertising messages to give her the reasons why claims are true—and she wants to see results. A testimonial advertisement might be the perfect tactic here—the "believe me because I tried it" approach, complete with whatever personal test results are appropriate.

Charlene, however, needs a little more dramatic claim to induce her to act. She's tried several shampoos, but isn't sure there's really any difference. Now, an exclamatory headline is probably in order—something similar to the Herbal Essence line: "You're Gonna Swear You've Got More Hair!"

And finally, Barbara may be the type of person who finds it hard to make decisions, and seeks continual reinforcement. The idea of clean, beautiful hair is enticing, but is a "new formula" really to be believed? In this case, a statement-of-fact is indicated—possibly with a "command" attached to it to help induce action: "This gentle-but-effective shampoo leaves you with hair that begs to be touched.

Experience a new kind of cleaning sensation this afternoon . . . and let *him* experience it tonight."

RELATIONSHIP TO SALES MESSAGE

Of course, attracting readers *to* an advertisement is one thing, while attracting them *through* it (to the actual product or store and to the sales message) is often a monumental challenge. Advertisements which shout: "Look at me! I'm clever! I'm amazing! I'm funny!" often wind up winning eyes and minds for a moment or two, but as soon as the "gimmick" is discovered, the show's over and readers hurry their separate ways. Or, as Alvin Hampel, creative director of the Benton & Bowles advertising agency, in New York, once observed, if audiences remember the *joke* (or the star jokester) but forget the *product*, the laugh's really on the client (and on the copywriter).

The trap to avoid here is "ad-itis": the process of calling attention to the *form* of an advertisement (the non-product parts), rather than to its *content* (the sales message and action-stimulus parts). On the other hand, dull (so-called "non-creative") headlines won't do the job either. So, when Pillsbury introduced its snack food, Wheat Nuts, the headline was *not*: "Here is a Product Which is Promised to be Eaten" . . . but rather: "New—and Guaranteed Not to Last!" Then, the body copy explained why.

EFFECTIVE HEADLINE WORDS

As we look for the "right words" to use in headlines, we'll find a virtual dictionary of possibilities. In fact, if we made a list of words to avoid completely, we'd no sooner go to press than some bright copywriter would find a way to use one of them very successfully. It's not so much *what* words we choose as it is *how* we use them that counts; some of the same words appear successfully in statement-of-fact, command, and question/riddle formats, and in relatively long and short headlines. Also, identical words, used in the same syntactical manner, may prove confusing and awkward: "Sweeten your two-calorie weight problem—with Will-Power," *or* may make a point in fine style: "Sweeten your diet meals—with two-calorie Will Power."

Granted, experience is still a great teacher, and there are a few headline-writing techniques that have proven effective for many advertisers. Just remember as you study them that by themselves they carry no merit badges; words can create powerful images, but in both positive and negative terms.

HELPFUL HEADLINES

Whatever their form, headlines should be friendly. Often, they come to the aid of readers seeking advice. Basic consumer wants and needs don't seem to change much as years, even decades, go by; and, in the final analysis, ads which cater to these motivations still outpull those that don't. After all, if a product is worth buying, it's certainly worth reading about, and paying attention to before the sale is made. Remember that one of advertising's major tasks as a marketing tool is to presell customers; few stores today have sales clerks behind every counter to describe every item.

Sometimes, help is in the form of a command, and sometimes it's more of an invitation. For example, a headline for peanut butter asked readers to "Crunch the Difference . . . New Extra Crunchy Jif," while one for hair dye was both reassuring and inviting: "If You've Never Colored Your Hair (Because You Didn't Know What to Expect), Find Happiness: The 'No Surprises' Haircolor." Or, the friendly, personable image of a store might serve as the heart of a headline: "Say Hello to Smilin' Joe, and Shake Hands With Savings—Joe's Meat Market." Notice that all of these headlines reveal—simply and clearly—both the advertiser's name and a suggestion as to the basic sales message.

SIMPLE HEADLINES

Simplicity can be a complicated matter for copywriters. Headlines which are easy to read and understand, and which make a sales promise sound easy to achieve have only begun to fulfill their assigned tasks; they must also find some clear, but unique, way to relate to prospective customers, lead logically into illustrations and body copy, and keep solidly within the advertiser's existing image.

Convenience is a very popular quality today—in product acquisition and use, in storage and re-use, and in terms of handling and servicing. Headlines that capitalize on one or more of these values without getting word-heavy or confusing make an important contribution to readership. For instance: "When a Big Cake is More than You Need, You Need Stir 'n Frost."

RELEVANT HEADLINES

A headline attracts readers because it's relevant to their lifestyles and demands (physical, intellectual, emotional, or whatever), not merely to the advertiser's sales objectives. Study the Creative

Strategy Statement for a corporate advertisement in Figure 6-1. In this case, a benefit-oriented headline seemed most appropriate . . . and the resultant advertisement appears in Figure 6-2.

FIGURE 6-1

Creative Strategy for General Electric Corporate Advertisement

1. *Target Audience:* Primary—35 to 64, home owners
Secondary—25 to 34, energy-conscious young adults

2. *Basic Company Attributes:* Able to generate nuclear fuel efficiently in large quantities
Concerned with America's energy needs
Constantly exploring new and better ways to provide and use natural resources

3. *Strategy Statement:* General Electric is geared toward progress in the field of energy production and conservation. The company believes that America's prosperity depends to a large extent on its wise allocation and utilization of electricity.

4. *Message Goals:* To alert current and prospective home owners and other concerned adults to the needs for and values of electricity;
To stress the importance of nuclear power and coal supplies.
To urge respect and public support for General Electric's efforts to produce and use electricity effectively.

Notice how this entire message is concerned with consumer welfare and prosperity. Even though a brand name item is featured, the advertisement shows readers how and why their attentive interest is warranted. "The company just wants to sell their products," is generally regarded as a negative reaction to an advertisement, whereas: "That's my kind of company—the one I want to deal with!" is an advertiser's "dream" response.

A familiar quotation may also be relevant to a particular creative strategy. For instance, "See you later, alligator" has been used in advertisements for I Zod (alligator-insignia) clothing. Or, a play on words may add relevance. "Women deserve lots of credit," claims a message for a credit card carrier case . . . while "Ready in a flash" is appropriate for a camera with a built-in flash. Levi's Womenswear advertisements have featured models who proclaim: "I'm having a fit" . . . and for years Reynolds aluminum foil has been known as "The best wrap around."

NEWS HEADLINES

Consumers are ever on the lookout for new products—or new product features—or new product uses. As far as we've come over the

FIGURE 6-2
Corporate Advertisement with Benefit-Oriented Headline

COMPLIMENTS OF GENERAL ELECTRIC COMPANY

years in product development (from instant coffee to instant cleaning), anything new is just naturally expected to be better; and, since "better," in terms of today's marketing concept, translates as "improved fulfillment of consumer wants and needs," the emphasis must be on the *value* of the "newness" from the product *user's* viewpoint.

Obviously, manufacturers can't afford to change products physically every time a new advertisement appears; so, copywriters must find different ways of presenting the same sales stories consumers have heard many times before. Headlines must *cue* readers that a message *is* different—and then follow through on its "consumer awareness" task. (See Marketing Outline item 62.) Examples from recent advertisements include: (1) "The New Colt. Isn't a Datsun. Isn't a Toyota. It's a Lot of Little Dodge"; and (2) "Introducing the Bathroom Cleanser That Clings . . . Amazing New Comet Liquid."

Headlines are valuable tools whose word combinations can spell the difference between a loyal convert and a lost customer. But how *long* should effective headlines be? Again, we can't prescribe. Headlines of more than twelve words may face practical problems of type setting (and be forced to "break" into a headline and one or more subheadlines)—and clarity and simplicity aren't usually facilitated through long, drawn-out attention-getters. In the end, the product, message-promise, and brand image must guide the action taken, although tricky, irrelevant headlines are rarely, if ever, appropriate.

TRANSITIONAL COPY

The second element to consider in developing print advertisements is transitional copy, including *overlines* (that precede headlines), *subheadlines* (that follow headlines), and picture captions. If the main headline does the complete job of message introduction, overlines and subheads may not be needed at all. But they can ease the transitional reading process, smooth out the flow and logic of the developing message, or, perhaps, whet the reader's appetite still further.

Research has found, in fact, that picture captions are read, on the average, by twice as many people as read the body copy of an advertisement.[3] Some copywriters even spread out their messages so each line appears with visual support.

THE LEAD-IN JOB

Recall the discussion of "participation" in Chapter 3. If transitional copy is to lead readers into the body copy, it often presents what social psychologists call "role-playing" situations. For example, a headline might query: "Out of gas at midnight?" And a caption under the accompanying illustration might invite readers to identify with the female driver: "Put yourself in her place."

As audience members play the role of the woman pictured, they slide naturally into the body copy, which might begin with the comforting thought that: "Help's just a few minutes away," and proceed to describe benefits of the particular auto service being advertised. Other headline/subhead arrangements might stimulate involvement with: "Can you see . . . ?" "What would you do . . . ?" or, "Sympathize with . . ." Each one seems to say to the reader: "*Come on—join in!*" (And so does the headline that says: "Fold this page in half to see how compact the product really is.")

Another popular involvement technique centers around what some educators and practitioners call the "How-To" approach. Imagine a headline that proclaims: "How to paint your house in one day"—while the subhead picks up the ball with: "And still have time for nine holes of golf!" (True, the headline may prove very tempting by itself . . . but the transitional bridge to the body copy makes the picture even rosier.)

A "teaser" headline, such as: "Don't Read This Ad *If* . . . ," can set the stage beautifully for transitional copy (". . . You Enjoy Waking Up Tired and Sore!") which, again, leads the reader down a clearly marked path to the body copy. As their curiosities are aroused, people are naturally inclined to keep reading.

THE INTEREST-HOLDING JOB

Transitional copy, along with illustrative material, is expected to maintain readers' interest long enough to get them into the body copy. Chapter 3 discussed a continuum of attitude strength, noting that firmly-held attitudes tend to resist change, and emphasized the importance of identifying specific consumer problems and situations. In other words, copywriters must recognize and relate to *existing* lifestyles before trying to change them in any way.

Audience involvement and interest-provoking techniques must keep pace with societal changes, too. Since today's consumers are learning more, traveling more, and trying more new things, the status quo and tradition no longer carry the importance they once did. So, if brand new products and ideas are presented in a meaningful, relevant way, consumers are often willing to experiment. The value standards presented in Chapter 3 still hold true, but they need to be housed in a little different environment. The cake that once tasted "just the way it did in Grandma's day" now has "all that rich, homemade flavor in an instant mix for today's active mom." And, even then, we have to remember that differing psychographics necessitate our carving our *several* mind's-eye positions for that cake mix:

(1) The lady with *money* first on her list of priorities says: "Keep it *cheap*." So, our headline/subhead appeal is: "Still Just a Few Cents Per Slice. So You Save With Every Serving."
(2) The mother whose greatest joy is pleasing her children says: "Should be *good*." And our headline idea is: "Specially Good Flavor for Specially Good Kids. They Deserve Its Homebaked Quality."
(3) The working woman indicates her time and effort worries when she asks for a kitchen job that's: "*No* trick . . . and *quick*." Thus, in this case our creative thrust is: "Ready in a Jiffy - With No Hassles. You Just Relax . . . and Enjoy."

Finally, regardless of psychographics, most people respond favorably to such "turn-on" words as "FREE," "NEW," "WIN," and "SALE." Retail advertisements, especially, stress price appeals.

BODY COPY

In body copy, we find *development* of benefit-promises, *explanations* of product feature-values, and *proof* of claims. It's important to stress, though, that copy is but another means to an end. The creative goal must not be ad-itis, but genuine product appeal; and the strongest kind of copy is built around what we'll call the X-Y-Z appeal.

THE STRUCTURAL CONCEPT

One of the copywriter's first questions, upon receiving a product assignment, should be: what is there to *exclaim* about this product, in terms of consumer wants and needs? In other words, what particular advantage, value, benefit, or reward does it offer that's (figuratively, at least) worth shouting about? Let's consider a chocolate-pecan cookie, made especially for kids by Kerry's Bakery (which uses as a slogan: "The Kind-to-Kids Company"). Now, suppose our copywriter samples one of these cookies, decides that the combination of sweet chocolate and crunchy nuts is delicious, and immediately checks the price to see if all that flavor shows up in the cost. But no! It's very reasonably "kid-priced"—and now we've found our *X claim* (the thing worthy of exclamation). Is this the only cookie on the market with both chocolate and pecans, or the only one that's relatively low cost? Certainly not. But that fact in no way alters the value of the *X claim*.

The copywriter's next question is: how come? What is it about these cookies that results in the *X claim* as we've identified it? The answer is the *Y factor*: the reason why the claim is true. And a little research reveals that Kerry's cares enough about kids to give them a double treat. They blend sweet, rich chocolate with the crunchy goodness of real pecans, all at a low price for hungry after-schoolers. Again, there's nothing particularly original here—but with a little creative flair, we can add the *Z* part of our X-Y-Z appeal: call it a *zipper*. This is the verbal and/or graphic device that zips up our sales proposition—packaging the *X claim* and *Y factor* in a distinctively different wrapping, so the product will stand apart from other cookies (even those with similar ingredients).

Picture, if you will, two little cartoon characters: one male and one female, dressed in royal "king and queen" garb. *His* display of ingredients and cookies (clearly showing the two-treats-in-one promise), and *her* attachment to her conspicuous purse, serve to support the *zipper* line: "A King of a Cookie—That's Within the Queen's Budget." Thus, a claim which wasn't unique to Kerry's becomes the coveted X-Y-Z appeal: something that does set Kerry's apart, just because no other company is making its promise in this manner. Most advertisers today are forced to use this "claim not currently being made by the competition" as the "original" part of their campaigns because unique *physical* features are hard to come by; furthermore, if a product is fortunate enough to have a tangible difference that proves successful, it isn't long before envious competitors jump on the imitation bandwagon.

DEVELOPMENTAL WRITING

Once an X-Y-Z appeal is firm, the copywriter must expand on it. He or she must describe and support this new creation—clearly and believably—without using what the late Leo Burnett, Chairman of the Board of the Leo Burnett Company, called "repetitious garbage and hogwash" in advertising copy. One of his choice examples of how *not* to write advertising copy took three forms, all based on a sales message for Green Giant Peas:

(1) *DULL RECITAL OF SELF-EVIDENT FACTS*
If you want the best in peas, you want Green Giant. Green Giant peas are carefully grown and packed to assure you of ultimate flavor satisfaction. These big tender peas are the best-selling peas in America because they are best liked. Get some from your grocer today.

(2) *HIGHFALUTIN' RHAPSODY OR PLAIN BOMBAST*
The big green jewel of the vegetable kingdom. You never knew a pea could be like this—dewy-sweet, June-morning fresh and overflowing with full pea flavor. This is no ordinary pea. This is a Green Giant pea, the big green jewel of the vegetable kingdom. Serve it with pride on a candlelit table and don't be surprised if your husband holds your hand a little tighter.

(3) *DEMONSTRATION OF WRITER'S CLEVERNESS WITH WORDS*
The peas plan that ends vegetable wars forever. The Green Giant, who is just about as big as a corn and pea man can get, has a plan that guarantees peas on earth forever—peas on earth, good will towards men. According to his plan, you just reach for a can of plump Green Giant Peas. They're so sweet and tender that the worst vegetable hater in the family will surrender and nobody will call it a-peas-ment. Get some from your good old grocer, like now.[4]

While a student of creative writing might find some real values in these "literary attempts," they're all sadly lacking in terms of selling discipline. So, we'll replace them with three more appropriate forms of presentation:

(1) THE PRODUCT TALE

First, we may decide to spin a tale around our product or company—to recount a success story (perhaps through a testimonial), outline a case history of product or service development (sometimes focusing on a specific societal value), or trace applications in different areas and across demographic lines. However we do it, we're usually involved with some kind of "time" pattern. (See Figure 6-3.) Notice that the headline, illustration, and slogan are very much a part of this sales story, too—reminding us that while we're discussing creative elements individually, unless they work, and flow, and *belong* together as one unit, we don't have an advertisement at all, but merely a collection of "pieces." (For our purposes, the "whole ad" is greater than the sum of its parts.)

FIGURE 6-3

Example of a "Product Tale"

Remember when you were in such a hurry to grow older?

At the time, thirteen seemed like a silly age. It was so. . .*young*.

And since growing up was taking so long, you decided to hurry nature along, and become Very Mature instantly.

As it turned out, the years didn't need any hurrying at all. The girl above trying to look like a Woman is *now* a Woman—and probably wondering, like yourself, how she got there so fast.

You can't postpone the future.

If all that time can fly by so fast, imagine how quickly the *next* several years will pass.

That's why we'd like to urge you to get ready for them.

And that's where Metropolitan Life can help.

We don't just insure your life. We help insure your future.

Let's say you're planning to send your children to college someday. If you take out your own Metropolitan policy, that can help pay for it.

Or maybe you've chosen a career instead, and you have an eye on a business of your own someday. Your Metropolitan insurance can help make that possible, too.

And, of course, men aren't the only people who retire. Women do, too. Your Metropolitan insurance can help make a secure retirement possible, too.

In fact, two out of every three dollars we pay out in benefits go to *living* policyholders to help pay for their future.

She who hesitates pays higher premiums.

At Metropolitan Life, we insure over forty million people. We've been helping people prepare for the future for 107 years. But while much has changed over that time, one fact about personal life insurance is always the same:

The sooner you begin, the less it costs every year.

See your Metropolitan representative. Soon.

Because the future gets closer every minute.

✪ Metropolitan
Where the future is now

COMPLIMENTS OF METROPOLITAN LIFE

(2) THE PRODUCT SCENE

Second, we might deal with product characteristics—features (both physical and psychological) which we can relate to one or more of our five senses. In short, we can *describe* our product—its make-up, uses, and advantages, in terms of benefits. (See Figure

6-4.) Here, we can zero in on tangible qualities, even though, as pointed out earlier, they may not be physically different from those of competitors.

(3) *THE PRODUCT CASE*

Third, we could *reason*—deductively (from a general situation to specifics), or inductively (from specific to general). Now we're talking about *explanation*—a logical type of presentation: because of A . . . therefore B; or, if you do A . . . you'll get B. (See Figure 6-5.) And, reasoning need not deal solely with rational evidence; it operates just as freely and effectively in an emotional realm, so long as the tenets of its argument are logical and its progression coherent.

Some advertisements combine two—or even all—of these writing techniques (depending on the particular X-Y-Z appeal involved). But what, you may ask, about the "purely persuasive" approach to copywriting? Ideally, all of the above approaches are persuasive. They may help expand consumer desire for a product by: (a) pointing out exclusive qualities that can be supported; (b) stressing contrasts with competing brands or with the *lack* of any such product (the effects of "non-use"); or (c) revealing an unexpected "plus factor." As a matter of fact, the whole advertisement should persuade readers to act, although we'll look at specific persuasive words in more detail shortly.

SEQUENCE OF THOUGHT

Even though advertisements are relatively short items (as opposed to feature articles and other types of writing), a coherent flow of ideas is crucial to success; unless thoughts move in proper sequence, readers get just as confused as they do with a poorly organized story. Granted, copywriters can't be certain that readers will look at every word of body copy, or every *line* in the exact order in which it's intended (because a reader's gaze is free to travel at will); but adherence to a few basic guidelines helps insure both understanding and response.

First, convincing logic involves the previously discussed "reason-why"—which may be rational ("enzyme E removes baked-on stains from dishes"), or emotional ("rainbow-colored notecards perk up your spirits and are fun to send"), or both. Body copy merely elaborates on the sales message suggested by other elements of the advertisement. Figure 6-6 is marked to show how the X-Y-Z appeal is developed throughout.

Looking at the matter a little differently, we find that body copy sequence depends to some extent on the setting in which the product

FIGURE 6-4

Example of a "Product Scene"

COMPLIMENTS OF RALSTON PURINA COMPANY

FIGURE 6-5

Example of a "Product Case"

PRESERVE YOUR CURVE.

You can hold onto the memories of good times gone. What's difficult is holding onto your figure. The right exercise can help. So can the right foods. That's why you ought to make a Dole® banana part of your everyday diet. It's sweet and creamy smooth. It satisfies your hunger. Yet a medium-size Dole banana has only about 101 calories and is 99.8% fat-free. Surprised? Not as much as you will be next time you try on that dress! Dole...a friend of the bride.

The Dôle Banana. As a snack, it's a natural.

COMPLIMENTS OF CASTLE & COOKE, INC., DOLE

appears. A *product-development* message involves something the advertiser did to or for the product before it reached the consumer:

HEADLINE: And You Thought All Tunas Were Alike.

COPY: Lots of people do. But see that Government seal on the Chicken of the Sea can? The one that isn't on any of the others? It means Chicken of the Sea tuna gets *more* than the minimum Government Inspection required by law. It means Chicken of the Sea gets voluntary, constant Federal Inspection for wholesomeness, cleanliness and proper weight—and has consistently good taste! No wonder only one leading tuna has a U.S. Government Inspection seal on every can. Only one leading tuna earns it.[5]

FIGURE 6-6

Example of X-Y-Z Development

HEADLINE: Ugly Stains Are Old-Fashioned!

ILLUSTRATIONS:

(Lefthand Side) *(Righthand Side)*

Living room scene. Child whose skin is heavily smudged sits on similarly-smudged sofa.   Living room scene. Child whose skin is heavily smudged sits on CLEAN sofa.

CAPTIONS:

(Above Picture): 1890   *(Above Picture)*: 1980

(Below Picture): Milk . . .   *(Below Picture)*: Milk . . .
Pop . . .   Pop . . .
Watercolor   Watercolor

(And *ARROWS* Indicate Stain Spots)   (And *CIRCLES* Indicate No-Stain Spots)

PRODUCT: (Large product insert near bottom: TUFSHIELD FABRIC PROTECTOR)

ACCOMPANYING
SUBHEAD: Tufshield's On-Guard!   **ZIPPER**

Y-FACTOR

BODY COPY: Yes, today's Tufshield, with its powerful, stain-resisting

X-CLAIM

formula, protects your upholstery from everyday smudges.

X-CLAIM

Spills blot away with a sponge because Tufshield lays down a

Y-FACTOR   **X-CLAIM**

tough stain protector—without changing the look or feel of

your furniture.

"Little accidents" may never be old-fashioned, but if

you've sprayed with Tufshield, freshly-spilled liquids

X-CLAIM

bead up and dab away: neatly and completely. But don't

wait. Try Tufshield now—*before* you need it! Tufshield:

ZIPPER

the easy way to guard your furniture.

A *product-use* message, however, demands emphasis on product functions and related customer rewards:

HEADLINE: We Traveled Coast to Coast on One Can of Lysol Spray.

COPY: 15 minutes from home, Tara had to stop. I used

Lysol Spray on surfaces to kill germs other people leave behind.

Every night we stayed in a motel, I was glad I packed the Lysol Spray. It freshened up stuffy motel rooms.

I found a great way to freshen air conditioned air. I sprayed Lysol in the intake vent.

In the bathrooms, Lysol Spray was a great help. I used it to kill athlete's foot fungus on the shower floors.

Lysol killed mold and mildew on shower curtains and tiles.

Lysol took stale odors out of closets.

From New York to California, there are a lot of uses for Lysol Spray.

Or, an *after-use* message calls for a look at results—minutes later, hours later, even days, weeks, and months later:

HEADLINE: She Conked Out But Her Hair Held Up.

COPY: After a long night's tour of nursing duty, your hair still looks great. Thanks to Final Net - the clear, concentrated mist from Clairol that you spritz on once to hold your hair all day. Final Net isn't an aerosol - it's nearly 100% holding power. So 8 ounces of Final Net goes as far as 15 ounces of aerosol hairspray. You may be too pooped to take another pulse, but your hair will still be holding up. Beautifully.

And, finally, a *product-extras* message focuses on product incidentals—such as the size, shape, or color of packages:

HEADLINE: Crisco Oil's New "Snap Cap" Puts the Lid on Messy Pouring!

COPY: The reason is Crisco Oil has a new "snap cap" with a specially designed edge that cuts off the oil before it drips down the bottle. That means the end of messy pouring forever! Crisco Oil gives you what no other oil can . . . fried foods that don't taste greasy, salad with no heavy oil taste, *and* a new "snap cap" that ends messy pouring!

As long as the copy sequence is logical, any of these settings can prove successful. The "development" approach might set the stage nicely for support of an X-Y-Z appeal, while in-use demonstrations speak for themselves. And, since results are such a vital part of many sales messages, the "after-use" framework is also loaded with potential, while notes on such extras as packaging and product premiums have merit if their appeals are clearly sales appeals and not mere frivolity.

Specific cautions here include: (1) bouncing the reader through the past, present, future, and back again, as this copy does:

When manual typewriters went out of style, cartridge machines took over, following widespread use of electrics. There are even correction ribbons—also on cartridges—and the future will see even more convenience features. Keyton's is always coming up with new ideas . . . but even their very first machines were ahead of their time, because . . .

(2) pushing the reader into obstacles which block the learning path, as this copy does:

You know, mountains are sturdy—well, so are Tracy's Travel Bags. They're firmly reinforced, much as your house is reinforced. And they withstand abuse. Just think how nice it would be if your furniture—and car—could stay free of scrapes and scratches! Tracy's bright colors remind you of a lovely spring garden. You can almost hear the birds singing . . .

and (3) running the reader ragged through an endless maze of clutter and trivia, as this copy does:

The reason this skin conditioner works so well is that the entire Silk 'n Sure staff wants to make certain you like and use their product. They really do. They try their best to put your interests first, and to give you just exactly the kind of skin conditioner you need. After all, sometimes you may stay out in the summer sun too long . . . or in the winter, it may be the brisk air on the ski slopes that chaps your skin—making it so rough and dry that you wonder if you can ever get it soft again. Of course, it does take a little time . . . but if you use Silk 'n Sure regularly—no matter what the season—you'll see a real difference . . .

The trouble with all of these examples is that "words" (and ideas) get in the way of the message. The X-Y-Z appeal and, actually, the entire brand selling story, get lost in the shuffle—literally buried under lines of copy which appear to be preoccupied with their own existence. Ad-itis? Absolutely.

MESSAGE UNITS

It often takes a long time to write a little "good copy." Writers may have to *wrestle* with a product, or fact sheet, or attitudinal study for a while before any real "message" comes through. Given that "magic idea," however, the challenge is to express it clearly—and enthusiastically; specifically—and personally; truthfully—but with an air of fascination or intrigue.

Phrases

In searching for that "right phrase," beginning copywriters may fall into the cliche-trap. Somehow, it's just easier to grab hold of a well-known (but overused) figure of speech, or proverbial line, than it is to create a new one. In fact, apprentice writers may find these cliches still "clever" . . . while experienced creative teams know they're usually used without regard for a specific advertiser's objective.

"Good English" is best defined as "appropriateness to the occasion"—and to the writer's purpose. There's no reason to *forbid* phrases like "good as new," "quick as a wink," or "easier said than done," so long as they appear *intended* by the writer and *fitting* in context.

An efficient use of cliches can facilitate the expression and reception of ideas, while a poor use inhibits both. As a rule of thumb (to coin a phrase), a copywriter should be wary of any idea that pops into mind too quickly; if a message is only a "conditioned response," chances are it doesn't hold much selling power.

Memorable phrases are often parts of slogans—company mottoes which appear on labels and packages, pens and calendars, and window displays and delivery trucks, as well as in advertisements: "Where America Shops for Value" (Sears Roebuck), "When You Care Enough to Send the Very Best" (Hallmark Cards), "Just Slightly Ahead of Our Time" (Panasonic), "We Are Driven" (Datsun), and "Nobody Can Do It Like McDonald's Can" (McDonald's Restaurants).

Sentences

As message carriers, opening sentences often answer questions anticipated from readers. For instance, the first line of body copy in a sewing machine advertisement might be: "*Yes*, all attachments are included in the price of the machine." Or, in an advertisement for a picture-hanging kit, the line might be: "*No*, you don't need any tools." Also, a single sentence may serve to: (1) relieve a burden ("When you shop Toby's for Christmas, your bills aren't due till March"); (2) restore a confidence ("Brandettes cereal has added all the vitamins and nutrients you've been asking for"); or (3) resolve a dispute ("A grueling eight-hour test proved the Century battery outlives other brands").

It may also be helpful at this point to examine some of what Bernard Gallagher would call "insincere" sentences—message units which serve to *distort* the intended effect:

(a) *MIRAGE*

This type of sentence "sounds great but says nothing." It tries to sell atmosphere without doing a thing for the product or brand name. Example: "The Dydi Dishwasher makes every home a dream home." (We might also add: "It'll wash all your cares away!")

(b) *PARASITE*

Here's a sentence which associates a brand name with some popular societal or cultural value—but provides no evidence that the value applies to the product. Example: "You need Coco's Cologne, because it's important to feel successful."

(c) *MUCH ADO ABOUT NOTHING*

Next is a sentence that tries to make a major sales claim out of an insignificant product difference. Example: "Raggety's Dust Cloths are so soft, the kids will love helping Mom clean house."

(d) *FRADULENT MEMORABILITY*

Finally, there's the sentence that strives for brand awareness through techniques unrelated to product value. Example: "Peter's Peppers: a name that's bound to make a hit—so big it fills a catcher's mitt!"[9]

Such double-talk does little to carry home a sales message. But what about humorous sentences? Can *they* lend emphasis and credibility? Of course—though they're extremely difficult to work with effectively. While most people don't mind being kidded, advertisements which make them look or feel foolish are losers. Yet, an on-target "hit" in a humorous vein (even if *rare*) can score points for memorability, brand preference, and even attitude change.

Paragraphs

Throughout our discussion so far, we've emphasized the importance of being creatively different—of developing psychologically unique claims, using original words and expressions. But how do we create whole paragraphs of copy, without sounding just like "all the other advertisements"—boastful of our product, inclined to be rambling, and downright dull?

Real originality is an accomplishment of the gifted few. Most of us are imitators, striving (unconsciously) to resemble chosen others. If the imitation is *conscious*, however—deliberate and purposeful—*and* coupled with "variations," we have a different story. Here, imitation can be useful. For example, the saying, "I'm stuck on you" predates most readers of this book . . . but Johnson & Johnson uses it in a 1980's style: "I am stuck on Band-Aid, 'cause Band-Aid's stuck on me!" And, the familiar song title, "Make Someone Happy" has been used with a twist in Betty Crocker Snackin' Cake advertisements: "*Bake* Someone Happy."

Finally, "The answer is crystal clear"—a line popular long before automatic dishwashers were developed—seemed ready-made as a headline for Palmolive's Crystal Clear detergent. Even an *advertising* slogan used often enough to be called a cliche can be "adapted" to suit a different selling purpose. Prudential Insurance's "Own a Piece of the Rock" became "Own Your Own Piece of the *Rockies*" when the publishers of *Forbes* magazine offered Colorado land sites for sale.

Sometimes an advertisement requires no body copy at all, since the message is understood perfectly without it. (See Figure 6-7.) Other sales stories do warrant more information and back-up support than subheads and illustrations can supply. In these cases, paragraphs might be built around the inherent value of a promised benefit or the product's physical qualities and uses.

Paragraphs of copy can help position products, strategically, as: (1) *convenience* goods (ones involving a minimum of buying effort); (2) *shopping* goods (ones requiring some "shopping around"—in order to compare prices, styles, or size and color selection); or (3) *specialty* goods (ones demanding extra effort to purchase—such as patronage of one particular store, or a follow-through in terms of a special-order request). Under today's marketing concept, one product is "better" than another only if it does a "better job" satisfying consumer demands. So, too, does a piece of merchandise find itself classified as one of the above—not as a product *per se*, but according to the way consumers perceive it. Advertising appeals may be quite different in each case—and slogans, spokespersons (if any), and even overall writing styles must be selected and "matched" with care.

PERSUASIVE WORDS

Now we need to examine specific words for their power to convince readers that the behavioral action suggested by a message (ultimate purchase of a product or service) is the most desirable course to

FIGURE 6-7

Advertisement With No Body Copy

pursue. But if whole advertisements are designed to persuade . . . how can we call on selected words to do the job? We can't. Once more, it's not so much *what* we say as *how* we say it that counts. For example, consider words that contrast with each other: (a) "locks freshness *in* . . . locks odors *out*"; (b) "*down* go the calories . . . *up* goes the taste"; (c) "*high* in quality . . . *low* in cost"; (d) "*hates* your dandruff . . . *loves* your hair"; (e) "*rough* on rust . . . *smooth* on skin."

These lines appear to summarize their respective messages in a neat, concise fashion; they don't push—but rather, *slide* readers into position for a call to action. Each one places the heart of an advertisement's benefit-promise squarely—succinctly, but creatively—before the audience.

Sometimes, persuasive words are housed in alliteration: (1) Hamburger Helper: "When You Need a Helping Hand," and (2) Tappan Gas Ranges: "From Tappan to Table—Up to Twice as Fast"; or in rhyme: (1) Pillsbury Plus Cake Mix: "Scratch Has Met its Match," and (2) Bounty Paper Towels: "The Quicker Picker Upper." Notice that all of these value-oriented slogans are friendly— and they carry a great deal of persuasive clout.

But total, genuine persuasion is a delicate task. Few manufacturers today expect a long-term brand commitment on the part of consumers because of five marketing factors noted recently by James Sheeran:

I. The sophistication of advertising appeals and media leverage;
II. The parity (sameness) of products in form, content, and promotion;
III. Intense price competition;
IV. Increases in point-of-purchase advertising and impulse buying; and
V. Abrupt changes in consumers' buying behavior.[10]

So even "brand loyal" customers must be persuaded to continue making a particular purchasing decision. In fact, Mr. Sheeran notes several different types of brand loyalty. *Intentional* loyalty is the strongest form—and the most highly prized by advertisers. Here, the consumer and product are "family" to each other—and "reinforcement" advertisements directed to these people regard them as such. Competing brands seeking a share of this consumer's dollar face a long, expensive, and probably frustrating communication (attitude-changing) task.

Artificial loyalty is a less intense affection for a given brand. Consumers in this category use the product (class) regularly, but may purchase any brand which is consistently available and satisfactory. Competitors wanting a piece of the buying action here must "try harder" than the brand currently being purchased, in terms of persuasion, but the job is far from impossible. Emphasis should be placed on the value of becoming a (newly) loyal customer, rather than merely on "trying something new."

*Voluntary non-*loyalty groups are shoppers who do not regularly buy any specific brands. Since they believe all products are pretty much the same, advertising messages directed to them often stress discounts, premiums available with purchases, coupons, or sweepstakes—short-term devices which stimulate immediate sales. These consumers have no particular attitudinal *or* behavioral loyalty to brand names.

Finally, *involuntary non-*loyalty individuals do have a high level of *attitudinal* commitment to specific brands, but do not make any extra efforts on their behalf. If a normally-purchased item is out of stock, they select a substitute rather than shop around. If the item is picked up by a relative or friend, and it happens to be a "different brand," no tears are shed. If a competing firm stages an enthusiastic in-store demonstration or offers free sample distribution, the buyer "gives it a try." In any of these situations, however, the conditions leading to non-loyalty may be temporary, and advertising communication efforts often carry a lot of swaying power.[11] In fact, a recent study found that a major function of advertising is to affect consumers' *perceptions* (images) of products and brands.[12]

The Second Person

One word regarded as critically important in advertising copy is YOU. Consumer-oriented copywriters cater to *your* wishes, speak to the difficulties *you're* encountering, and appeal to the plans *you've* made, or to the hopes *you'd* like to see realized. Somehow, the emotional impact (and persuasive power) is a lot greater here than it is when readers are directed to "please *the* family tonight" or to buy from a company which has "the gift-buying public" in mind.

News

"New" has already been discussed as a word-motivator, but we've also seen how reliance on superlatives and words which exaggerate a product's differences and performance can detract seriously from news credibility. Readers who accept a superlative claim: "The newest, most revolutionary cleaning development in history!" are often disappointed after product purchase; and at that point, the copywriter has probably lost the chance to stimulate any repeat buying.

Price

Price appeals carry their own kind of action incentive—and it's a positive one in most cases (except, perhaps, when it comes to sophisticated fashion and other high-class, specialty goods). In a recent study conducted by the Cahners Publishing Company, 98% of the respondents indicated that pricing information in advertisements affected their product selections.[13]

The majority of today's newspaper advertisements feature prices (in both headlines and body copy), since newspapers are a local medium and cost variations across retail establishments are deemed worthy of emphasis. In magazines, a national medium, we're more apt to find dollar figures omitted from advertisements, although many a copywriter sees fit to mention a product's "reasonable price" and "low cost features," or the fact that it represents a "valuable investment" and is, therefore, a good bargain."

Positivism

Long before Norman Vincent Peale proclaimed the power of positive thinking, copywriters had learned that consumers were more apt to read advertisements dealing with hopeful solutions than they were those dealing with discouraging problems. (One exception may lie in the area of problem *prevention*, where negative appeals might seem relevant.) Also, positivism can be related more directly to "future planning" than it can to "past regretting." For example, the Savings and Loan Foundation, featured in Figure 6-8, centered a recent Christmas campaign around: (1) the spirit of giving (positive and cheerful); (2) in a "free" context (positive and very appealing); (3) with a child's education as a theme (relevant and important); (4) all tied together with a creative twist ("Give a Future . . . " and "a gift that can't be broken or lost").

Comparativism

Often, a comparison with competitive products is used in advertisements—even a literal, side-by-side, feature-by-feature comparison which has been ethically acceptable (and legally protected) since the early 1970's. Points of contrast and superiority (faster and safer . . . cleaner and softer . . . thinner and sweeter) can help build an X-Y-Z appeal, and unusual or dramatic claims ("decorates beautifully while it repairs completely" . . . "a single application

FIGURE 6-8

Example of Positivism and Future Planning

THIS HOLIDAY GIVE A FUTURE.

THE SAVINGS AND LOAN FOUNDATION COLLEGE SAVINGS PLAN.
It can be tax-free!

This holiday, give a very special gift. One that your child will never lose, break or tire of. Give him the promise of a future by setting up a Savings and Loan Foundation College Savings Plan. The interest earned can actually be tax-free.

We have a free booklet that explains the simple details. So this holiday, make your family's future a little brighter. With a Savings and Loan Foundation College Savings Plan.

Member Association Name and Address

Member Federal Savings and Loan Insurance Corporation
Member Savings and Loan Foundation, Inc.

COMPLIMENTS OF THE SAVINGS AND LOAN FOUNDATION, INC.

protects for months" . . . "survives the 'torture test' without wilting"), if properly documented, can lend an air of originality and exclusivity. Further, the FTC has encouraged the use of comparative messages which enhance consumers' information-gathering activities. The specific words used, however, must be checked carefully for confusing implications and misleading overtones.

It's estimated that between 7 and 25% of all advertisements in the major media today feature some form of product comparison. And, research has found that comparative messages may *help convince* shoppers to try a new brand of product, but also may prove more confusing and less credible than other messages overall.[14] Clearly, even when they're toned down, advertising claims are not blindly accepted by today's consumer. And when they're used to set one brand directly apart from named competition in an advertisement, the reader balks still more, and the copywriter's persuasive task grows increasingly difficult (though *not* impossible given appropriate talent *and* a deserving product offering).

ACTION-INDUCING WORDS

Up to this point, effective copywriting probably sounds like it requires a lot of *painstaking efforts*, but stand by for the clincher: all of them are *futile* unless the final copy element hits home. Interest in a product may be keen, and the desire for benefits intense; but if acquisition is too *difficult*, consumers will rarely make the effort. In most cases, the line of least resistance prevails: simply operated products are preferred over complex ones, easy-to-follow instructions are chosen over intricate ones, and a convenient store, service, or brand of merchandise is selected over one that's hard to find.

Some advertising creative efforts are designed to move goods, such as appliances, slowly but steadily over time, while others must move items, such as perishables, in a hurry. In either case, however, the *consumer's* position must be recognized. (At a traffic light, the pedestrian has the right of way, and in advertising, the *consumer* has.) The more "push" the copywriter feels compelled to give, the more reason-why support had better be given, too.

Though scholars claim that "spoken" advertising dates back to the age of cave dwellers, most early efforts (of the street vending variety) were focused on "direct action"—calling for immediate sales. This form of advertising, asking potential customers to "buy now," or "do it today," later became known as *hard sell* (regardless of whether or not it included any of the "shouting" or so-called "brow-beating" often associated with this technique). Unfortunately, because so many direct-action advertisements do feature a fast-talker or super-salesman approach, the term "hard sell" is often erroneously associated with anything loud or pressured. The old adage still rings true for many car dealers, furniture outlets, and discount stores:

> "He who whispers down a well
> About the goods he has to sell
> Will never reap the golden dollars
> Like him who shows them 'round and hollers!"

Still, both hard sell techniques and their soft sell counterparts (which ask readers to "remember a name," or "think about buying" sometime in the future) serve important functions in advertising today. Newspaper (retail) advertisements tend to be hard sell, since the buying urgency is strong: quantities may be limited, sales may be short-lived, and goods may be perishable. Magazine advertisements, conversely, are usually soft sell; readers don't "shop" national magazines like they "shop" local newspapers (for daily food specials, for example), and national advertisers are more interested in establishing regular (consistent) buying patterns than they are in making immediate, one-time sales.

PUTTING THE PRINCIPLES IN PERSPECTIVE

No matter how many guidelines we present, we're not going to establish any ideal way to write advertisements. Some sales messages will hit home without incorporating many of the concepts we've discussed; others will miss their marks entirely, even though they adhere rigidly to the "rules." The point is, basic creative *training* (acquired, perhaps, from reading and performing simple, repetitive writing tasks) can only call attention to these rules. Genuine *education* gives us the reasons behind the rules, and helps us apply them to varied situations. But it's *experience*—personal involvement with the advertising world—that teaches us how and when to follow rules and how and when to break them. On-the-job learning, often coupled with scientific research, reveals the conditions under which creative prescriptions need to be: (1) rigorously adopted; (2) partially applied—as media or audience characteristics permit; or (3) modified in some way to meet seasonal demands, special sales requirements, or competitive actions.

In any event, words alone are rarely enough to meet modern advertising communication demands. Every day it seems we need more information about more kinds of merchandise—faster and more conveniently than was true yesterday. And, in many cases, it would just take too many words to do the job. So, in the next chapter, we join forces with non-verbal creative tactics.

STUDY QUESTIONS

1. Name two separate functions of advertising headlines.
2. List and discuss four headline-writing guidelines designed to help copywriters choose the "right words."
3. Identify and discuss the functions of three types of transitional copy.
4. Explain the meaning behind the three parts of the X-Y-Z appeal. Of what value is this appeal to advertising copywriters? And to advertising's audiences?
5. Once an X-Y-Z appeal is established, what are three different ways a copywriter might "expand" on it?
6. Describe four settings in which a product might appear in an advertisement, that affect the sequence of body copy.
7. Should cliches be avoided at all costs in advertising copy? Why or why not?
8. Give some examples of "insincere" sentence units, also known as "double-talk."
9. What determines whether a product is a convenience good, a shopping good, or a specialty good?
10. How does consumer brand loyalty affect a copywriter's choice of persuasive tactics?
11. Discuss some differing functions of "hard sell" and "soft sell" calls to action.

ENDNOTES

1. John M. Keil, "Can You Become a Creative Judge?" *Journal of Advertising*, Winter, 1975, p. 30.
2. David Ogilvy, "How to Create Advertising that Sells," *The Wall Street Journal*, June 15, 1972, p. 9.
3. *Ibid.*, p. 9.
4. "Keep Listening to that Wee Small Voice," issued by the Committee of the Board on Improving Advertising, American Association of Advertising Agencies, 1962.
5. From a magazine advertisement for Chicken of the Sea Tuna.
6. From a magazine advertisement for Lysol Spray Disinfectant.
7. From a magazine advertisement for Clairol Final Net Hair Spray.
8. From a magazine advertisement for Crisco Oil.
9. See Bernard P. Gallagher, "The Gallagher Report," Vol. XIX, No. 40, 1971.
10. James J. Sheeran, "The Four Faces of Brand Loyalty," *Scan*, Vol. 27, No. 4, p. 11.
11. *Ibid.*, pp. 12-13.
12. Leonard N. Reid, and Lauranne Buchanan, "A Shopping List Experiment of the Impact of Advertising on Brand Images," *Journal of Advertising*, Spring, 1979, p. 28.
13. *How Important To Readers Is The Mention Of Price In An Advertisement?* Cahners Advertising Research Report, No. 115.1, Cahners Publishing Company, New York.
14. See Terence A. Shimp, and David C. Dyer, "The Effects of Comparative Advertising Mediated By Market Position of Sponsoring Brand," *Journal of Advertising*, Summer, 1978, pp. 13, 17-18; and Thomas E. Barry, and Roger L. Tremblay, "Comparative Advertising: Perspectives and Issues," *Journal of Advertising*, Vol. 4, No. 4, 1975, pp. 17-18.

7

CREATIVE TACTICS FOR PRINT MEDIA: LAYOUT EXECUTION AND PRODUCTION

All members of an advertising creative team should be able to *visualize* ideas and design concepts. Even those who claim to have no artistic ability must be able to "see" (in a mind's-eye view) a variety of ways to illustrate the "good taste" or "high quality" of an apple pie. For example: (1) a beaming family enjoying the pie; (2) an apple tree filled with succulent fruit; (3) a chef preparing the pie; (4) an animated, A-#1 apple revealing its composition; and (5) empty pie plates being passed for second helpings. In addition, copywriters need a working knowledge of print layout and production techniques to assist them in their role as communicators.

The layout itself provides a graphic representation of all the elements which will appear in the final printed advertisement, while a separate *copy sheet* contains all words which are to be set in type. Actually, there is a fair amount of overlap between these two pages in terms of content, though their forms are decidedly different. We'll examine both in detail shortly, but first let's see how layout technique, working together with copy elements, performs a number of valuable communication functions. Certainly, it can help attract and hold reader attention and interest, by emphasizing the selling story in a stimulating and aesthetic manner. But also, it can guide readers' eyes through an advertisement in the direction prescribed by the copywriter, and help them focus on key message elements. An *ineffective* layout may still result in registration of attractive pictures, colors, or designs . . . but if the *product* gets lost, ad-itis scores an unfortunate victory.

Pictorial material for layouts may be created specifically for advertisements (ordered from commercial photographers or commissioned artists), or it may be clipped from a supply of "stock art" (sometimes literally called "clip art"). Much retail advertising depends on the use of already-existing artwork because of time and cost limitations. Hence, "mat books," containing hundreds of illustrations, headline material in various type styles and sizes, plus all sorts of geometric borders and frames, are published every month, and may be thought of as a kind of library of layout materials from which advertisers borrow as the occasion demands. The savings in time and effort are tremendous, but advertisers who subscribe to this service must also realize that many of their competitors do, too. Advertisements may, therefore, have a look of "sameness" about them, although a talented copywriter can overcome this handicap with a fresh copy thrust, an original theme line, or an imaginative campaign slogan.

When *original* artwork is involved, it's usually ordered in a fairly large size, and then scaled down to fit specified layout dimensions (which are often too small to permit an artist to work within them comfortably). Photographs, likewise, may be "cropped," or edited down to meet space (and particular shape) requirements. And sometimes the same advertisement appears in different sizes in different publications. A full page in *Newsweek*, for example, is much larger than a full page in *TV Guide*.

LAYOUT: THE NOUN

As noted, a layout is the visual plan for an advertisement which houses all graphic elements (in varying degrees of finish or polish), as described below:

(1) *The OVERLINE/HEADLINE/SUBHEADLINE(S):* because its type size and style, and even its manner of wording, is often quite different from the body copy, and because headline material is such a critical communication tool, this creative element is considered a part of layout as well as a part of copy;

(2) *One or More ILLUSTRATIONS With or Without Captions and/or Bold Price Displays*: these form the "heart" of a layout, and usually provide the greatest degree of reader interest;

(3) *One or More BLOCKS OF RULED LINES*: although the body copy of an advertisement doesn't appear on the layout, these "blocks" indicate where the copy will go and how much space it will occupy;

(4) *Occasional COUPONS, BORDERS, and Other DECORATIVE*

ELEMENTS: these items are not required, but may be included if they help further the advertising message; and

(5) *The ADVERTISER'S LOGOTYPE or SIGNATURE ("LOGO" or "SIG")*: layout designers take care to see that this vital element is prominent, although it often winds up in the lower righthand corner of advertisements.

Not all layouts include all five of the above, but the majority contain most of them. (Note: while every advertisement is required by law to include the advertiser's name, if it appears in "illustration" form, as it might on a product package, an additional logo is not essential.) Also, there are five major layout *stages*, at least the first two of which even "non-artistic" creative people may be expected to produce:

(a) The *thumbnail* is a miniature layout—often no more than one-quarter the size of the finished advertisement (sometimes less). It's almost a doodle-sketch—a quick transfer of image from mind to paper—showing members of creative and account teams where elements might be placed, and indicating the content of illustrative material. Some creative people "think" in thumbnails (and, hence, make many of them before deciding on a specific approach to develop). Others omit this stage of layout design completely;

(b) The *rough* layout is "rough" in some respects, but very refined in others. It is exactly the size of the actual advertisement . . . and all of the elements (all *type* beyond the body copy, all pictorial material, and *blocks* instead of body copy) are in the exact size and shape, position, and proportion to one another as they will be when the advertisement ultimately appears in a newspaper or magazine. The amount of graphic detail in a rough layout, however, varies considerably. Headlines, captions, and signatures may be lettered in with a pencil, while illustrative material is sketched—even traced—and perhaps "shaded" a bit. Then, again, if the *following* layout stage is omitted, the *rough* will incorporate more polish;

(c) The *finished* layout *may* be the first one prepared—if the designer is an experienced art director or highly skilled layout artist. On the other hand, especially in the case of retail stores, other local businesses, and some industrial firms, it may be the *last* layout stage encountered before production. It is one step up the ladder from the *rough*, but still shows only "blocks" instead of body copy. The specific type style desired, however, is probably shown more clearly, color may have been added, and pictures are sharper, more "finished";

(d) The *comprehensive* layout ("comp") is frequently prepared (at cost) in ink, water color, or other art media, by advertising agencies for client approval. Body copy is often (though not always) included here, and the entire advertisement appears on a heavy, cardboard surface called bristol, or art board, so it can be handled easily at client presentation sessions. The layout resembles the final advertisement in every possible detail (though still is not suitable for camera reproduction);

(e) The *camera-ready pasteup*, or *mechanical*, isn't really a layout ("plan") at all, but the end result of the preceding layout stages. This, in fact, *is* the final advertisement as it's been prepared for photoengraving and ultimate distribution to the media.

Now, assuming we're dealing with a *rough* layout (the one usually prepared by students of advertising copy and layout), let's see how the actual layout page compares with its corresponding copy sheet. Study Figures 7-1a and 7-1b carefully, and note that:

(1) both pages show all headline material, although the *layout* shows it in its proper size and position, while the *copy sheet* merely records it, and indicates the nature of the type (to be discussed presently);

(2) both pages deal with illustrative material, although the *layout* presents it graphically, while the *copy sheet* merely describes it;

(3) both pages are concerned with copy, although the *layout* merely indicates its presence with ruled lines, while the *copy sheet* includes all of the actual words. Note, too, that the copy blocks on the layout are keyed (by letter) to the copy sheet;

(4) both pages show the advertiser's logo, although the *layout*, again, reproduces it graphically, while the *copy sheet* simply lists it.

LAY OUT: THE VERB

To lay out an advertisement is to assemble pieces, in much the same way you complete a puzzle. In this case, however, there is no "perfect" solution—but, rather, a series of possible "fits" which are in keeping with a given creative strategy. Listed below are five major design principles—guidelines for arranging layout elements on a page. They're not hard and fast rules which must be followed for every advertisement, but they have proven effective in terms of reader attraction and message communication.

BALANCE

Balance in a layout lends a sense of stability. Unbalanced advertisements may look top-heavy or one-sided, and the reader's

FIGURE 7-1a

A Copy Sheet to Accompany the "Rough" Layout

HEADLINE: Finish First with the sport of the 80's
(FRANKLIN TYPE . . . WITH 6-POINT LEADING)

SUBHEAD: The Datsun 200-SX Hatchback

ILLUSTRATIONS: Car positioned at focal point, with runners and track for added attention. Driver points UP to the headline, and also shows "#1" (as reinforcement). Three inserts support the copy (bucket seats, 5-speed transmission, and alloy wheels), and lead the reader's eyes through the three copy blocks.

COPY A: The 1980 Datsun 200-SX Hatchback finishes first as the sport of the 80's. Its sleek sporty new style and standard features give you the look and feel of total control. Ease into its lowback bucket seats and take control of the powerful fuel injected engine. And if you want to relax a little more, the seats recline fully to give you added comfort for long hauls.

COPY B: Take those trips worry free with the 200-SX's superior gas mileage—28 mpg in the city and 40 mpg on the highway. With Datsun's fuel injected engine, you'll get more power from less fuel—and that means more miles to the gallon. You'll finish first with standard features like 5-speed transmission with overdrive and full instrumentation.

COPY C: Get an even sportier look with extras like alloy wheels. Drive yourself into first place and finish first with a real winner—The Datsun 200-SX Hatchback. Start this decade with the #1 sport of the 80's.

LOGO: #1 Datsun . . . We Are Driven

reaction is one of discomfort. *Formal* balance is a symmetrical arrangement: the top and bottom halves of the layout, or the right and left sides, are identical in terms of elements. The feeling created is one of formality (sometimes dignity) . . . and while few advertisements today feature *exact*, (mirror-image) symmetry, a number of them—especially business advertisements—use at least semiformal displays to portray (reinforce or change) company images.

The layout in Figure 7-2 is symmetrical. Notice how it enhances the feeling of "togetherness" in terms of advertising elements and message delivery, and how it helps communicate the simple, direct sales story.

Informal balance results in more varied layout arrangements, and is often more in keeping with modern, casual lifestyles. Nonsymmetrical advertisements are still balanced, but this time it's an *optical* balance. The headline, illustrations and copy blocks may be placed in various spots—not in a systematic, right-left, or top-bottom fashion. The overall effect, however, is one of equal weight on each side. The vast majority of advertisements in this book are informally balanced.

FIGURE 7-1b

A "Rough" Layout to Accompany the Copy Sheet

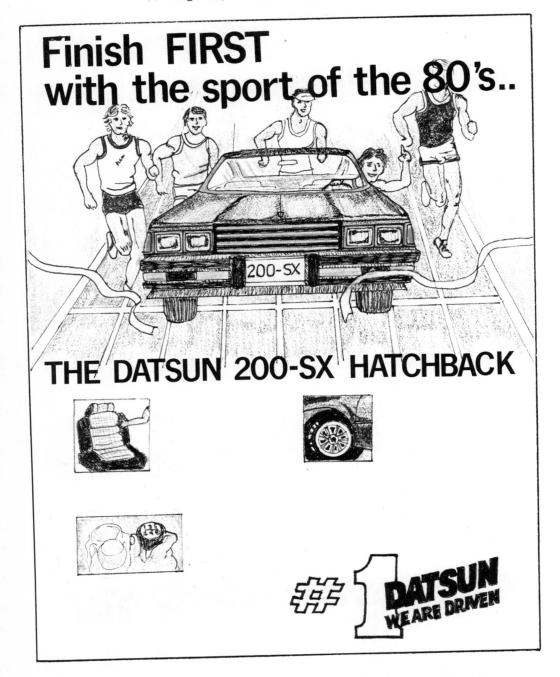

FROM THE PORTFOLIOS OF JEFF HARDIN, CAROLYN F. O'SHAUGHNESSY, AND BARBARA ROWAN REYNOLDS

FIGURE 7-2

Formally Balanced (Symmetrical) Advertisement

9 ways to liven up the burgers this holiday weekend!

1. Pizza burger (Hamburger with shredded mozzarella and pizza sauce)

2. Dill burger (Hamburger with whipped cream cheese and fresh dill)

3. Chef salad burger (Hamburger with Julienne ham, cheese, green pepper, turkey)

4. California burger (Hamburger with lettuce, tomato and mayonnaise)

Dixie Belle burger 5. (Hamburger with a slice of tomato under mayonnaise, mayo browned with burger)

Bacon burger 6. (Hamburger with bacon, tomato, pepper and Swiss cheese)

Bavarian burger 7. (Hamburger with cole slaw, poppy seeds, salad dressing)

Chedda-burger 8. (Hamburger with a slice of Cheddar cheese)

9. Coca-Cola
Coke adds life...

Copyright © 1978, The Coca-Cola Company. "Coca-Cola" and "Coke" are registered trade-marks which identify the same product of The Coca-Cola Company.

The "optical center" of a layout (often called the focal point) is the spot where the reader's eye normally comes to rest, upon exposure to the advertisement. It's often slightly above and to one side of the exact geometric center, and is the point around which designers arrange layout elements to achieve a balanced effect. Since virtually all advertising strategies call for emphasis on a sales message, creative teams must be wary of "irrelevant" focal points (no matter how "entertaining" they might be). As a centralizing concept, the optical center sometimes *runs away* with the entire advertisement (and with readers); if it's unrelated to the product message, therefore, the sales communication effort fails completely.

The "optical weight" of any layout element is a result of its size, shape, and color. Large items, irregularly shaped items, and dark items tend to appear heavy, and their counterparts light. Also, placing an element farther from the optical center tends to increase its weight, so (1) a small element placed away from center can balance a larger one closer in; and (2) a large element done in a light tone can balance a smaller, darker one, when the two are equidistant from center.

CONTRAST

Contrast —in the size, shape, color, tone or texture, and direction (horizontal, vertical, diagonal) of layout elements—adds visual interest when used sparingly. It also creates confusion when used indiscriminately. An easy way to tie key layout items together, so readers will relate one to another, is to use an advertisement's *only color* for *them* (and for nothing else). Or, perhaps attention is drawn to the *only circles* in a collection of rectangles . . . or to the *only* *"standing"* (tall) elements in a group of "sitting" (short) ones. Even white space in an advertisement can contrast with colored objects and black type—setting them off, giving them an air of importance, and helping balance the layout in the process.

MOTION

Motion is the feeling of aliveness—even among static visual elements. In fact, some *idea* of movement is implicit in nearly everything we see. It not only provides interest, but also contributes significantly to establishment of a sequence or pattern for eyes to follow in progressing through an advertisement. Normally, as Americans, we read from left to right and from top to bottom, and wise layout designers take that into account (because forcing readers to read "against the grain," so to speak—against their lifelong conditioning—is *not* the way to ease them into a sale!)

Also, eyes tend to move from points of maximal attention to those of minimal attention (beginning, usually, with the optical center): from larger elements to smaller ones, and from items of greater color intensity to those of lesser intensity. And, as discussed above, since the layout artist knows that eyes "associate" elements of the same size, shape, or color, he or she may "key" specific items accordingly. Or, a desired eye path may be indicated through use of more obvious "pointing devices" such as a finger, a knife, and a pair of eyes—and also the corner of a box, the slant of a road, and the positioning of a foot about to take a step.

A couple of recurring challenges facing layout designers are (1) to direct the reader's gaze to all items *in order of their importance* to the sales message, and (2) to keep that gaze *within* the advertisement (instead of pointing it off the page: side, bottom, or top).

PROPORTION

Proportion deals with: (a) the relationship between layout elements in terms of size; (b) the ratio of individual elements' lengths and widths; and (c) the total amount of space occupied by the elements as opposed to the white space around them and to the size of the entire advertisement. Generally, the most effective relationships are those which seem least obvious to readers. If there is too great a variation in size between any given items, or if there are simply too many variations, the eye may register confusion—an awkward feeling, perhaps—and very probably a conscious awareness of the *items per se* (ad-itis again).

Displeasing proportions are usually those which are dull: for example, a layout which is exactly "top half *picture*" and "bottom half *copy*," or one which contains only four 3″ x 3″ squares—one housing the headline, one an illustration, one the copy, and one the logotype. On the other hand, the advertisements used as examples in this text demonstrate a wide variety of interesting proportions— divisions between illustrations and type which give layouts both a dynamic quality and an air of congeniality that invites readers to get involved.

UNITY

Unity is achieved when a layout's separate elements appear optically "tied together" as a unified whole. While "white space" may make a valuable contribution to advertising design, it shouldn't be conspicuous between major items on the page. It does serve to isolate a particular item or items . . . and can lend an image of prestige, in part by preventing any feeling of element "clutter." Also, it can become its own kind of "image trademark" for a brand or store. (See again Figure 4-6 on page 79.)

Simple borders around advertisements often support feelings of unity—literally "fencing in" the elements of each message. And physical space isn't the only concern here; *theme* harmony is another aspect of unity. The separate units of a layout arrangement must be psychologically part of the same concept. (Note: two marks of a beginning copy and layout student are, first, an advertisement prepared with a "hole" (or large blank space) in the center, and second, a message with no unifying theme (to tie together the claims made and benefits presented).

The advertisement in Figure 7-3 is unified around the concept of TWO: the *word* "two" in the headline and body copy, two dogs' faces, two bowls, two subheads (each of which contains two words), two pieces of food, and two "pointer-lines."

Finally, similarities in type style (between headlines and logos), in color (between a graphic symbol and a package), and in shape (between pictorial elements and a trademark or product display) enhance a layout's singleness of purpose. For one example, see Figure 7-4. (Note that this same "similarities" idea served a slightly different purpose in our previous discussion of contrast and motion.)

LAYOUT FORMATS

From a wide range of potential layout formats or styles, we've selected a few for comment which appear quite consistently year after year. No serious student of advertising creativity should feel limited to these, but must be alert to a host of others, and be encouraged to experiment with new ideas.

The *conventional*, or *classic* layout features an illustration in the upper 60-70% of the space available, with a headline and copy blocks arranged below. Or, the headline (and sometimes the copy) appears superimposed over the picture's background, and is placed both above and below the key scene. While messages presented in these layouts are generally straightforward and explanatory, however, they need *not* be dull or unoriginal.

The *all-type*, or *type-heavy*, layout contains little or no pictorial material. When stores run clearances on hundreds of items, for example, they often request a "sale headline," plus a series of copy blocks, each accompanied by a bold "numbers" display (either prices or discount-figures), and a department or category-of-merchandise listing. (See again Figure 4-7, on page 80). This approach is usually ideal for communicating a large amount of important detailed information.

FIGURE 7-3

149

Unified Advertisement

FIGURE 7-4

Trio of Advertisements Using Graphic Symbols

The *poster*, or *picture-dominant*, layout is the opposite of the above, with a large illustration covering all or nearly all of the advertisement. A diamond merchant might feel that a close-up of a newly-engaged couple—their faces radiant as he slips a ring on her finger—carried sufficient emotional impact to require no verbal sales pitch (except, perhaps, for one small line near the bottom: "And Aurora Loves Her, Too. Aurora Diamonds.")

The *Mondrian* layout emphasizes rectangular forms and interesting lines (as did its namesake, Dutch painter Piet Mondrian). The *multi-panel* layout is a comic strip, or other picture-caption arrangement. *Omnibus* and *circus* layouts include many different items—which appear in a "helter-skelter" arrangement in the first case, and in a "noisy celebration" in the second. A hodgepodge of shapes and sizes, reverse-type blocks (white on black), exclamation points, and headlines which shout for attention, are often part of these advertisements.

Figure 7-4

So how to choose? The nature and number of elements to be arranged in the layout will be an important influencer, as will the overall size of the advertisement. And the creative team must never lose sight of the original campaign plan. Does the strategy call for bold, pictorial communication with an emotional punch (*conventional*)? Or, perhaps a sequence of graphic ideas is needed (*multi-panel*). A strategy involving a serious corporate message about energy problems might suggest *all-type*, while an end-of-the-month sale may demand *omnibus* treatment.

THE PACKAGE-ILLUSTRATION LAYOUT

An introductive product-communication strategy frequently calls for a *package dominant* picture in advertisements, since a primary

Figure 7-4

goal is to show readers what the new product looks like (so they can pick it off the store shelf). If the type is easy to read, the package face may carry all of the information otherwise placed in paragraphs of body copy. Or, sometimes a two-page spread features the package (alone) on one page, and informative copy on the other, along with possible graphic inserts showing usage/benefits.

In certain cases, a package is featured throughout an advertising campaign, because the package *is* the product: the Sunkist orange, the Idaho potato, the Dole banana. (See again Figure 6-5 on page 124). And, products wrapped in see-through containers provide ready-made package display illustrations: a bottle of perfume or liqueur, a package of cold cuts or cookies, a jar of salad dressing or syrup.

Package "functionalism" provides a practical reason to highlight the container in an illustration. Pump sprays, dispenser boxes, and built-in applicators are popular examples. In addition, *size* may be seen as a function: tiny packages promise portability, and giant ones indicate bonus quantities. And, finally, the package may appear in every campaign advertisement *as* the signature/logo.

THE ORIGINAL-ART LAYOUT

Drawing and painting styles for layouts include both *line art* and *toned art.* In the first case, solid lines or blocks appear on a plain background with no intermediate tones between black and white (although line *color* is no problem as long as two colors don't fall on top of each other). The work may be done with pencil, pen, crayon, charcoal, or chalk. In the second case, there is a range of intermediate values from either white or light gray to dark gray or black, and popular examples include photographs (both color and black-and-white), colored drawings and water-color paintings, and etchings and engravings. Granted, not every reader will appreciate quality artwork, but if it establishes and promotes the specific image called for by a creative strategy, it may well be worth its price.

Shading forms range from airbrush and silhouette techniques, to "natural" (screen and halftone) and "synthetic" (Ben Day tint) methods. Generally, the effects desired here are those of depth and dramatic appeal.

ENHANCING READERSHIP

Regardless of the format you choose, you can often increase both the amount of time readers spend with it, and the amount of interest it generates for your product and message. How? By following a few tips on layout size and color, and on the use of pictures and copy blocks.

LAYOUT SIZE AND COLOR

Although decisions regarding the size and color of advertisements are often based largely on cost, a couple of points are worthy of note. Recent research has confirmed what studies have found for decades: first, that readership increases proportionately with advertisement size. Half-page layouts outscore quarter-pagers by 36%; advertisements filling two-thirds of a page outscore those filling one-third of a page by 38%; and two page spreads outscore one pagers by 89%.

Looking at the matter another way, assume that a three-quarter-page layout is the "norm." That is, this size draws an "average" amount of readership. Then, dropping down to a one-quarter-page size cuts reading in half—and going to two pages more than doubles it.[1] (Note: these page divisions, along with the "gatefold"—a multi-sided fold-out—are most common for magazines; newspaper advertisements are generally measured by columns or parts of a column, and by *agate lines* (fourteen to the inch, frequently in groups of 300, 600, and 1,000).

Two-color advertisements outpull their black-and-white counterparts, in terms of readership, by 13%, and four-color layouts improve scores by an additional 10%.[2] To the extent that a similar style (and/or size, and/or color) is established for a series of advertisements, however (over a period of months, or even years), it becomes an identity factor assisting in the recognition of successive messages. Hence, even the advertiser who can't afford color may achieve a valuable audience mind-position.

Sometimes, of course, a creative strategy may dictate a dramatic change in layout design, size, color scheme or color *effects*: natural, or highlighted. For instance, the goal might be to reverse a negative brand image, or to develop a new company philosophy. Or, an advertiser may wish to cater to audiences in a market segment which hadn't previously been reached.

PICTURES

Pictures should convey as much of the total X-Y-Z appeal as possible, portraying the product, service, or store involved clearly, and in a style consistent with the images of both advertiser and medium. Also, layout artists must take care to see: (1) that important pictorial elements aren't cropped (cut off) in order to fit available space, and (2) that elaborate border designs and artistic flourishes don't crowd and clutter that same (precious) space.

COPY BLOCKS

Because copy blocks are traditionally the least interesting parts of an advertisement, a layout designer often guides readers to them by using: (a) asterisks or little dot-bullets; (b) numbers; or (c) large initial letters (the first letter of the first word in each paragraph)—as well as the various "pointing devices" discussed earlier.

In addition, all but the shortest of copy blocks should be *broken up* with subheads, white space, indentations, boldface type, and even underlining. And, copy set *flush left* is much easier to read than copy set *ragged left*—regardless of whether the right side is flush or ragged (mainly because readers are accustomed to the flush-left arrangement). Finally, column widths shouldn't normally exceed the approximate width of a newspaper column—except, perhaps, in the case of unusually large type or short copy.

MECHANICAL PRODUCTION

What follows is a non-technical presentation of some rather technical print reproduction procedures. Since this book is neither a graphics primer nor an advertising production manual, we'll examine these areas only briefly—as they relate to strategic concerns and to the use of our Tactical Check Chart. The student seriously interested in pursuing advertising mechanics is referred to some current texts in this field.[3]

The process of reproducing words and pictures from copy sheets and layouts may itself influence the communication effects achieved; so, mechanical production must be a part of advertising strategy from the onset of creative activity. Costs, of course, play an important role, too, because they may prohibit the use of original artwork or color. And media choices have a bearing because both printing processes and paper stock are involved.

PRINTING PROCESSES

Multiple copies of an advertisement are produced through the transfer of ink from a printing surface to sheets of paper. There are several different transfer procedures, however. First, in *letterpress* printing, sometimes called *relief* printing, raised surfaces carry the ink and deposit it, under pressure, on paper. An example is an ordinary rubber stamp used in offices and homes for dates, costs, and other clerical notations. This traditional method of printing is most frequently used by advertisers in metropolitan newspapers, and large-circulation magazines such as *Reader's Digest*, *Time*, and *Ladies' Home Journal*. From an artistic point of view, the impressions made are very sharp and precise, but only considered "high quality" with coated, or other smooth-finish, paper (because this method of ink transfer is especially sensitive to paper texture).

Second, in *gravure* printing, a much thinner ink sits in a depressed "pocket" in each printing plate, and is picked up from there by the machinery involved. Sunday newspaper supplements, and portions of *TV Guide*, *Family Circle*, and *Good Housekeeping* magazines are printed by gravure, as are a number of catalogs, labels, and even packages. This method offers maximum fidelity in specialized art forms, because the thin ink closely approximates the artist's original medium. On the other hand, this same ink may give line art or type matter a "ragged edge" appearance. Also, gravure printing is expensive unless the number of copies run is very large (since the printing cylinder carries a high initial cost).

Third, *offset lithography*, or *planographic* printing, features a printing element which is neither raised nor depressed. Both an ink-attracting and an ink-repelling substance lie flat on each plate, but only the former one covers the images to be transferred to paper. This type of contact surface is known for its resiliency, so offset is used effectively on a wide variety of paper textures. Most direct mail materials are now printed by offset, as are the majority of small and medium-sized newspapers and magazines, and many cartons and other packaging materials. Initial low printing plate costs make offset economical for small press runs, and the sharp, precise impressions often rival those of letterpress on a wide variety of paper choices.

Fourth, *silk screen* printing is used for posters, display materials, and packages, especially when small quantities are needed. In this procedure, paint or ink passes through a fabric or metal mesh which contains a design (so the mesh serves as a kind of "stencil"). Most advertising printing, however, uses one of the three previously discussed processes.

PAPER

The reproductive quality of any advertisement is ultimately influenced by the paper on which it's printed; some knowledge of paper characteristics, therefore, is helpful to creative teams. In direct mail, advertising designers have control over the weight, color, finish, and texture of papers used; when it comes to newspapers and magazines, however, the problem is one of adjusting creative elements to existing (predetermined) production situations.

Book Paper

Except in the case of newspaper printing, "book papers" are the most widely used printing stocks in advertising. *Antique* paper has a rough texture, while a *machine* finish provides a moderate degree of smoothness. The *super-calendered* variety is a "slick" paper (used in most magazines), and *coated* (or *enamel*) stocks, in both dull-coated and glossy finishes, are the most highly processed and expensive.

Newsprint

Since newspapers are read and discarded quickly, the paper used is generally the cheapest available. Newsprint is porous, and has a relatively uneven surface compared to more highly processed papers. It's suited only for letterpress printing, although a firmer variety of paper, similar to newsprint, has been developed for use with offset.

What effect have all of these considerations on decisions made by layout artists? First, if a paper stock conveys a rich appearance, as opposed to a cheap one, this "image" may easily rub off on (or become part of) the message carried. Second, some advertisements may be clipped and saved by readers and, hence, must appear on a fairly durable kind of paper. Finally, the quality of type and picture reproduction—based both on the printing process and on the paper stock—may determine to a large extent the detail and number of type faces and illustrations selected.

TYPOGRAPHY

As a tactical activity, the choice of type faces plays an important role in layout development and production. Basically, typography is just a vehicle for transmitting a verbal message; but its physical features can contribute a great deal to the communication of mood, image, and credibility. Both the designs and the arrangements of letters draw psychological responses from audiences—and there are probably as many different reactions as there are readers to make them. In addition, there are an estimated 1,500 different type faces.[4]

Type Groups

ROMAN type is a simply designed, not very ornate style of letters whose strokes show (1) non-uniform widths, and (2) small "appendages" (called serifs) at many of their ends. It's an easy-to-read type, used today in commercial printing more extensively than any other design. Subgroups of Roman include *Old Style*, *Modern*, and *Transitional*. The first is characterized by slanting or curved serifs and little contrast between thick and thin strokes. The second has straight serifs and a pronounced difference in stroke thickness, and the third represents a compromise between the other two. In addition, there are literally hundreds of Roman type *families*—all variants of the basic design (in terms of the weight, width, and angle of letters), and part of the working vocabulary of printers.

BLOCK or *CONTEMPORARY* type features letters without serifs (sans-serif)—or occasionally with *square* serifs—and a uniform thickness of strokes, plus a mechanical precision not found in Roman type. The capitals have a block-like appearance, increasingly popular in advertising, especially in "display" lines (headlines and captions). A substantial amount of body copy is set in Block type, too, because its uncluttered design gives it a "streamlined" look many advertisers appreciate. Then, again, some typographical experts complain about the plain, even monotonous, appearance that results from large masses of Block type.

ITALIC type faces are merely italicized versions of standard Roman type families. The strokes are simply lighter in weight (giving the appearance of a fine pen), and letters are slanted to the right. Occasionally, an advertiser may set an entire piece of copy in an Italic face, although it's difficult to read in large quantity. More often, a word or phrase is set off in Italics to lend emphasis.

SCRIPT and *CURSIVE* faces resemble handwriting, and are sometimes used for headlines and captions (and also slogans), particularly when the advertisement calls for a graceful, or feminine, effect.

Some miscellaneous types include TEXT, or OLD ENGLISH, a heavy, ornate style used only rarely in advertisements to establish an association with centuries past. And, *ECCENTRIC*, or *NOVELTY*, type faces range from circus-poster styles to the overly romantic and exotic. Figure 7-5 identifies some popular advertising type styles, and presents them in a variety of *sizes* (our next topic of discussion).

But do advertisers really care about the specific type selected for them? Is the associated image an important strategic concept? Take a look at Figure 7-6.

Type Measurement

The standard unit of type size is the "point"—a measure of the height of the slug on which the letter was cast in traditional metal type. There are 72 points to the inch, but each point *includes* the size of the non-printing "shoulder" of the slug. Thus, it's incorrect to say that printed type which measures ¼ of an inch is 18-point type (even though 72 ÷ 4 = 18). The type size in this case would actually be *larger* than 18-point.

Type used to set body copy in an advertisement is usually 14-point or less, and "display" type, normally appearing in headlines and captions, is 18-point and above. When a layout designer deviates from these norms, it must be with a specific sales communication goal in mind, or ad-itis gains an upper hand.

FIGURE 7-5
Example for Type Sizes and Styles

14 point 18 point 24 point 30 point 36 point 48 point

60 point 72 point

Franklin Extra-Condensed 48 point

Serif Gothic Heavy 48 Poin

Casual Reverse 30 point size

Dom Casual Bold 30 point size

Dom Diagonal 30 point size

STENCIL

STENCIL OUTLINE 30 POINT SIZE

COMPLIMENTS OF KNOXVILLE PRINTERS, INC.

FIGURE 7-6

Typography and Image

COMPLIMENTS OF LOEWS HOTELS

The width (horizontal space) occupied by a line of type is measured in "picas"—and there are six of them in one inch. Printers use points and picas to prepare cost estimates for type-setting jobs. Extra *spacing*, often placed between lines of type, is called "leading" (pronounced "ledding"), and varies in thickness.

When multiple lines are set evenly on both right and left sides, they're said to be "justified"; otherwise, they're set "ragged" (ragged left and/or ragged right). Finally, the *depth* of copy space occupied is measured in "agate lines," of which there are 14 to a "column inch" (an area measuring one column across and one inch down). Obviously, some messages which can be conveyed in a 1,000-line advertisement (an area approaching half a page in a standard newspaper) would have trouble in a space one-quarter that size or less. Still, a creative strategy need not be scrapped just because the advertiser suddenly runs short of funds or decides for some reason to cut back. Effective communication occurs through small-space advertisements every day. For instance, Figure 7-7 shows a creative way to announce a pre-inventory sale in just a fraction of the space filled by large, multi-item advertisements.

FIGURE 7-7

Small Space Advertisement with a Creative Flair

Parks Belk

Counting! Counting! We hate
to do it, but it's time again...

**Parks-Belk
will be closed
for inventory
Wed., Jan. 30**

C'mon in and take it off our
hands Monday and Tuesday
during our big Pre-Inventory
Clear-Away. You'll find racks
and stacks of fabulous
values throughout the store.
And hurry: the more you buy,
the less we have to count!

COMPLIMENTS OF PARKS BELK CO.

Type Selection

The choice of type for a given layout (in terms of size, style, and spacing) is governed by two primary considerations: reading ease, and the image of the advertiser and message. Each is important enough to warrant individual attention.

Reading Ease. Type must not interfere with an advertisement's sales story any more than unnecessary pictures or words should. "Gimmicks" usually do more to divert reader attention than to direct it. Examples are: (1) a change in typeface in the midst of a headline; (2) artistic, but hard-to-decipher type colors *over* background colors; and (3) type set on top of already "busy" picture-details. And, body copy set in sans-serif type is difficult to read because the letters appear closer together than they do when the little serif "tails" are included.

Type legibility is affected by five basic factors, the first of which is *size*. Normally, the larger the type, the more visible it is; however, practical advertising considerations prohibit setting all of the type in every advertisement in "display" size. Then, too, psychologists maintain that the human eye moves through a magazine or newspaper in a series of "jumps" (fixations)—and not in one smooth, continuous flow. And, not every eye takes in the same number of words at each stopping point. While very large type may be easily *seen*, therefore, it may not be the most satisfactory in terms of reading (and comprehension). The average person is most accustomed to text matter in type ranging from 8 to 12 points.

The second factor affecting reading ease is *letter design*. Audience familiarity plays a large role here, and Roman and Block type styles are especially legible because they're so often encountered. The contrast between lower case and capital letters is important, too; since lower case has a greater variety in shape (height and contour), it lends itself to faster reading than does an "all capitals" design. But do all creative strategies call for "speed reading"? Of course not. The easier it is for readers to take in an entire message, however, the greater the chance that message will (1) register the advertiser's name and basic claim, and (2) start the wheels of action rolling.

The third item to consider is the *weight* factor. As a rule, the heavier the letter image appears on paper, the more legible it is. But if the imprint is so heavy it overshadows the white space which would otherwise surround it (and set it off for easy reading), it may become *less* legible. Also, an extreme contrast between type and the paper it's printed on may call attention to the letters per se—another example of ad-itis.

Bolder types, rather than lighter ones, are often needed against a background color other than white, since *value contrast* (darkness/lightness) affects legibility also. Finally, as was true in the case of letter design, audience familiarity with black-type-on-white-paper has a lot going for it. Repeated studies have found that legibility declines in a "reverse type" (white on black) situation.

The fourth consideration is *line length*. Lines which are too short make for choppy reading, forcing eyes to swing back and forth too often to be comfortable. And long lines cause eye strain because of the span involved. So what's the "proper" length? It all depends on the type size, but a traditional guideline is 39 characters (letters, numbers, or whatever) per line for ideal legibility. In practice, lines ranging from about 28 to 55 characters—filling, in most instances, between two and four inches of horizontal space—are read without difficulty.

Sometimes a strategy calls for the "listing" of items, features, or other copy points; but, obviously, they can't all be "run together" in continuous lines. In such cases, *numerals* create a feeling of importance (whereas the "bullets" mentioned earlier, along with asterisks, do not). Then, too, normal punctuation is recommended for the natural, sincere impression it creates; an overuse of exclamation points or word-emphasis (underlining or italicizing) may backfire, since it calls attention to the fact that the writer's ideas were "unexciting" enough to need artificial boosters.

Our fifth concern is with *leading*. Both type size and type design affect the amount of leading needed to assure easy reading (remembering that readers feel no compulsion, as a rule, to read beyond the headline material). Most typographers follow the policy of leading body copy one or two points, although very large type sizes and long line lengths may require more.

In almost all cases, extra leading is required between paragraphs which aren't indented . . . and, as previously noted, copy blocks should be "broken up" before they become long and cumbersome. (Unfortunately, the more a layout resembles a standard textbook page, the less appealing it is!)

Advertiser-Message Image. In addition to its other duties, the type in a layout should help reflect an appropriate company atmosphere and project the spirit of the message delivered. It must be in harmony with (1) the product's image, as revealed in the copy, and (2) the other physical elements arranged by the layout designer and specified by the medium involved. For example, if an advertisement is trying to convey the sturdiness of a large machine or appliance, a delicate script or lightweight Roman type would hardly be appropriate. By the same token, messages dealing with perfume and lingerie would find that boldface type or a design with heavy strokes in its letters all but destroyed any aura of sensuality or femininity which might otherwise be produced.

By its own appearance, therefore, type can create feelings of formality, or chic modernity, or bargain basements. It may suggest speed and power; shyness and withdrawal; confusion and intrigue. But how does it work in conjunction with the rest of the layout? First, a contemporary Block face would be out of place next to "scratchboard" illustrations—facsimiles of old-fashioned, wood-cut techniques. Similarly, heavy type designs would clash with feathery, transparent, water-color pictures. Also, in a long, narrow layout, it may be wise to choose tall, thin type—to carry out the spatial theme—while in layouts with curved and/or circular elements, type with a less rectangular look may provide the best aesthetic fit.

What about mixing different typefaces in one advertisement? The experts say "go ahead"—with the following cautions: (1) a maximum of three or four faces should appear in one layout (although *fewer* in a small advertisement); (2) only faces which blend well together belong together; and (3) all faces used should help communicate the desired advertiser image, and should not call attention to themselves. (See Figure 7-8.)

Finally, some advertisers feature different type styles in different seasonal/holiday/special-event communications. Others strive for a consistency (familiarity) of type across all messages—and across

164

FIGURE 7-8

Type Style Used as Message Enhancer

campaigns. Even television commercials may help carry the ball here—by focusing, for example, on a distinctive type style in words printed (superimposed) on the screen. We'll examine this procedure in detail as we move into a discussion of creative strategy and tactics in the broadcast media.

STUDY QUESTIONS

1. What's the difference between LAYOUT, the noun, and LAY OUT, the verb?
2. Name the five elements comprising a layout.
3. One layout stage is known as a *thumbnail*. Name and describe four other stages.
4. What are the similarities and differences between a layout and a copy sheet?
5. List and describe five major design principles used by layout artists in the arrangement of layout elements.
6. Differentiate between a *conventional* layout and an *omnibus* layout, and between *line art* and *toned art*.
7. How does layout size and color affect readership?
8. List four different printing processes—and give one characteristic of each.
9. Why should creative personnel be concerned with the paper on which advertisements are printed?
10. What's the difference between Roman and Block type groups?
11. What do we mean when we say that "display" type is "18-point" and above?
12. What are two basic considerations which govern the choice of type for a given layout?

ENDNOTES

1. *How Advertising Readership Is Influenced By Ad Size*, Cahners Advertising Research Report, No. 110.1, Cahners Publishing Company, New York.
2. *How Advertising Readership Is Influenced By The Addition Of A Second Color*, Cahners Advertising Research Report, No. 111.1; and *How Advertising Readership Is Influenced By The Addition Of 4-Color*, Cahners Advertising Research Report, No. 112.1, Cahners Publishing Company, New York.
3. See: Bahr, Leonard F., *Typographia*, Harper Woods, Michigan: Adagio Press, 1976; Bockus, H. William Jr., *Advertising Graphics*, 3rd edition., New York: Macmillan, 1979; Broekhuizen, Richard J., *Graphic Communications*, 2nd edition, Bloomington, Illinois: McKnight, 1979; Ernst, Sandra B., *The ABC's of Typography*, New York: Art Direction, 1977; Lewis, John Noel Claude, *Typography: Design and Practice*, New York: Taplinger, 1978; Patterson, Donald Gildersleeve, and Tinker, Miles A., *How to Make Type Readable: A Manual for Typographers, Printers, and Advertisers*, New York: Harper & Brothers, 1975; *Pocket Pal*, New York: International Paper Company, 1974; Swerdlow, Robert M., *Introduction to Graphic Arts*, Chicago: American Technical Society, 1979; Turnbull, Arthur T., and Baird, Russell N., *The Graphics of Communication; Typography, Layout, Design*, Holt, Rinehart and Winston, New York, 1975.
4. Arthur T. Turnbull, and Russell N. Baird, *The Graphics of Communication*, Holt, Rinehart and Winston, New York, 1975, p. 37.

8

CREATIVE TACTICS FOR BROADCAST MEDIA: COPYWRITING AND AURAL/VISUAL PLANNING

Leaving printed messages behind us for the moment, we enter the equally challenging world of broadcasting. Here, we'll find, as we did with newspapers and magazines, that while differences between the two media affect creative strategy and tactics in important ways, radio and television are at least fraternal twins in many advertising campaigns. Their electronic capabilities, and their persuasive functions and limitations, often give them separate *roles* but common *goals* as members of an advertiser's marketing/communication team. So, we'll consider commercial writing in this chapter—for both radio and TV—and leave production concerns for Chapter 9.

Radio messages are, of course, combinations of aural effects only: words, sounds, and music. But effective radio commercials develop pictures in listeners' minds—scenes which can be as vivid and imaginative as anything seen by the human eye (and a lot less expensive). On the other hand, TV combines the sights of print and sounds of radio with the drama of motion pictures, as well as the personality of face-to-face selling. Unfortunately, however, ad-itis runs as rampant in the broadcast media as it does in print—if not more so, since radio and television are regarded primarily as entertainment vehicles.

Broadcast copywriters, unlike their print counterparts, control the focus of audience attention. Listeners and viewers aren't free to scan messages at will, or to study selected lines or illustrations. Once they've chosen to tune in, they see and hear the exact words, scenes, and special effects the respective advertisers have approved—in a specified order. The creative challenge is to make messages exciting enough—in a sales-oriented way—that audiences do more than just "enjoy."

Our first concern is with creative elements in radio (and TV's audio track), followed by those of TV's visual channel. Remember, as you read, that the Tactical Check Chart, in Appendix II, contains a list of the developmental approaches we'll discuss, but that no method should ever be selected before the creative strategy has been consulted (and, in all but the simplest cases, studied thoroughly).

SOUND COMMUNICATION

Americans are primarily eye-oriented. We're taught from early childhood to read words, to look at pictures (both still and moving), and to study with our eyes—everything from puzzles and diagrams, to interior arrangements and designs for new fashions and cars. Gradually, we get accustomed to receiving the majority of our sensory impressions through our eyes, and become conditioned to directing our attention toward visual stimuli. On the other hand, most people agree that *listening* is an easier task than reading— even though it may be more difficult to comprehend without support from visual material. So, the copywriter has "captive ears" if he or she can but make the listening job a pleasant—and simple—one.

RADIO'S HEADLINERS

Since there's no bold type or graphic eye-grabbers in radio, the task of attracting an audience falls to the very first sounds presented in a commercial. Examples run the gamut from screeching tires and exploding cannons, through trumpet fanfare, drums, and cymbals, to actual shouting matches between carnival-barker-type participants. Occasionally, an advertiser will try reverse tactics: a hushed "pssst," a soft, rhythmic heartbeat, or even a lullaby. Then, too, a number of commercials simply begin with hoped-for verbal appeal in a "Here's news" line or a "Need help?" query. Our concern, however, must be not with gaining attention per se, but with (1) reaching our chosen audience (that select group of listeners indicated in our master strategy), and (2) doing so in a manner conducive to the informational/persuasive task confronting us.

In other words, we start (as always) with a creative strategy. Let's suppose our goal is to position Hot & Spicy's Apple Pie as an out-of-the-ordinary dessert—appropriate as a "reward" for something well done. Now, look at the following "attention-getter" (opening line) tactics for a radio commercial for Hot & Spicy:

> After a long morning of tedious frustrations, a tiring afternoon filled with emergencies and complaints, and a bone-chilling ride home when the car heater went out . . . a different kind of dessert treat is not only well-deserved, but probably about the best thing to be thought of all day.

There are 50 words here—not one of which names the product or describes it in any way. Furthermore, the lines together provide little more than a commentary on a rather gloomy day of living. The *sales spark* in this partial message is completely buried . . . though we *can* pull it out—and express it in just 15 "radio style" words:

> A tough day, and a cold winter evening—two great reasons for a special dessert.

Or, we can be even more specific . . . and still stay within 15 words:

> A tough day, a chilly night, and you're ready for Hot & Spicy's Apple Pie.

Selling time is so short on radio, we can't afford to waste precious, brand-differentiating seconds.

Now, what about the opening line's job of defining a target audience? Continuing with our message for the "special dessert," we know we're addressing people in a cold-winter environment and people who have difficult days. But are they business executives or homemakers? Or what about students and their teachers? Secretaries, truck drivers, sales clerks, or, perhaps, volunteers in community projects? (See Marketing Outline item 37.)

All of these people, along with countless others, are frequently faced with more than enough demands and pressures to qualify for the "tough job" label. Yet, no one commercial can appeal equally to such diverse interest groups—even though the *product* can and does. Hence, we look for more specifics in the message—words (and maybe accompanying sounds and music) which suggest more clearly and directly which wants, needs, and attitudes (not necessarily job types) the advertiser is hoping to reach. A second version of the same commercial (with slightly different phrasing or effects or both) might aim toward another attitudinal segment, and a third version toward still another. Granted, probably none of the three would *alienate* people in the market for this product, but each would appeal specifically to a given lifestyle (while, perhaps, providing positive reinforcement for others).

AUDIENCE PARTICIPATION

Involvement is an important attention- and interest-holding technique in the broadcast media, just as it is in print. But now we're talking about a much more personal situation. A radio (or TV) announcer can actually talk to listeners—questioning them personally about a problem, or explaining a sought-after item or effect in a highly emotional context. Sing-along music and jingles invite audience participation, and familiar sounds: (1) a crying baby, (2) a roaring engine, or (3) a fizzing soda poured over ice, help set a mood, establish a locale, or enhance a copy point. And the more closely these effects are tied in with the heart of a product story: (1) a loving way to soothe a baby's cries, (2) an auto mileage-performance booster, and (3) a cool refresher on a hot afternoon, the more help they will be in triggering a response.

Examine the commercial in Figure 8-1. The jingle and background effects support the message beautifully—but never overpower it.

FIGURE 8-1

Radio Commercial for Nix Cough Drops

SOUND: *GROUP OF PEOPLE COUGHING . . . UP, UNDER, AND OUT AS JINGLE BEGINS*

JINGLE: If coughing's your worry
And you're out of tricks:
Get help in a hurry—
Just reach for the Nix!

MUSIC: CONTINUES UNDER

ANNCR: A nagging cough's a continuous cycle—the more you cough, the more you irritate an already scratchy throat . . . and the greater you find the urge to cough again. Nix Cough Drops give you the double relief you need to soothe rough, irritated membranes and stop your cough before it starts. That's right . . . Nix is really two kinds of medication combined in one easy-to-take drop: it's a lozenge for your throat and a real medicine for your troublesome cough. No messy liquids to measure, and no capsules or tablets to swallow. Just dissolve a Nix drop in your mouth and powerful pain relievers rush to calm that annoying tickle. So next time a nagging cough pops us . . .

SOUND: *COUGHING RETURNS, THEN OUT, AS MUSIC COMES UP*

ANNCR: *. . . pop in a Nix. It's two-way medication for two-way relief.*

JINGLE: *Get help in a hurry—
Just reach for the Nix!*

ANNCR: *Nix Cough Drops.*

SOUND: *MUSIC OUT . . . FOLLOWED BY "SIGH" OF RELIEF*

Similarly the spraying sound behind the commercial in Figure 8-2 is actually part of the sales story. And it's woven into the message fabric simply and memorably. Neither commercial uses production as a substitute for a selling idea (in which case the effects would become mere gimmicks), but, rather, as a message carrier—and an interesting (and informative) one in both cases.

FIGURE 8-2

Radio Commercial for Klene Spray Disinfectant

SOUND: *SLOSHING WATER, SCRUB BRUSHES AGAINST ROUGH SUR-FACES . . . AND A TIRED FEMALE VOICE PUFFING AND PANTING (UP & UNDER)*

ANNCR: Tired of fighting the dirt war against household germs? Then get rid of worn-out ammunition (*SOUND OUT*) . . . and *listen*:

SOUND: *SPRAYING SOUND*

ANNCR: . . . to the sound of Klene. Yes, Klene Spray Disinfectant's on *your* side when it comes to tracking down harmful bacteria in your home. (*SNEAK IN MUSIC: ARMED FORCES DRILL - WITH RAT-A-TAT-TAT*) Its anti-germ action lasts a full seven days, so you spend less time and money fighting "germ warfare!" Just use Klene Spray once a week and keep every room in your house fresh—free of pesky germ build-up. Just a press of a button replaces the old scrub-by-hand disinfectants, so your job's easy. And Klene even destroys germ-*causing* particles, so hard-to-reach corners—even closets—stay *odor*-free, too. Before you go to battle against germs and odors, call in the specialist. You'll have a cleaner, fresher home with Klene Spray. (*MUSIC OUT*) Pick up a can today . . . and listen:

SOUND: *SPRAYING SOUND IN, AS MUSIC OUT*

ANNCR: . . . to the sound of Klene.

THE X-Y-Z APPEAL ON RADIO

Now let's study Exhibits 8-1 and 8-2 again, in terms of their X-Y-Z appeals. Recall from Chapter 6 that we're looking for: something to "exclaim about" (X); a why-factor (Y); and a zipper-line (Z) to tie it all together in a unique fashion. In the Nix commercial, we have the following:

X = a one-step way to get relief from coughs and throat pain;
Y = because Nix combines two kinds of medication in one drop;
Z = two-way medication for two-way relief: when you're out of tricks . . . reach for a Nix.

And in the Klene commercial, we have:

X = an easy, economical, powerful way to disinfect your home;
Y = because Klene kills germs and odors *and* their causes;
Z = listen to the sound of Klene.

Both claims are clear, appealing, and "different" enough to hold listener interest. The first is primarily a *product scene* presentation, with a little of the "case" (reasoning) approach thrown in; the second is the reverse—a *case* first, and a descriptive scene only secondarily. Finally, both messages feature a product-in-use sequence.

Regardless of the medium involved, the X-Y-Z concept helps copywriters establish and maintain a singleness of purpose. Radio audiences are often distracted ones, however (doing, saying, and thinking other things while they listen)—more so than their print media cousins. So it's important to consider copy in a little different way when it's received by the ear instead of the eye.

THE SOUND OF WORDS

Each word must be weighed for its potential contribution to the selling power of the commercial, and for its "goodness" (clarity, simplicity) of sound. "Rich, creamy sauces" somehow has a much truer ring to it than: "smoothly delectable spreads with an appetizing consistency," or "tantalizingly tempting toppings"— even though the latter might be deemed "clever" alliteration.

Whistle-through-the-teeth words are obviously taboo—as are "hissing" S's and tongue-twisters such as: "Come crunch Kris's crispy Kracker Krisps today!"

THE SOUND OF VOICES

"Write to express, not to impress" has always been good advice for advertising copywriters—and in the case of radio commercials, we must *speak* to express (a message's X-Y-Z appeal), not to impress (listeners with the pear-shaped tones or melodic voice of an announcer). While the need for proper casting is obvious, the successful radio copywriter learns to appreciate the "personality values" of human voices, and to incorporate them into message designs long before production stages begin.

How many real "differences" are there in terms of vocal patterns? We won't even hazard a guess, but just one talented performer, by the name of Allen Swift, has been called the Man of a Thousand Voices. As we begin the decade of the 1980's, he's heard on nearly 200 separate, vocally distinct radio commercials for a wide range of products.

THE SOUND OF SOUNDS AND MUSIC

Mind images created by non-spoken parts of an audio track can be bright, positive, and spirited (birds chirping, car engines humming, and instruments beating out a lively rendition of "Happy Talk") . . . or tearful, lonely-and-depressed, and solemn (soft sobbing, the howling of wind and animals, and a few bars of "Pomp and Circumstance"). Generally, both music and sound effects can help keep commercial copy "flowing," by accenting key points or serving as a background for them; by providing smooth introductions and transitions between speakers or message segments; and by creating symbolic images: sluggish sounds for sluggish moods; creaking, thumping, rumbling sounds for an air of suspense; and peppy whistling for a feeling of confidence and success. In addition, they can *replace words* as an advertiser's aural logo, and can exemplify selling points and benefits (often through product-in-use sounds). (See again Figure 8-2, on page 171.)

Music may be composed and arranged specifically for an advertising campaign (at considerable expense), or a popular tune (words, music, or both) may be adapted to fit a particular series of commercials. (Examples might include flying "Up, Up and Away"; bouncing along to a "Mexican Hat Dance"; and galloping off with the "William Tell Overture.") In any case, as one of the largest industries in America, music plays an important—if often unacknowledged—role in American lives. It has proven a powerful selling tool for giant auto makers, fast-food establishments, and small packaged goods, and it may deliver a rational sales message or communicate on purely an emotional level. But it's also easy to *misuse* music in commercials—and to defeat a selling purpose. Let's "note" a few guidelines.

First, music can enhance an image of leadership in a product category. For example, Hershey's chocolate used an "anthem" behind its successful "Great American Hershey Bar" theme. Second, music provides a natural tie between the two broadcast media in a campaign. General Foods made a 60-second version of its TV song, "Tastes Like That Good Old-Fashioned Lemonade," and carried it successfully into radio.

Third, music helps build a distinctive brand personality. Even with Dial soap's relatively new "Startin' Out Dial" campaign in full swing, the "Aren't You Glad You Use Dial" song claims high commercial recall and credibility. Similarly, the child-sung "O-S-C-A-R" tune for Oscar Mayer bologna has given the product firm lodging in the minds of school kids and their lunch-making parents.

Following multiple exposures to a musical theme or jingle, many consumers find themselves absentmindedly humming the tune around the house—or mentally tapping it out while they shop.

There's an enduring quality here that sometimes pays large, even if unseen, dividends in terms of brand positioning. In most cases, experts agree that both the brand name and the sales promise belong in musical lyrics. That way, a "commercial" is delivered every time people sing the song. And, as always, the idea must be simple and clear before it can be remembered.

Now look at Figure 8-3. In a way, it seems the product was *made* to fit the music—instead of the other way around.

FIGURE 8-3

Musical Commercial for 3-Way Complexion Lotion

JINGLE: (*MODERN ROCK BEAT*) *Here's a little notion*
To set your world in motion
It's like a magic potion
3-Way Complexion Lotion. (MUSIC UNDER)

ANNCR: If you want excitement in your world but are stopped—

SOUND: *MUSIC RUNNING DOWN AND STOPPING ABRUPTLY*

ANNCR: —by a skin problem, let 3-Way Complexion Lotion help. It washes your face better than soap, softer than cream. Just follow these three easy steps for a smooth, clearer complexion. First . . .

SOUND: *CHIME*

ANNCR: . . . apply 3-Way to your face. Massage it in, and feel it loosen hidden dirt. Second . . .

SOUND: *CHIME*

ANNCR: . . . rinse the lotion off. It leaves your skin soft and moist—never dry. Third . . .

SOUND: *CHIME*

ANNCR: . . . reapply 3-Way and leave it on as a make-up base or night lotion. It keeps on penetrating to soothe away dryness and help clear surface blemishes. Before you know it . . . (*SNEAK MUSIC IN*) . . . your skin will be clearer, smoother. Just right to start your world moving again.

JINGLE: *It's like a magic potion*
3-Way Complexion Lotion

ANNCR: Try some today . . . for tonight.

Some sales stories demand either more delicate or more rigorous copy than could readily be set to music. For example, a life insurance company might not welcome a sing-song aura attached to its accidental-death-policy messages. And, it's unlikely that a commercial designed to clarify misunderstandings about a bank's investment plans would do so through tuneful ditties—again because of the inappropriate image which could result.

Finally, when the heart of any commercial message—its X-Y-Z appeal—*is* set to music, two precautions should be observed. First, enunciation must be very clear; sometimes the melody predominates and the words are lost to listening ears. Second, the sales idea must take precedence over the song, so the audience doesn't remember a "nameless" tune.

Whatever the form of production, it's interesting to note that practitioners in this field often acknowledge the receipt of more helpful suggestions from art directors than from copywriters. Clearly, it's *pictures* (albeit mental ones) which must be communicated.

SPECIAL ROLES FOR MUSIC

When product messages are made available to retail outlets for purposes of local store tie-in, "doughnut" commercials may come into play. This *cooperative* advertising situation often involves a nationally produced jingle or sales-message-in-song—say, for a shampoo—at the beginning and end of the commercial. The middle portion is filled with soft background music only (or, sometimes, left completely silent), so a local message can be inserted. Sometimes, it's pricing news (a week-long special on the shampoo offered by a particular drug store), and sometimes it's just store information (location, hours of operation, and/or other shopping incentives). Hence, the musical part forms a ring (or "doughnut") around the spoken words in the center (in the "doughnut hole" position).

The same situation may occur when a chain such as J. C. Penney or Sears Roebuck gives local stores a chance to incorporate messages around a standard (nationally aired) musical theme or jingle. And, of course, the jingle itself continues to provide a memorable means for communicating brand or company image, and for reminding listeners of names and claims.

In a "sandwich" commercial, the local message fits between a standard, *spoken* open and close. But if the store involved has a musical theme or jingle, it may be incorporated into this middle "filling" (or layer) of the sandwich, along with additional verbal appeals. (Note: while the above discussion normally applies to *radio* commercials, the same ideas can be related to TV.)

USING THE HUMAN VOICE EFFECTIVELY

Radio commercials can milk the cow that jumps over the moon, or shine the ocean floor, with just the right blend of fantasy and credibility to help sell Dell's Dairies and Pratt's Polishes effectively.

Or they may become hopelessly bogged down in the sounds of heavy barnyard hoopla, machines, and orchestral crescendos and stingers. It all depends on the creative team's priorities: does the sales message, or entertainment, come first?

Also, as noted previously, even unobstructed, heart-of-the-sale copy, if poorly written, can bore both radio and TV audiences into non-listenership (mental tune-out, physical tune-out, or both). Consider, however, the skilful way Pan American Airways tackled the communicative-appeal problem of rising costs. Commercials featured family members sadly wishing they could afford a trip abroad—but the setting was *ten years in the future*. The thrust of the lament was: "Why didn't we go to Europe back in ᵢₙ(current year) when prices were reasonable!?" The overriding sales appeal, of course, was "Don't put off that trip" (or, "Now's the best time there is."), and the whole message proved both a creative and a sales-inducing twist on the woes of inflation.

Another example comes from a Small Fry boutique in Claremont, New Hampshire. The store decided that man-or-woman-on-the-street interviews were overused in radio commercials—and, hence, rather stale in their appeal. So, more "appropriate" tactics gave audiences a *kid*-on-the-street interview—with the ideal mix of humor and factual information needed to help sell children's clothing effectively. (See Marketing Outline item 24.)

The job of establishing and maintaining credibility is just as important in broadcasting as it is in print. The commercial which begins by asking an audience of dieters: "Want to lose five pounds this week—safely and easily at no cost?" may set the wheels of desire in motion . . . but it also opens the door to the need for some very specific product (and brand) particulars. Anything which sounds too-good-to-be-true faces a critical proving ground before it can hope to be accepted. So, this particular message might continue with a hard-hitting, free-trial-guaranteed-results story: "Try the Slim Trim Body Shaper free in your home for a week. A few minutes a day is all it takes with Slim Trim—plus a few simple menu plans—and you're on your way. Say goodbye to five pounds . . . or return the Body Shaper without paying a cent."

Notice, however, that the "sensational" approach drops the believability ball right at the start:

"Ladies and gentlemen, stand by for a miracle! Now you can trim away your unwanted pounds and never gain them back! Eat everything you like and still stay thin! Yes, there's absolutely nothing to it with the Slim Trim Body Shaper . . ."

By the time all the "holes" in this type of message have been plugged:

". . . of course, you *do* have to increase your exercise as you increase your intake of calories . . . and of course, you can't eat *much* of some foods . . ."

. . . the audience has tuned out in disappointment and/or disgust.

In addition, conversational style—complete with its short sentences and fragments, its contractions, its active pace, and its overall "punch" and "sparkle"—just naturally *belongs* in the "talking" media of radio and TV. And what about the "call to action" in commercials? Although it need not always pack a hard-sell immediacy ("rush out and buy"), as it often does in radio, the intended response must be clearly motivated and easy for listeners to make.

Compare the following:

NOT:	*. . . BUT RATHER*:
Send your request to Informative Services, Incorporated, Post Office Box 31857, Grand Central Station, New York, New York, 10020, and as soon as you receive your samples by mail, select the one you want and take it to Randy's Redemption Outlet, 4639 Main Street, right here in Jonesville; then, place your order, and wait for the call which tells you the shipment has arrived.	Stop by Randy's Redemption next time you're on Main Street, for information on how to order. Or, call Randy today—he's in the white pages of your phone book.

An extreme example? Perhaps. But even a so-called "simple" close, which briefly and effectively summarizes the X-Y-Z appeal: "So, for a party-pleasing dessert that whips up fast, get Frost Cream Delight; choose from three cooling flavors at your grocer's today" . . . has been known to drag out as follows (in the hands of a novice copywriter):

So if you drive over to your favorite supermarket sometime today . . . or just about any convenient grocery store . . . and ask the clerk in the frozen foods section for a carton of Frost Cream Delight, in any one of three different flavors, you'll wind up with a dessert that is bound to please the guests at your next party.

With this foundation behind us, we can now apply some of the print copywriting principles discussed in Chapter 6 to radio and TV. Once again we must emphasize, however, that these guidelines do not comprise a formula which guarantees successful commercials;

they do represent some approaches which have proven effective across countless product classes and throughout many years of advertising.

KEEP NEWS FRESH

Radio and TV have proven to be valuable information sources, as well as entertainment outlets. Indeed, they're credited with being up-to-the-minute news providers 24 hours a day. Hence, commercials which proclaim something different are expected to deliver it: "A unique combination of seasonings makes this dressing delicious on both fruits and vegetables." On the other hand, idle use of the word "new" hinders both its immediate credibility and its acceptance in other messages as well: "a glue with hundreds of new uses in your home."

BE CONCISELY CLEAR

Broadcasting's time restraints prohibit the enumerations of items which often appear in newspaper advertisements. Long lists of features, ingredients, and uses are boring to the ear and quickly forgotten. Even printed lists superimposed on the TV screen are dull. So, copywriters use collective words which specify product and user concerns, but which also summarize what might otherwise be unwieldy word-element collections. Examples are: "make-up articles," "travel needs," "camera accessories," "picnic items," and "beach necessities."

KEEP MESSAGES PERSONAL

Since spoken words are more intimate than written ones, the use of the second person in most broadcast copy is even more critical than it is in print. Occasionally, a case can be made for extensive use of the first or third person, as long as certain precautions are observed. An exclusive boutique might use the "we/our/us" approach to invite loyal customers to a special sale:

The birthday's on us. We've collected sample merchandise from our agents worldwide for a week-long birthday showing and sale. Each piece was chosen with our very special clientele in mind . . . because we're fussy. Come join our celebration: we may be getting older, but we're looking better than ever.

Compare this example, however, with a "pushy" first-person appeal from a sporting goods store:

> Hurry in to buy some of our magnificent sports apparel. We spend a lot of time and effort getting it all together, and, of course, we love to sell it to people. Our survival depends on making money, so come in and help us stay in business. We've got the best . . . so don't shop anywhere else.

The impersonal "he/she/they" attitude (often expressed also as a "the" position: easy on the hands . . . available from the nearest store . . . perfect for the children's toys) generally sounds cold and aloof. Once in a while, though, it can help devalue something which is being discouraged: "The friend who recommended that cheap detergent needs *your* friendly advice: one bottle of Jubilee cleans 50% more dishes." Or: "They said it couldn't be done . . . but Bowen's Bakery wasn't listening. They said no one could put sweetbread quality and taste in a low-calorie loaf . . . but Bowen's did it anyway."

SAY/PLAY IT AGAIN

We spoke briefly in Chapter 6 about the need for verbal and pictorial elements to reinforce each other in a printed advertisement—in effect repeating the sales message in two different visual channels. In the broadcast media, since commercials are fleeting, it's even more important that the advertiser's name and X-Y-Z appeal be expressed throughout a message, and through repeated airings of the commercials in a campaign.

A good exercise might be to list, first, a complete X-Y-Z appeal—with all three parts clearly labeled—on a sheet of paper. Then, for each part, write down half a dozen different ways of saying exactly the same thing (and notice the different "pictures" that come to mind):

X = SuperFruit nuggets satisfy your craving for sweets without added sugar or sugar substitutes.

Y = Only natural fruit juices are used.

Z = Sweeten your day the SuperFruit way.

OTHER POSSIBILITIES FOR X

1. Goodbye candy snacks . . . hello SuperFruit;
2. Keep snack time healthy;
3. A sweet little munchie that's not sugar-heavy;
4. A sweet fruit snack—not a junk food;
5. How sweet it is: but naturally so;
6. A fruit snack for your favorite sweet tooth.

OTHER POSSIBILITIES FOR Y
1. No added chemicals—just the juice from fresh fruits;
2. Minus added sugar: a plus for your diet;
3. Lower in calories than sugared candy, but still deliciously sweet;
4. No artificial sweetners—just real fruit flavor;
5. Naturally sweet, so there's never a sticky, syrupy taste;
6. Nothing masks the flavor of your favorite fruit juices.

OTHER POSSIBILITIES FOR Z
1. A SuperFruit treat is SuperFruit sweet;
2. The healthy treat that's oh, so sweet;
3. Put the SuperFruit snack on your health track;
4. A super kind of sweet in a fruity kind of flavor: SuperFruit;
5. It's fruit! It's super! It's SuperFruit!
6. It's naturally sweet . . . and sweetly natural. It's Superfruit.

Finally, depending on the length of the commercial involved, select the expressions which seem to offer the simplest, yet most distinctive, way to tell the selling story. Often, the zipper line is repeated two or more times *verbatim* (for impact), while the X and Y appeals are varied (to help maintain interest).

BEWARE THE VAGUE SHADOW

Because commercials are short, copywriters are inclined to lace them with simple terms which occur so often in daily conversation that they've lost whatever "specific" meaning they may once have had. It's *hard* to avoid using them (they're a lot like shadows), and, admittedly, you'll find them on pages throughout this text: words such as 'good,' 'better,' 'best,' 'great,' 'greatest' (and others, but especially those five).

Imagine each of these in a line from a commercial: (a) smells *good*; (b) a *better* kind of travel package than you thought possible; (c) the *best* way to beat the heat; (d) tastes *great*; and (e) the *greatest* support your feet have ever known. In each case, the copywriter should ask WHY—and HOW—and then let copy provide answers. For example: is it a hearty brewing process that causes the ("good") aroma? And a delicate blending of herbs that causes the ("great") taste? Here are the beginnings of pleasing, motivating mental images.

Even a more specific claim such as "fast and easy" for a dessert doesn't really come to life for listeners until it's explained: not in a *clock's* (fast time) or a *mechanic's* (easy-to-operate) terms . . . but in the prospective customer's terms. Is it faster than frosting a cake? As easy as boiling water? Then say so! Similarly, rather than claiming a product is a "real treat," try for a more visual, active picture: a party-pleaser . . . a mid-morning refresher . . . or a cooling, summertime snack.

On the other hand, every rule has its exceptions. Tide detergent took an overused saying: "The best (whatever) on earth," and turned it into a very effective, appropriate slogan: "TIDE: The Best Detergent On American Soil." Here's an example of a "best" that's clearly "better."

TREAT FIGURES LIKE FIRE

What about numbers on radio? In a word: beware. Addresses, phone numbers, and sets of figures detailing package weights, serving sizes, and nutritional contents usually prove very cumbersome. Ears haven't got memories . . . and the notion that listeners sit beside their radios with pens in hand, ready to take down information, is pure myth. Of course, a memorable price tag or vitamin percentage, a 50% savings spectacular, and an address which corresponds to the current calendar year can all be considered exceptions to the non-numeral rule.

But a word to the wise is: don't count on the numbers game to score with listeners. Rather, use an occasional figure to dramatize an important part of an X-Y-Z appeal—and leave the rest to visual representations: (1) "Come to Shelly's today—across from Potter Park"; (2) "Imagine: twice as much iron in one teaspoon as you're used to getting in a whole glass"; and (3) "call one of Zell's seven outlets—they're all as near as your yellow pages."

In the case of TV, numbers written on screen *can reinforce* the audio track—but the majority of TV commercials are only 30 seconds long; "too many numbers" can bog down an otherwise smooth-flowing message.

PROMISE POSITIVES

Thinking back to our discussion of "positivism" in Chapter 6, we now ask: do listeners really react differently if an announcer tells them to "remember" something than if he or she advises: "don't forget"? Or, what about "shop today," as opposed to "don't wait until tomorrow"? Or, "you'll be glad," versus "you won't be sorry"?

We have no universal "proof positive" that a negative approach is inherently a turn-off; but, human nature being what it is, we'd be hard pressed to find an advertiser who would seek a negative *image*; and it doesn't take a psychologist to know that a constant barrage of negative *anything* (words, gestures, expressions, or the like) surrounding a company or product is bound to set off unfavorable vibrations. (As another example, think of someone you know who frequently complains, rarely smiles, and always seems to see the black cloud instead of the silver lining. Now, even though this person may be an intelligent person, a brilliant artist or technician, and maybe a trusted friend, ask yourself how much more pleasant it would be if his or her disposition were positive and optimistic. You might not let such a concern affect your friendship or respect—but there's that (however slight) aura of negativism to contend with just the same.)

In a nutshell, advice to radio and TV copywriters is: *try* the positive before deciding you're content without it. At least experiment with a "faces will beam" line before proclaiming only that your product will "wipe away tears of sadness," "erase sorrowful expressions," or "get rid of gloomy looks." And listen to the sound of "each bite will delight" before insisting that "none of the ingredients can fail to please."

URGE A RESPONSE

Advertisers use radio and newspapers, in the majority of instances, to encourage direct action from audiences. Both of these media are locally oriented, and frequently use "hard sell" (do-it-*now*) tactics. The challenge for copywriters is to make it *easy* for consumers to respond—in a hurry, but without any uncomfortable pressure; to leave them with a feeling of excitement, but not anxiety; to urge but not to push.

Even in the occasional soft-sell radio commercial, listeners must know precisely what they're expected to do (even if it's only to "think" or "remember"). An out-of-the-way restaurant in one city believed its isolated location was a plus factor: it was a peaceful setting that gave customers a chance to unwind. The closing line of its radio commercial, however, advised listeners—somewhat mysteriously—that: "We're hard to find . . . but worth it." There was no mention of directions or of an address.

Television and magazine advertisers are more apt to ask for indirect action—the "soft sell" approach. They frequently ask audiences to "keep this name in mind," to "come in next time you're looking for bargains," or to "check this one out before you buy." Unfortunately, however, a surprising number of advertising messages include *no* calls to action—hard sell *or* soft sell. Apparently, copywriters are afraid of sounding "dictatorial" (although your authors still maintain that reference to a "suggested response" is a basic part of the persuasive communication process).

Now let's look at specific formats for radio commercials. Then we'll "cross over" the audio track—and move into the visual concerns of TV.

RADIO COMMERCIAL FORMATS

Radio copywriters develop their sales messages in a variety of formats, featuring one or several commercial speakers. The critical thing to remember is that *realism* helps sell . . . and whether or not all characters and situations are realistic, the delivery of product copy had better be. Messages which sound artificial or overly rehearsed are boring—and easily ignored.

SINGLE-VOICE COMMERCIALS

One-speaker messages may be delivered in several different forms: (1) a straightforward, often factual, no-frills presentation of product developments or benefits, which may emphasize competitive advantages; (2) a hard-sell, carnival-pitch, which features a "hurry-hurry-hurry" approach—often to the "biggest savings show in town" (or something similar); (3) a personality commercial, wherein a celebrity (or, in a lighthearted vein, perhaps, a comic impersonator or "storybook character") delivers the message, and lends his or her image to the product and sales story; and (4) an actual testimonial or endorsement of a product, service, or store, made either by a "star" or by an unknown individual with whom the audience can easily identify: a busy homemaker, an anxious traveler, or a successful business executive.

The advertised item, the target market, and the X-Y-Z appeal to be conveyed all play important roles in determining which of the above formats is selected for a given commercial. But the skilled copywriter keeps an open mind to "competitively unique" possibilities which may help strengthen a brand's positioning efforts.

MULTIPLE-VOICE COMMERCIALS

When two or more speakers take part in a radio commercial, they may: (1) carry on a dialogue (discussing a product's features and uses, as well as their own problems and needs); (2) interview one another (about anything from shopping habits and brand preferences, to job activities and vacation plans); and (3) engage in a mini-drama (resolving a dilemma, introducing a new service, or explaining the reasons behind a product's value).

Dialogue

Dialogue may lead into or grow out of a more standardized "announcer-delivery"; or may fill the entire commercial; or may serve as "bookends" to the message, both preceding and following the announcer's part. Unfortunately, though, unless it's handled expertly, dialogue often sounds very stilted:

MARY: Joan, have you heard about the simple but effective rug shampoo called Repel?

JOAN: Why, no, Mary . . . how ever do you use it?

MARY: Just hold the can six-to-eight inches from your carpet and spray with a slow, sweeping motion until evenly wet.

JOAN: My! That is wonderful, Mary! How long does it take to dry?

MARY: Just thirty minutes. Then you simply vacuum off the white powder which has formed—and the job is complete. Use it on upholstery and pillows, too, if you wish.

JOAN: Well, I certainly do thank you, Mary. That's exactly the product that I have been searching and waiting for. I'll be sure to buy some new Repel on my next trip to the store.

Can you imagine using Mary's explanation—or receiving Joan's reaction—in an exchange with any of *your* friends? The sequence loses credibility steadily from beginning to end, and sounds dull, flat, and impersonal, even though the second person "you" appears frequently. The message should surround the dialogue, instead of being squeezed in between irrelevant chatter. Now, hear and feel the difference in the dialogue below:

JOAN: Hi, Mary—cleaning house? (*SPRAYING SOUND*)

MARY: (LAUGHS) No, Joan . . . just *spraying* my carpet clean. With Repel.

JOAN: But now it's all *wet*!

MARY: Only for half an hour. Then it's once over with the vacuum and I'm through. (*SPRAYING SOUND*)

JOAN: Hey—not on *pillows*!?

MARY: Sure—and furniture, too. I just spray Repel (*SPRAYING SOUND*) . . . and relax. Simple?

JOAN: I'll say—and that's *my* kind of job: *repelling* extra work! (BOTH LAUGH)

ANNCR: Try Repel—the simple way to spray-clean.

Interviews and Dramas

Interviews can carry product stories effectively—if they stay within sales-message bounds, and don't wind up merely exchanging trivial chatter. Problem-solving dramas may also be powerful action-inducers if they're developed with audience predispositions in mind. The more listeners can identify with the characters and situations portrayed, the more receptive they're likely to be.

HUMOR IN RADIO COMMERCIALS

Evidence from a majority of recent studies shows that humorous appeals rarely increase an audience's retention of a sales message. Further, humor as a creative tactic doesn't often boost a commercial's persuasive powers. It *can* stimulate audience "liking" for a message source (the spokesperson, or voice-of-the-advertiser) but can also backfire, giving this individual or company an insincere or superficial image.

Still, radio listeners do appreciate an occasional lighthearted presentation, and it's often an effective attention-getter. The question is: does the use of humor lead to positive product-message reinforcement (for example, accurate listener recall) or does it detract from the real "selling" information, by focusing on itself (the joke-for-the-sake-of-a-joke)?

Once the copywriter is sure that humorous tactics are called for by a specific creative strategy, two possible approaches are: (1) a miniature playlet, involving a conflict and resolution, and (2) a more extemporaneous drama/discussion which may develop as a "story," but may also simply describe or explain a product or process. The first case usually involves either humorous *characters* (who appear in a "normal" situation) or a humorous *situation* (which unfolds around "normal" characters). The second case may require a series of edits (so the actual message is assembled after the recording has been completed) and the addition of a number of special effects (so-called "audio dimensions").

In both instances, however, copywriters must relate to audience needs and experiences, must treat their products respectfully (having fun *with* them, but never discrediting them), and must make all copy honest, simple, and direct. Figure 8-4a shows the Creative Strategy and Figure 8-4b an actual commercial for Schieffelin and Co. (Blue Nun wine) campaign. This radio spot exemplifies, in your authors' opinion, one of the best uses of humor in commercials in recent years.[1]

MULTI-MEDIA CAMPAIGNS: RADIO'S ROLE

Radio is often called the "reminder" medium—because it reminds listeners not only of products and X-Y-Z appeals, but also of the advertising for those products in other media. The same jingle running in a TV spot is often used on radio also—and media continuity is enhanced. Some advertisers (especially local ones) lift their entire TV commercial audio tracks (with or without jingles)

FIGURE 8-4a

Creative Strategy for Blue Nun

TARGET AUDIENCE:	Primary: 18-34 Secondary: 35-52
BASIC CLAIMS:	Delicious tasting Imported Correct with any dish
OBJECTIVE:	To position Blue Nun as an all-purpose dinner wine that goes as well with meat as it does with fish.
RADIO STRATEGY:	Use Stiller and Meara in a dialogue situation where wine is an integral part of the (recognizable) setting.
EXECUTION TECHNIQUE:	Provide humor through entertaining characters who use frequent twists of meaning in their conversation. Emphasize campaign slogan: "Blue Nun is a delicious white wine that's correct with any dish," and repeat product name several times.

and use them as radio spots (called, literally, "lifts"). The cost savings here is obvious, and once the visual portion of the message has become well established (through repeated exposure), radio's "reminder" capabilities go to bat for clients in fine style.

Often, in these situations, the TV commercials feature an off-camera voice or voices. Hence, viewers may already be used to hearing the message without actually seeing the speakers. On other occasions, TV audio (and even copy from printed media) may be adapted to radio by changing a few key words. For example: "*Look at all the designs you can make* . . ." (on TV) might become: "Create a design to fit *your* lifestyle . . ." (on radio).

Finally, radio can take a product displayed in full color in a national magazine and "localize" it—giving it a friendly, personal image by tying it in with advertising for a retail store. On the timely medium of radio, words like "this morning," and "waiting for you right now" take on added value because the listener often hears them while driving to the very store where the product is sold. If it's a frequently-purchased, low-cost item (as are many products advertised on radio today), chances are the brand name is already well known, thanks to other media; so, radio simply capitalizes on this knowledge.

Can radio say the same thing about a product that other media say? In most cases, yes—but the way radio says it may be quite different. If a scene which is readily apparent in print or on TV takes half a minute just to "set" clearly through words and sound effects, the radio copywriter must find another approach. On the other hand, a slogan such as, "You can't beat Crest for fighting cavities"

FIGURE 8-4b

Radio Commercial for Blue Nun

ANNCR: Stiller and Meara.

STILLER: Good evening, Miss. Will you be dining alone?

MEARA: (IN TEARS) Yes.

STILLER: What can I get you?

MEARA: Manicotti.

STILLER: Oh, I'm sorry we're all out.

MEARA: No. I mean Carmine Manicotti. He just broke our engagement. He had his mother call and tell me.

STILLER: Oh, the swine.

MEARA: No, she was very sweet about it.

STILLER: No, I meant Carmine. Anyway, may I suggest the Surf and Turf tonight?

MEARA: Is that some new singles bar?

STILLER: No, the Surf and Turf is our new delicious combination of lobster tail and filet mignon. Perhaps to raise your spirits, a very special wine.

MEARA: Can I get a wine that goes with seafood and meat?

STILLER: Certainly. May I bring a little Blue Nun to your table?

MEARA: I'm sure she'd be very sympathetic, but I'd much rather be alone.

STILLER: No, Miss, Blue Nun is a wine. A delicious white wine that's correct with any dish. It goes as well with meat as it does with fish. And, perhaps after dinner, cantaloupe.

MEARA: I don't see cantaloupe on the menu.

STILLER: No, that's me. Stanley Cantaloupe. I get off at eleven. Maybe we could go out on the town.

ANNCR: Blue Nun, the delicious white wine that's correct with any dish. Another Sichel wine, imported by Schieffelin and Co., New York.

Compliments of Schieffelin and Co.

can run easily in any medium. And, of course, *time* is a critical factor. The majority of radio commercials today are either 60 seconds or 30 seconds in length, but some may be as short as 10 seconds.

MULTI-MEDIA CAMPAIGNS: TV'S ROLE

Television is known as the "impact" medium. Even though it appeals directly to only two of the five human senses, seeing and hearing, wise copywriters use its powers of impact to involve viewers in tasting, smelling, and touching as well. In most print advertisements, the entire message is exposed simultaneously—without any mystery or dramatic effects.

But in TV, a suspenseful "curiosity over what's coming next" can run continuously if the copywriter uses television's unique capacity to control the flow of audience attention. Suppose, for example, that a scene opens with a close-up of a woman crying. Attention is aroused: is she hurt? Sick? Frightened? Then the camera pulls back slowly—and we see she's peeling onions (with an old-fashioned onion peeler, of course). The two-scene sequence is crucial here if the desired effect is to be achieved; if the opening shot were a medium shot of the woman peeling onions and crying, the "drama" would be lost.

After the "problem" peeler is introduced, the advertiser's own brand (say, Willy's Onion Wizard) and the solution to the homemaker's dilemma can appear. But to introduce this latter item *first* in the sequence (for instance, as a title: "Willy's Onion Wizard Presents," *superimposed over* the medium shot above) would, again, seriously decrease the value of the "crying" idea as an attention-getter.

TV COMMERCIAL FORMATS

As was true in radio, TV sales messages may be delivered in a number of different styles, utilizing a wide variety of production techniques. Four basic formats, however, were examined by Therence Shimp in a study of hundreds of national TV commercials, and they'll serve as guidelines for our discussion.[2]

FOCUS ON AN INDIVIDUAL

In this first category, the most popular approach is the *endorsement*—made by a "typical consumer." Granted, a person-on-the-street commands a much smaller commercial fee than a professional actor or actress does, but the emphasis on "real people" has also proven very popular with viewers. Problems concerning artificial situations in these commercials, as well as stilted dialogue, are noteworthy—but, then, Mr. and Ms. American aren't really expected to be polished product presenters. As long as the audience identifies with them, their messages often prove both credible and memorable.

Celebrity endorsers are also numerous: film and TV personalities, singer/musicians, sports figures, and others register quickly with viewers, since they tend to "fascinate" every time they perform. Stars *are* effective sales communicators, too, *if* they shine for their respective *messages*, and not for themselves alone. If there is a realistic, believable relationship between a celebrity and a product, and if that relationship is nurtured (not flaunted) through natural, need-fulfilling copy, the association can become a powerful, image-enhancing tool for the advertiser.

Also, celebrities may appear in commercials which focus on their *personalities*, rather than on any personal product endorsements. The value of celebrity-pull, alone, may be disputed—but when, for example, a Jerry Lewis telethon for Muscular Distrophy draws over $30 million from the American public in 20 hours, even skeptics have been known to tip their hats.

Recent commercial examples include: (1) Ricardo Montalban's "aura of sophistication" going to work for Chrysler Cordoba's Corinthian leather; (2) Juliet Prowse's renown as a dancer supporting her "good fit" message for L'eggs pantyhose; (3) Muhammed Ali's "rough and tough" character pitching Delco products and the D-Con roach exterminator; (4) Dick Cavett's perceptive, inquisitive nature complementing the informative content of *U.S. News and World Report* magazine; and (5) Karl Malden's "law enforcement vibes" tying into the "protection" theme of American Express Traveler's Cheques. Understandably, a number of East and West coast talent agencies now specialize in matching advertisers to stars. There's no guarantee, however, that any celebrity can be persuaded to appear exclusively in commercials for one company. Some experts believe that multiple exposures for a variety of products and services weaken a star's selling power, while others feel that as long as the performer remains high on viewers' popularity lists, he or she will continue to score points for associated brand names.

Before deciding one way or the other, ask yourself, first, if your message has a strong selling idea *without* any celebrity (it *should*), and second, if any one of a dozen stars could fill the bill equally well. If so, it's probably wisest to forget the celebrity idea; chances are, it's the personality slot alone that audiences will remember.

The same careful consideration should be given to voice-over announcers (who don't appear on camera), since the top 25 or so artists in this field command hundreds of thousands of dollars per campaign. (Note: flat, or scale, two-hour recording sessions are billed at $100 and more for radio, and $200 and more for TV.)

Next in line are straight, on-camera spokespersons—actors and actresses who haven't achieved star status. As many as one-third of today's TV commercials utilize such presenters—either by themselves, or in conjunction with real-life characters. It's generally agreed that while the "pro's" add precision and polish to commercials, amateurs contribute a sense of spontaneity and innocence. And some advertisers—ranging from fast food restaurants to laundry detergents—feel that a blend of the two provides the ideal sales communication vehicle. Examples are: a professional off-camera delivery over an actual in-home scene, or an interview situation in which only the interviewer is an actor or actress by trade.

FOCUS ON A STORY

The second format category includes commercial dramas—little playlets—which come in two forms: one with off-camera announcers and on-camera pantomime, and the other with on-camera performer/speakers. As the story unfolds, so does (1) a problem requiring use of the advertised product for its solution; or (2) a chance encounter with the product which leads to its acceptance and continued use; or, less often (3) an avoidance of the product which leads to discomfort or discontent.

Narrative commercials generally feature off-camera messages delivered over a little case history—of a product, service, or store. Frequently displayed are (1) the "involvements" of an advertiser in consumers' lives; (2) the track record an advertiser has acquired over time; and (3) the philosophies behind an advertiser's offerings . . . and the images the company has developed and maintained.

A simple one-day's television monitoring activity will reveal that approximately 75% of all commercials fall into the "individual" and "story" format classifications.

FOCUS ON THE PRODUCT

Third, we must examine the full-fledged product-orientation—featuring the TV medium's prized *demonstration*, as well as various other types of product display and/or performance. It's important to note that both "individual" and "story" presentations can and often do incorporate demonstration; in fact, up to a third of all commercials on the air today do. We're concerned here, however, with the messages which do nothing but focus on the product.

Automotive spots are often good examples, as are do-it-yourself items (designing, assembling, mixing, applying, repairing). And, a demonstration of how and why a product works (of its construction, as well as its operational features) may lend credibility to a claim otherwise deemed exaggerated.

A commercial's "setting" is often a critical concern when the focus is on a product (and/or on its package). Sometimes the item appears all by itself—in limbo. It may seem to float in space (picture a dark chocolate cream puff flying over a pale blue sky), or be "spotlighted" (imagine a sparkling gold watch hanging suspended in a dark studio, with a beam of light focused on its face). In other cases, scenes may be shot: (1) in fully-lit studios featuring table-top product demonstrations; (2) in realistic interior situations (in homes or stores); (3) on actual exterior locations (from the woods to city streets); or (4) in imaginative settings (dream worlds, futuristic locales, or storybook lands).

In each case, before a decision is made, message strategy must be checked. Is the plan to set the product off—in effect, to isolate it from potentially distractive elements? Or should a "contrast" of some sort be dramatized: heating vs. air-conditioning; plane travel vs. road travel; hand-made designs vs. mass production. How about symbolism: hearts and flowers; a wholesome, earthy quality; or a youthful, energetic activity? Special circumstances might even dictate extraordinary appeals—such as product torture tests.

Harry Wayne McMahan, a well-known TV commercial consultant, advocates what he calls the product-as-hero format. Webster's New World Dictionary commercials gave their product a genuine personality when they showed pages flipping over and talking by themselves. And, one of New York's Citibank commercials featured quarters dropping into a glass (like pain-relief tablets): "For those little financial headaches." Pies and pastries can make and bake themselves, while golf and tennis balls come to life to present their own sales stories, and animated faces appear on all kinds of products to focus viewer attention on the heart of the buying situation.

Sometimes, the product itself doesn't "do" anything. But an air of suspense—or delight—builds *around* it: thanks to a spotlight or sunbeam, a mysterious wand or mystical genie, a creeping shadow or twinkling star. Then, again, a special "package" may be created around the product: an unbreakable carton, a container which can later be used as a dish or glass, or a decorated dispenser-box. Finally, advertised brands can compete with competitors and "win." They can rescue consumers in distress, or rise to the top of an elaborate in-store display—above all of their lower-placed brothers and sisters.

FOCUS ON A TECHNIQUE

Our final consideration is the "production" emphasis. Animated fantasies can carry viewers to the land of jolly giants, playful tigers, and tree-dwelling elves, while comedy routines find Jonathan Winters costumed as a never-ending assortment of people, places, and things. Special effects, in both audio and video tracks, pop in and out of magic shows, and take viewers on interplanetary adventures (which result in "revolutionary" new electronic devices, vehicles, and even desserts).

Sometimes, visual symbolism plays an effective role here, too. For instance, when gasoline moves through its pump—into a very expensive *champagne glass*—viewers get the point immediately. Or, consider the objective of a regional dairy: to position its ice cream as the one *kept cold*. TV commercial tactics? A technique that placed earmuffs around the ice cream cartons as they moved from the plant to the delivery truck and store.

THE X-Y-Z APPEAL ON TV

Now it's time to examine a full 60-second TV commercial to see how its X-Y-Z appeal is developed. When you study Figure 8-5, don't worry about the technical production lingo, since it will be discussed in Chapter 9. Rather, as you examine each shot, try to think of other ways the product might have appeared and other ways the sales message might have been presented (especially in some more common *30-second* forms). And remember that an advertising campaign consists of a series of different advertisements and commercials, even though the basic message may remain the same.

The first scene captures the audience—not just mothers, but busy ones: those who need a helping hand in the kitchen. Attention is aroused through well-matched audio and video, and we're on our way.

The value of Pyfer's story is clear in the second and third shots: here's an easy way to give families needed nutrition . . . along with hearty taste. But is the audience "involved"? Check the copy—and the clear-cut reward being promised. If, as noted earlier, our mothers really seek the "line of least resistance" when it comes to problem solving, this commercial's off to a fine start; it's laying the groundwork for a simple, sure-fire solution to dinnertime worries.

The fourth through the seventh scenes get the adrenalin flowing. The need is apparent, and the benefit within reach. Now the appeal is enhanced: anyone for vitamins? How about freshness? *Sure* there's desire here—plenty of it (especially with the "no extra work" feature thrown in). Notice that the X-Y-Z appeal (fresh potato flavor without fresh potato work—thanks to Pyfer's special cooking and packaging processes) appears more than once—in more than one form—but remains honest, believable, unmistakable.

The eighth and ninth shots tie up the sales package with some strong ribbons: a perfect creation for the dinner table . . . and

FIGURE 8-5

Form for a TV Storyboard

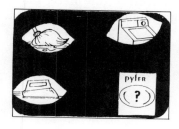 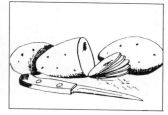 

FADE IN CU ANIMATED EYES WHICH POP OPEN IN SEQUENCE TO MOP-IN-USE, WASHER SPINNING, IRON-IN-USE, AND EMPTY PLATE WITH "?" WHICH TURNS INTO PYFER BOX ON CUE	CUT TO CU POTATOES BEING SLICED; ZOOM IN ON PILE OF THIN SLICES	HORIZ WIPE TO MS PYFER KITCHEN; CHEFS WORKS AND MACHINERY MOVES
ANNCR: Here's eye-opening news for busy homemakers with dinner-time worries: Pyfer's potato flakes.	All the nutrition of fresh potatoes, thin-sliced to retain flavor.	Pyfer's special chef turns these crisp slices into tasty, delicate flakes -- so your cooking job's easier.

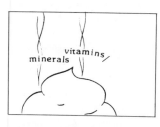 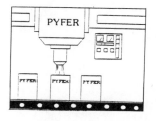 

ZOOM IN TO CU ONE POTATO AND MATCH DIS TO ANIMATED POTATO WHICH SHOWS ITS CONTENTS	CUT TO MCU LAB AND ZOOM IN ON MACHINE WHICH PRESSES FLAKES AND SEALS BOXES WHICH "BULGE" WITH FLAVOR	DIS TO CU ANIMATED PYFER BOX WHICH ALTERNATELY "EXPANDS" TO SHOW POTATO INTERIOR AND GOES BACK TO ORIGINAL
The vitamins and minerals your family needs from potatoes...	...stay sealed in Pyfer potato flakes -- along with explosive taste appeal...	...in a package of real potato flavor.

194

Figure 8-5

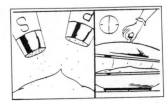

CUT TO MOM'S KITCHEN
WITH CLOCK IN BKGD;
CU OF HANDS POURING
AND STIRRING; ZOOM
IN ON FLAKES

Just add Pyfer's
potato flakes to milk
and heat. They're cut
thin so they cook up
fast -- with all
their vitamins
inside.

DIS TO CU HAND PUTTING
LID ON PAN; HOLD AS
CLOCK MOVES 1 MIN;
WIPE ON CU HANDS WITH
SEASONING

Then, cover your pan
and wait one minute.
Season to taste...

IRIS (CLOCK) WIPE TO
MCU FAMILY AT TABLE
GLEEFULLY EATING;
SUPER "PYFER" OVER BOWL

...and watch your family
dig in! They'll love
that mashed potato
goodness...and you'll
love knowing each
fluffy forkful...

CUT TO CU MOM EATING
POTATOES AS THOUGHT
BALLOON APPEARS: REAL
POTATO NEXT TO BOWL
SHE MADE; ZOOM IN ON IT

...is loaded with food
value -- like just-
picked potatoes.

CUT TO MCU PYFER CHEF;
WIPE ON SPLIT SCREEN:
CU POTATO "FIXINGS"
AND LARGE SUPERED "X"
OVER PREPARATIONS

Pyfer's chef assures
you of high quality
nutrition; you get
fresh potato flavor
without fresh potato
work.

CUT TO MCU STORE SHELF
AS LARGE AND SMALL BOXES
ZOOM TO CAMERA WITH
PRICES FLASHING; BOXES
HOLD IN FG AND SUPER
"REAL POTATO" OVER EACH

Get Pyfer's mashed potato
flakes today. Two
convenient sizes, two low
prices, and the same real
potato goodness -- from
Pyfer.

beaming family approval. And while we know it's *Mom's* prize, there's never any doubt that *Pyfer's* is the winner. People appear in this commercial, but the product and X-Y-Z appeal dominate.

An active recap of the sales message, and lively, relevant copy set the stage for final curtain. Conviction is there, and both the tenth and eleventh scenes capitalize on it. Then: the last scene and the last word are, once again, "matched" for impact.

Was this commercial plan the best one possible for Pyfer's? No one can say for sure—but few would quarrel with the direct manner in which it applied the guidelines we've presented so far.

COMPARATIVE COMMERCIALS

Chapter 6 discussed the mention and display of competing brands of products in advertisements, and noted some related concerns for copywriters. In the perishable medium of television, the chances for viewer confusion over which brand is actually being advertised intensify; thus, while some product messages continue to thrive in this format, a large number of advertisers avoid it entirely.

Studies examining the extent of comparativism in TV commercials have found figures as low as 3% (messages which are "completely comparative"—second by second, brand name by brand name), and as high as 18% (messages which, at the very least, *imply once* a "comparison with unnamed brands").[3] Results reported by Lamb, Pride, and Fletcher, however, support those made by a variety of others: approximately 8% of the commercials on the air today assume a "mainly comparative" format. Further, they can be broken down into two types: (1) *associative* commercials, which point out similarities between the advertised brand and competitors; and (2) *differentiative* commercials, which point out differences.

Finally, there are three levels of comparative intensity: (a) the *low* level, which involves no mention of names, but refers to the "leading brand" or "major competitor"; (b) the *moderate* level, which does include names, but doesn't compare on a point-by-point basis; and (c) the *high* level, which mentions names and compares feature by feature. The most frequently used type is the *high intensity*, *differentiative* commercial, and the items most often presented in comparative formats are drug products, followed by household items, foods, personal care products, and durable goods.[4]

HUMOR IN TV COMMERCIALS

How widespread is the use of humor in TV commercials? It all depends on how we define "humor." If we mean elements which provoke *hilarity* among viewers, we're undoubtedly talking about something less than 5% of all commercials on the national airwaves today. The ability to make masses of people laugh is a rare one at best—and the more diverse the audience is, the more difficult the task becomes.

In a recent study of 2,000 commercials, however, a research team broadened the definition of humor to include the mere use of one or more verbal gimmicks: puns, understatements, either single-voiced or dialogue-exchanged jokes, and audio/video situations involving satire, irony, or something ludicrous. But even in this instance, less than 15% of the messages qualified as humorous, and in more than half of these cases, the humor was clearly product directed, and not there solely for attention-getting or entertainment purposes.[5]

Clearly, selling is a very serious business, and, as an indispensable selling *tool*, advertising is obliged to treat it with respect.

LOCALIZING A NATIONAL CAMPAIGN

Before moving into broadcast production, a brief word is in order concerning two special strategic situations in advertising. The first involves the "localizing" of a national campaign. TV viewers across the country are familiar with Wendy's Restaurants' "Lots-Of-Napkins" campaign launched in the late 1970's. Facing strong competition from McDonald's and Burger King, Wendy's chose a positioning strategy centering on its hamburger product, rather than on its speed/efficiency of service, varied menu, prices, or other features.

Two of the many commercials from this campaign appear in Figures 8-6a and 8-6b. Notice that (1) an "ingredient" story ties in beautifully with the hot-and-juicy *meat* theme, (2) the (unique) napkins story is shown in several different settings, and (3) the same Wendy's logo appears at the end of both of these commercials (and, in fact, nearly all others in this and later campaigns).

National commercials for Wendy's have also featured the celebrity appeal of Jonathan Winters. But let's look now at the way these message ideas appeared in one specialized market. The Honolulu agency for Wendy's, Starr/McCombs, adapted the national campaign plan to a local situation (home-grown ingredients and friendly service), and personalized it still further by using a popular local entertainer, Danny Kaleikini, as celebrity spokesman.

This commercial appears in Figure 8-7. Notice again the presence of all three story-lines ("ingredients," "hot and juicy," and "napkins"), and the incorporation of the familiar logo shot at the end. Also, the "you're gonna love" copy line was picked up from the

FIGURE 8-6a

National TV Photoboard for Wendy's

**THE
WENDY'S
NATIONAL
ADVERTISING
PROGRAM,**
INC.

"TWINS"
30 Second TV

(Music: "Wendy's Tune")
Wendy's presents,
hot and juicy hamburgers.

If you've ever had a dry,
chewy hamburger.

you're gonna love Wendy's
hot and juicy hamburgers.

Wendy's hot and juicy hamburgers.
Juicy meat. Juicy toppings.
And lots of napkins.

COMPLIMENTS OF WENDY'S INTERNATIONAL, INC.

FIGURE 8-6b

National TV Photoboard for Wendy's

THE WENDY'S NATIONAL ADVERTISING PROGRAM, INC.

"256 WAYS" 30 Second TV

(Music: "Wendy's Theme")
Wendy's presents, juicy toppings.

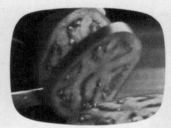
At Wendy's...

we take all the great hamburger toppings...

and fix them in 256 different combinations.

We fix the toppings 256 ways...

but at Wendy's...

we fix the meat only one way, hot and juicy.

COMPLIMENTS OF WENDY'S INTERNATIONAL, INC.

national commercials, and the *tag line* (address/location of one or more Wendy's restaurants), though not shown in Figures 8-6a and 8-6b, is frequently inserted by local stations across the country which air national spots.

The X-Y-Z appeal is clear and strong here, even though all three parts aren't spelled out in the audio track:

X = a hot and juicy hamburger you'll love
Y = Wendy's uses only fresh meat and toppings, (and doesn't believe in dry, chewy burgers)
Z = (so juicy you'll need) lots of napkins

COOPERATION BETWEEN ADVERTISERS

The second situation to examine involves a commercial sponsored by two different advertisers. We've already discussed the cooperative plan under which a national manufacturer joins forces with a retail outlet carrying that particular product. In resultant advertising messages, the manufacturer asks consumers to "buy my brand," and the retailer follows through by requesting that they "buy it at my store." Sometimes, however, two advertisers sharing a slightly less obvious purpose produce an advertisement. For instance, a soft drink or potato chip manufacturer and a company making thermal coolers or paper napkins might co-sponsor a message dealing with picnics. (And, either the two former or the two latter advertisers in this case might also get together.)

Another example is shown in Figure 8-8. In Hawaii, tourism (including travel to and from major islands in the Hawaiian chain) is the number one industry. It makes "good marketing sense," therefore, for an interisland airline and car rental company to co-produce a commercial. Notice, too, that the message is again delivered by local celebrity Danny Kaleikini, who does, in fact, travel extensively throughout the islands on the entertainment circuit.

Can you find the complete X-Y-Z appeal here? (Give it a shot on your own before looking at the explanation below.)

X = an all-in-one package: a fly/drive combination plus attractive coupons—all as convenient as your telephone
Y = the spirit of friendship and a background of very successful business combine to produce a valuable customer package
Z = make your next trip beautiful . . . and: "*You're* Number One"

A nationally-run commercial for Budget Rent a Car, shown in Figure 8-9, plays up the "You're Number One" theme throughout.

FIGURE 8-7

Example of a Local TV Photoboard for Wendy's

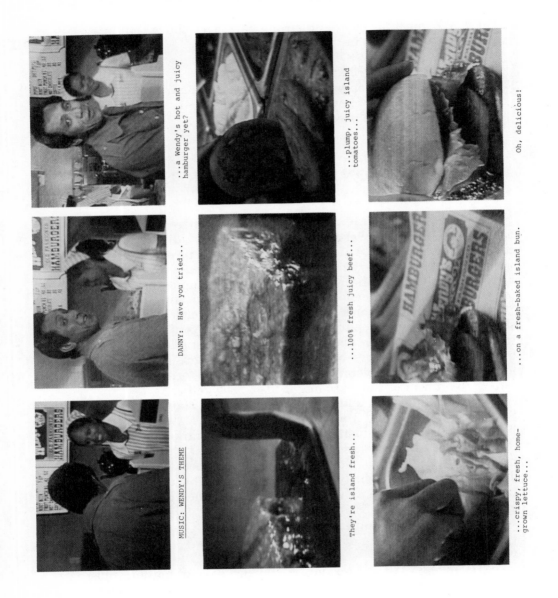

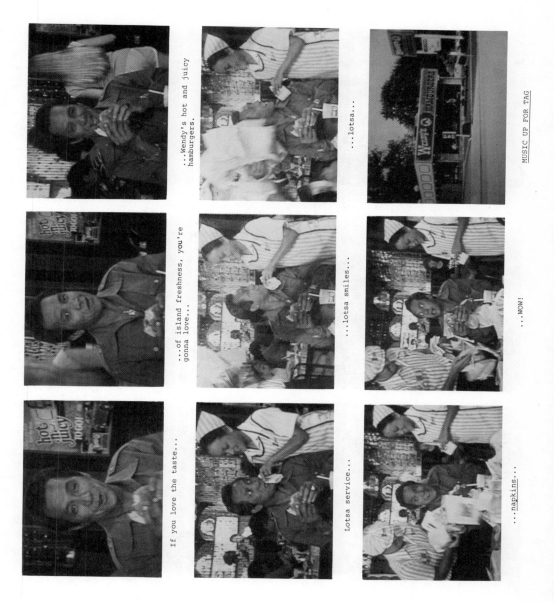

FIGURE 8-8

Example of a Local TV Photoboard for Budget Rent a Car

DANNY: Aloha, Hi! Danny Kaleikini here. Wherever I go in the Islands...

...my friends from Budget Rent-A-Car and Aloha Airlines are always there.

FLT ATT: An airline with the Spirit of Aloha.

CAR ATT: The leading car rental company in the Islands.

DANNY: And a Budget coupon booklet...

...with free admissions...

...to all of Hawaii's...

...leading attractions.

Make your next trip...

...beautiful. For
reservations...

...see your travel agent, or
call 836-1111.

That's Aloha Airlines. Where
you're number one.

COMPLIMENTS OF FAWCETT MCDERMOTT INC.

FIGURE 8-9

National TV Photoboard for Budget Rent a Car

1980 Network TV Commercial "Elevator"

GIRL: Going up?

ANNOUNCER: Move up to Budget Rent a car . . . where you're number one!

MAN: I had no trouble getting here. Budget made it easy.

MAN: They gave me this card already printed up with exact directions. Now that's a real service for travelers.

ANNOUNCER: Budget Rent a Car proves you're number one!

MAN: I can't believe it! Hertz charged ten dollars more than Budget for the same one day rental on the same size car.

MAN: And Budget's right inside most airports.

ANNOUNCER: At Budget,

you're number one!

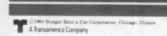

©1980 Budget Rent a Car Corporation, Chicago, Illinois
A Transamerica Company

Printed in U.S.A.

COMPLIMENTS OF BUDGET RENT A CAR CORPORATION

But in this case there is no cooperative arrangement. A discussion of Budget's services, costs, and convenience fills the spot.

Now it's time to examine radio and TV script and storyboard forms in detail. And, in Chapter 9, we'll examine some production activities which are counterparts to the production concerns discussed in Chapter 7.

STUDY QUESTIONS

1. It's not enough for radio's "headliners" (opening words and/or sounds) to gain attention. They must do it with *what two very specific goals in mind?*
2. How can the "sound" of words and voices affect a radio audience's reaction to a commercial?
3. What two precautions should be observed when a commercial's X-Y-Z appeal is set to music?
4. What is a "doughnut" commercial?
5. How do copywriters get around the use of "lists" of items or features in a radio commercial? Give specific examples.
6. How can copywriters take the "push" out of a hard sell line—without losing the appeal to urgency?
7. Name and describe four different commercial formats—two for radio and two for TV.
8. Why is humor frequently avoided in radio and TV commercials?

ENDNOTES

1. See J. Douglas Johnson, ed., *Campaign Report Newsletter*, January, 1979, American Association of Advertising Agencies, New York.
2. Therence A. Shimp, "Methods of Commercial Presentation Employed By National Television Advertisers, *Journal of Advertising*, Vol. 5, No. 4, Fall, 1976, pp. 32-34.
3. See especially S. W. Brown and D. W. Jackson, "Comparative Television Advertising: Examining its Nature and Frequency," *Journal of Advertising*, Vol. 6, No. 4, Fall, 1977.
4. Charles W. Lamb, William A. Pride, and Barbara E. Fletcher, "A Taxonomy for Comparative Advertising Research," *Journal of Advertising*, Vol. 7, No. 1, Winter, 1978.
5. Patrice Kelly and Paul Solomon, "Humor in Television Advertising," *Journal of Advertising*, Vol. 4, No. 3, 1974, pp. 32-34.

9

CREATIVE TACTICS FOR BROADCAST MEDIA: SCRIPT AND STORYBOARD EXECUTION AND PRODUCTION

Radio commercial scripts may take any of a variety of forms, but a popular one appears in Figure 9-1. Everything not spoken over the air (all "instructional material" for speakers and engineers) is capitalized, and sound effects and music are (additionally) underlined. It's generally felt that upper-and-lower case letters are easier than all-capitals to read (by speaking talent), and that all other material should be set off from copy as clearly and completely as possible.

A few basic radio production terms may appear in these scripts and should be noted before progressing further. They're also used in the audio portion of TV scripts and storyboards, so will be useful to us there, too. In many cases, the lingo is self-explanatory (and sometimes abbreviated):

BRING BKGD MUSIC UP
FADE VOICES DOWN AND OUT
HOLD TRAFFIC SOUND EFFECTS (SFX) UNDER ANNCR

In others, a word of explanation is in order:

FIGURE 9-1

Example of Radio Script Form

SOUND:	*OFFICE NOISES (TYPEWRITERS, TELEPHONES) UP & UNDER*
ANNCR:	When you leave the noises at work . . .
SOUND:	*CROSSFADE SOUND OF CHILDREN ARGUING AND CRYING*
ANNCR:	. . . only to find new ones at home, snap in—a Snap-ette!
SOUND:	*SEGUE BEAUTIFUL MUSIC AND HOLD UNDER ANNCR*
ANNCR:	And *relax* . . . because a Snap-ette tape is the perfect remedy for those end-of-the-day blahs. Each tape is filled with the sweetest sounds this side of slumberland. And the nicest part is . . . *(MUSIC OUT)* it works in a . . .
SOUND:	*STINGER "SNAP" AS ANNCR SAYS:*
ANNCR:	. . . *snap*! Get Snap-ette tapes at any record store.

to CROSSFADE is to decrease gradually the volume of one sound or piece or music, while simultaneously increasing the volume of another;

to SEGUE is to switch from one sound or musical selection to another abruptly—without fading up or down;

and a STINGER is an "accent sound" which punctuates a word or line of copy.

In television, things get a little more complicated. Copywriters, of course, aren't expected to be experts in TV production, but they do need a working knowledge of basic techniques if they are to translate creative strategies into convincing audio and video channels. Figure 9-2a illustrates a television commercial script. Each scene—or "frame" is presented in "video-ese," and its accompanying copy appears in the audio column alongside. Notice that the visual instructions contain three different types of material (often, again, abbreviated): (1) transition information (explaining how viewers will be carried from the preceding scene to the existing one); (2) composition information (explaining the shot's perspective—from long-distance to close-up, or from wide angle to narrow); and (3) a basic description of the scene's elements and actions.

The TV *storyboard* that accompanied this script is shown in Figure 9-2b. Copy appears as before, but this time it's accompanied by a kind of "comic strip" sequence of pictures. Now the film or videotaping crew can visualize more readily and completely what the copywriter (and his or her partner in art) intend to convey.

FIGURE 9-2a

Example of a TV Commercial Script

CLIENT: Parks-Belk
PRODUCT: Men's Suit Sale
LENGTH: 30 sec.
AIR DATES: April 27-30, 1980
STATIONS: WCYB, WJHL, WKPT

AUDIO: Carl Swann/Disco Cut #2
                Jingle Bed
PRODUCER: Louisville Productions
DIRECTOR: Bob Pilkington/Gary Clem
WRITER: Anne Koehler/Phyllis Atkins
TALENT: James Bailey; Tom Chapman

PRODUCTION NOTES: All video to be chromakeyed over slide of Men's Dept. Bristol store. Model facing camera as if in front of mirror. Use stop-action changes of suits on model for magical effect. Chromakey suit changes to tape of Tom's reactions as amazed customer.

VIDEO	*AUDIO*
(1) FADE IN MLS JAMES IN NAVY SUIT AS TOM ENTERS RIGHT. LOGO SUPERED AT LEFT. (2) SUIT CHANGES TO BEIGE. TOM REACTS, MOVING LEFT, GETTING EXCITED. (3) BROWN SUIT. TOM REACTS.	<u>MUSIC INTRO: THEME PHRASE, 2 SEC.</u> ANNCR: Parks Belk does it again! It's *the* suit sale. Parks-Belk's big annual suit sale and it's now! This week!
(4) BLUE SUIT; REACTION. KILL SUPER.	Now's the time to buy your suits at sale prices. You'll love these vested suits with the new narrow lapels . . .
(5) SUPER $69.88 AND HOLD. (6) SUIT CHANGE TO TAN STRIPE; RE-ACTION.	And just look at the price . . . only sixty-nine eighty-eight. Great suits at a great price!
(7) KILL SUPER. TOM ON LEFT FOR FINAL SUIT CHANGE, GRAY PIN-STRIPE (MS). JAMES EXITS RIGHT, TOM FACES CAMERA.	Hundreds of suits sale-priced for just sixty-nine eighty-eight!
(8) TOM, BACKVIEW CU WALKS ON SCREEN, NOW WEARING GRAY SUIT. SWAGGERS, PROUD; 3 BELK SUIT BOXES IN ARMS (MLS). (9) TOM EXITS RIGHT.	Get one or a whole closet full . . . but hurry! At this price they'll go fast.
(10) CUT TO SPLIT-SCREEN EFFECT: LOGO SUPERED WITH 4 STORE NAMES ON LEFT SIDE; TOM, PLEASED, ADMIRES BOXES FROM BOXED-INSERT ON RIGHT SIDE OF SCREEN. (11) STORE HOURS SUPER ON, FLASHING.	It's the *suit sale*, this week at these Parks-Belk Stores. Now open Sunday, one till six.
FADE TO BLACK.	

FIGURE 9-2b

Example of a TV Storyboard

COMPLIMENTS OF PARKS BELK COMPANY

WHERE TO BEGIN

Some advertising agencies always start with a storyboard; then, after the commercial format is pretty well established and approved, a script *may* be prepared to accompany it. If the commercial is going to be filmed, it may be turned over to the production house purely in storyboard form; and, in this case, the agency might never call for a standard script, because the film company will prepare a highly technical "shooting script" from which to work. On the other hand, if the commercial is going to be videotaped (as most local spots are), the two-column script may be all that's required. If an additional storyboard is prepared, its purpose is often to help the advertiser client visualize scenes, and to assist the TV director in staging them. Both scripts and storyboards thus play important communication roles . . . but one doesn't necessarily precede or follow the other.

Now let's discuss video terminology in detail.

SCENE COMPOSITION

Camera shots must be considered from two different perspectives—one stationary and the other moving. First, simply by changing lenses, a camera operator may show the same subject or scene (1) from a distance—in a *long, full, cover,* or *establishing* shot (all basically the same); (2) part way in—in a *medium long shot,* a *medium shot,* or a *medium close-up* (each one bringing viewers a little closer to the target); or (3) up close—in a *close-up* or *tight shot,* or an *extreme close-up.*

Each successive change shows viewers more detail, bringing them, in essence, closer to the "stage" or performance. In addition, a high or low camera angle can create the effect of "peering down on" or "gazing up at" an object or person. Some cameras are equipped with a floating vertical pedestal, permitting shots from a very elevated angle/peak. The camera cue in this case is simply "boom up" or "boom down," and the object being viewed will appear to shrink and grow accordingly.

When a character dominates a picture, the camera may take a *head shot,* a *chest* or *waist shot,* or a *knee* or *full* (head-to-toe) *shot.* When more than one individual is involved, there is the *2-shot* or *3-shot,* the *group shot,* and the *over-the-shoulder shot* (behind one character, "looking toward" another).

CAMERA MOVEMENT

Second, a camera may move—to lead or follow some talent action or the unfolding of a scene or message (for example, a display of ingredients or a collection of merchandise). One way is by *panning,* a term which refers to a swiveling of the camera itself, left to right or right to left, while the (movable) *base* of the camera apparatus remains in one spot. The effect is similar to that achieved by looking through a swiveling telescope (whose "standard" remains stationary). And, when the movement is *up and down,* it may be called *tilting,* although "pan up" and "pan down" are acceptable terms, too. A very slow pan results in almost imperceptible traveling, while a "zip pan" swings the camera so fast the picture blurs (to show, perhaps, the way a series of tasks appear to a harried secretary, or to a headache-sufferer).

Of course, the farther away the scene gets from the lens, the fewer the details which viewers can decipher. So, sometimes the entire camera *and* its base are moved: *trucked,* or physically pushed across the floor, again in a left or right direction, to precede or keep up with movement across a set. (Note: when the movement is more circular, it may be referred to as an "arc right" or an "arc left.")

When the desired movement is forward or backwards, or *into* a scene and *away* from it, a zoomar camera lens accomplishes the task. It zooms in and out from a long shot, through a medium shot, to a close-up, and back again (at controllable speed), maintaining perfect focus. Or, roughly the same effect is achieved by physically pushing and pulling—or *dollying*—the entire camera/base toward and away from the scene portrayed. In this case, a little more time and effort are required—to keep movements smooth and focus sharp—and resulting angles and perspectives may be slightly different from those obtained by zooming.

Some of the above actions may be accomplished simultaneously. For instance, a table-top demonstration strategy might ask the camera operator to "zoom in on the display of ingredients while panning right to the product package."

OPTICAL SCENE CHANGES

Panning/tilting, trucking/arcing, zooming, and dollying all result in a change of scene for viewers. And, they're all accomplished through some form of physical action (from "finger/hand manipulation" of camera lenses to full-body movements). It's also possible, however, to bring the viewing audience a new picture electronically, while all cameras and their operators remain motionless.

A simple button-punching technique in the control room (or a film-editing procedure in the laboratory) may show viewers, in a very few seconds, *first*, the picture held by Camera One; *second*, the picture held by Camera Two; and *third*, the same Camera One picture again. When the switch is made as quickly as the snap of a finger, it's called *cutting* or *taking*: "cut to 1, cut to 2, cut to 1" (or "take 1, take 2, take 1"). When it's made more slowly, so that Camera One's shot disappears gradually while Camera Two's shot just as gradually takes it place, the term is *dissolve*. Thus, we might have: "take 1 . . . dissolve 2 . . . dissolve back to 1."

Or, the scene change might be a little fancier. A new picture may literally *wipe* the old one off the screen: horizontally ("wipe right" or "wipe left"), vertically ("wipe up" or "wipe down"), diagonally ("wipe across"), in a circular fashion ("iris"), or in any of a variety of other ways.

Dissolves and wipes generally indicate a greater passage of time and/or change of locale than "cuts" do. In a cake mix commercial, cuts would probably be used between shots of a mother and daughter at work in the kitchen, while a dissolve transported viewers "back to Grandma's house" at cake-making time—and then home again. Finally, when Mom's mix goes into the oven, a clock-sweeping wipe would permit the finished cake to appear—all in 30 seconds.

Rarely does a picture vanish completely during a commercial—leaving a blank screen in its place before another shot appears—but under unusual circumstances, *fade in* and *fade out* might be used. (Consider, for example, the *leap* in time from cave dwellers' "wheels" to automobiles of the 1980's.) Also, the opening shot of most all commercials begins with a fade in (from, literally, "nothingness"), and the closing shot fades out at the end.

OTHER TECHNIQUES

Four additional terms are used so often they deserve mention here. A *superimposure* ("super") is two shots presented on top of one another: words over pictures (see again Figure 8-8, on page 202), or even pictures over pictures. It's an excellent way to reinforce spoken copy or to emphasize a package.

A *split screen*, on the other hand, is two or more scenes shown side by side. Used frequently to compare products or activities, or to show relationships across time and locations, two-way split screens are a lot easier to follow than are three- and four-way (though the latter may be used, when strategically sound, to gain attention in an opening shot, or to recap an X-Y-Z appeal in a closing one).

A *freeze frame* is a stationary ("frozen") shot which, more than likely, has been moving, but is suddenly halted in its progress across the screen. Again, it's used for emphasis—to focus and hold viewer attention on a key message ingredient.

And, finally, a *matte shot* appears to viewers as if through a telescope or pair of binoculars, a keyhole or porthole, or any other device which limits viewing to one person at a time. These effects are easy to achieve by placing a "cut-out" (matted) form in front of the camera lens.

After commercials have been produced on film or tape, photographed versions of them, called photoboards, are sometimes provided for client and agency files. As "still forms" of the finished moving pictures, they're obviously much more convenient to handle (and to discuss and compare). Figures 8-6a, 8-6b, 8-7, 8-8, and 8-9, on pp. 197-204, are photoboards.

PRODUCTION CONCERNS

Three major considerations crucial to every production decision in broadcast advertising are the *time* involved, the *effort* required, and the *dollars* available. (Remember them through their first letters: TED.) So important (and often inseparable) are these items that it's safe to say they sit on every dotted line where production signatures are affixed, and on the shoulders of everyone who must negotiate production terms.

Specific figures in these areas vary greatly, according to: (a) market and station sizes, and audience composition; (b) the specific product, service or store concerned; (c) the cast, crew, production locale, and facilities available; and (d) overall campaign strategy (objectives). Actual numbers, therefore, will not, as a rule, be quoted. Comparisons will be made, though, so readers may appreciate the relative magnitude of each of these factors in various production situations.

THE COMMERCIAL SETTING

Rarely today are radio and TV commercials presented live. (Possible exceptions might occur in local news and talk programs, and are generally kept very simple.) Rather, audio tape, videotape, and film pretty much fill the airwaves. All are readily available and easy to work with, and they put so much less strain on participants (both cast and crew) than was true decades ago in live, on-air work, that their value is beyond question. Gone are the days of canceled celebrity appearances in commercials because of travel scheduling problems and conflicting commitments, along with the constant worry over flubbed lines and last-minute equipment failures. The term "live *action*" is still used in television and film today, however, to differentiate actual "talent" (people) performances and natural scenes from animation and other mechanical and electronic effects.

Broadcast production is deeply involved with drama and the other performing arts. Unfortunately, however, the glamor and excitement associated with "show business" may overshadow the fact that it can be as technical and demanding as typography and photoengraving.

Production methods available often influence (and even dictate) the creative approaches used in writing. Equipment and facilities not only affect the exposure and interest levels of a commercial, but can materially alter the nature of the message delivered. Both print and broadcast production are creative *interpretations* of writers' and artists' ideas—not just executions of them.

RADIO'S PRODUCTION ELEMENTS

Recall from Chapter 8 that advertising messages on radio build "mind pictures" through voices, sound effects, and music, all of which may direct attention, establish mood, and give each sales story a unique personality.

In choosing commercial talent, casting directors listen for *personality* voices; vocal quality and inflection may, in fact, prove as important as the actual words in terms of message communication. Does a creative strategy call for the Voice of Authority to explain a scientific development or a new safety feature? Or, is a wildly exuberant, genuinely concerned, or softly romantic tone needed—as, for example, in commercials for the circus, for life insurance, and for perfume respectively?

The vast majority of today's radio commercials include some form of music or sound effects: to emphasize a point and/or to help sustain a mood. Music, by itself, may be particularly helpful when local talent proves less than expert at delivering lines of copy. A musical background keeps the commercial moving despite otherwise awkward pauses in a spoken message.

Libraries of such "stock" music are readily available, if originally-composed scores or jingles aren't required. When the latter *are* needed, studio personnel must usually allow time for several separate recording sessions. But regardless of how music and other effects are used, production crews remain attentive to volume levels, rhythms or beats, and the exact placement and duration of each element of sound. For example, if a door *opens* to an auditory wind and rain storm, unless it then *closes* (to lose the storm), the noise itself must diminish if lines of copy are to be heard.

The Recording Process

The radio field crew's stock-in-trade is the tape recorder—an instrument which seems to become more automatic every year. Compact, hand-held cassette recorders with built-in microphones and self-threading tapes permit more than an hour's worth of recording time for just the press of a button. Battery operated, they come complete with automatic adjustments for different sound levels—so on-location commercials are easily recorded. And the "real thing" is increasingly popular with commercial producers today (that is, *natural* sounds and voices), although some in-studio production may be included also (and sound effects libraries are commonplace). Examples might include recordings made on a farm (for "country-fresh eggs"), at a ball park (for the crowd's "favorite thirst quencher"), or in a traffic jam (for the car "built for today's driving problems").

In the control room at a radio station, both standard, reel-to-reel and cassette recorders are often found. In some cases the former serve reinforcement, or "back-up" roles, and in others, an editing function. (See Figure 9-3a.)

FIGURE 9-3a

Control Room with Seven Audio Recorders at KRFC, San Francisco

PHOTO COURTESY OF AMPEX CORPORATION

Now, to get an idea of the variety of considerations involved in audio production (for a radio commercial or for the sound track of a TV spot), look at Figure 9-3b. And notice at the bottom that both the client or agency and the station must approve the order.

Local and National Campaigns

As noted earlier, radio is primarily a local medium, but many national advertisers use it to supplement, and to localize, their campaigns in other media. Radio stations generally produce commercials for their local clients, while national spots come already packaged (by recording studios commissioned by advertisers and their agencies). In the case of *cooperative* advertising, where both a national manufacturer and a local store are involved (for example, "Buy delicious Kraft cheese . . . at your friendly A & P store") the commercial arrives at each station "almost complete." The last ten seconds of the tape may be left blank, or may contain only a musical "bed" over which any announcer can insert appropriate local store information.

While TED concerns may appear to be less in radio than in TV, specially-created sound effects and musical tracks can weigh heavily in terms of time and effort; also, decisions regarding celebrity participation can affect dollars in a major way. Then, too, since radio spots are often scheduled more frequently than TV spots (because of lower time costs and the music-and-commercials format of many stations), advertisers usually demand several different versions of their commercials, so listeners don't tire of hearing the same one every few minutes.

A recent radio campaign for American Express involved production of 2,500 different spots. The massive undertaking (with logistics comparable to a Hollywood extravaganza) included taped interviews with some 2,000 restaurant proprietors in 51 markets (all completed within a six-week time span). Eight writer-producer teams scurried around the country, talking with restaurateurs about the "fine dining" at their respective establishments. Altogether, more than 31,000 commercials were aired in this campaign, on 230 AM and FM stations.

TELEVISION'S PRODUCTION ELEMENTS

As noted, television is a lot more than radio copy with pictures added. While the audio track serves a supplementary role, TV commercials which take full advantage of their medium's potential tell their sales stores in active, *visual* ways. When the heart of the

FIGURE 9-3b

KGMB & KGMB-TV Audio Production Order and Charges

KGMB & KGMB-TV
AUDIO PRODUCTION ORDER AND CHARGES

Issued by:_____ Date_____

Person Handling Session: _____ For: _____

CLIENT:_____ (   ) Radio

AGENCY:_____ (   ) Television

ADDRESS: _____ (   ) Other Stations

Contact: _____ Phone:_____

Production Studio (A or B)_____Day/Date_____ Time _____

TV Control Room Reserved (day & date) _____ Time _____

No. & Length of Commls.

60	30	20	10	other

Tape Editing _____

1/4" Tape _____ Cartridge _____ Other_____

Talent Requested:_____ _____

Background Music Requested:_____

Background Music Used: _____ _____ _____
        Album   Side   Cut

Need by: _____ Time _____ Deliver To_____
    Day & Date

SPECIAL INSTRUCTIONS:

Production Studio Rental _____ Charges _____

Tapes_____Length _____ Charges _____

Carts_____Length _____ Charges _____

Talent _____ Charges _____

Other_____ Charges _____

TOTAL

Completed_____ Date_____ Time_____
      Signature

Client/Agency Approval_____ Station Approval_____

sales message is in the *audio*, the video may be nothing more than "magazine pictures" on the air. But if sound alone can communicate an X-Y-Z appeal, why not use radio (and save thousands of dollars)? Of course, the answer may have something to do with TV's reach, or with its general audience appeal; but from a purely creative standpoint, the production called for in Figure 9-4 doesn't justify use of the television medium.

FIGURE 9-4

Example of Weak TV Visual Appeal

CUT TO CU PRODUCT

He'll love Dago
Doggies...

DIS TO CU OF
"SHIMMERING" 33¢

...and for a third
of a dollar...

DIS TO CU DOG'S FACE

...he'll have the
cleanest teeth in town!

Compare these limited-appeal frames, however, with a vastly improved set in Figure 9-5. Now both audio and video tracks share the job of sales message communication—in a dynamic, viewer-involving manner.

FIGURE 9-5

Example of Strong TV Visual Appeal

CUT TO CU DOG BITING
EAGERLY INTO DAGO

He'll love Dago
Doggies...

DIS TO CU ANIMATED
DOLLAR BILL SPLITTING
INTO THIRDS; FOCUS ON
CENTER (DOG'S FACE)

...and for a third of
a dollar...

DIS TO CU DOG ADMIRING
MIRRORED REFLECTION
AS LIGHT SPARKLES
AROUND TEETH

...he'll have the
cleanest teeth in town!

Audio Production

All of radio's music, sound effects, and voice combinations are available in television's audio track as well. The "music for commercials" business alone now involves annual expenditures in the hundreds of millions, and seems to run the gamut from pop tunes to classical music. (A recent Mercury Cougar theme was based on Beethoven's Sixth Symphony.)

An effective jingle may be produced for less than $1,000—or may run $4-5,000. If it's "big music," such as the "I Love New York" melody behind that state's massive promotional campaign in the late 1970's, the stakes increase. Creative fees can easily run to $10,000, and that same figure may be required for each orchestral track produced. Well over half of all prime time TV commercials today do incorporate music, but many don't include lyrics.

Buying existing music and/or lyrics, either of which may be parodied, can cost anywhere from $15,000 to $100,000 and beyond, but can also do "great things" for an advertiser. For example, a popular lyric during World War I, "Pack Up Your Troubles in Your Old Kit Bag," was changed to fit a Union Carbide product six decades later. "Pack up your garbage in a new Glad Bag" ran successfully for several years.

In terms of talent, movie and TV stars, along with recording artists, popular athletes, and lovable children, are but a few of the commercial presenters available. While emotional rapport with the audience is important in message delivery, however, the problems involved with ad-itis have already been discussed. From advertising's point of view, the value of faces—and voices—lies in their ability to project a unique *selling* personality effectively.

Budget restrictions, of course, will shorten considerably the talent roster from which an advertiser may choose. Professional actors and actresses belong to performers' unions (the Screen Actors Guild, the American Federation of Television and Radio Artists, and the Screen Extras Guild); they're compensated not only for their time and effort in *making* commercials, but also for their *appearance* in these commercials (both radio and TV) every time the spots are run. And Hollywood *stars*, along with athletic heroes and other celebrities, usually negotiate their own compensation packages— far beyond the limits specified in union contracts. Production crews have their own unions, notably the International Alliance of Theatrical Stage Employees, the International Brotherhood of Electrical Workers, the National Alliance of Broadcast Employees and Technicians, and the Directors Guild of America.

When amateurs are involved—such as the "man in the car," the "woman in the office," or the "family at home"—payment for services is in the form of a personally negotiated "talent buy" (usually a one-time package). Afterwards, if participants find they like the acting business, they are invited to join a union.

Video Production

The visual portion of TV commercials reaches viewers from any of three different sources: live camera pick-up and slides, videotape recordings, and film. Especially handy today are video cartridge tapes: self-threading, self-cueing, automatically rewound tapes of varying lengths which are real TED savers. These "carts," as they are called in the trade, permit local advertisers to produce a series of commercials at far less cost than would be involved if each spot were produced separately on film.

For example, a standard commercial "open" and "close" for a sporting goods manufacturer filmed, perhaps, in the main plant might be preserved on carts (both audio and video material). Then, different in-studio sets (featuring golf equipment, tennis outfits, and camping gear) could be recorded on *separate* carts—televised scenes with camera-action only (no sound). Finally, selected sequences, assembled into a series of individual messages, could use the stock open and close, while an announcer read a new piece of copy whenever the advertiser felt it was time for a change.

In other situations, too, at least part of a commercial may be shot on silent *film*. The corresponding audio copy is recorded separately and then "dubbed in" over the action. Such a procedure, referred to as "recording wild," would undoubtedly be followed if a storyboard called for lines to be delivered by *airborne* talent (divers, ski jumpers, parachutists, and the like). In addition, as was true in radio, some national advertisers localize their commercials by providing silent film or videotape to stations, which then use their own announcers for the copy. And on the horizon, according to experts, is the widespread use of film carts.

Standard optical devices such as dissolves and wipes may be supplemented by a variety of imaginative techniques. Consider, for instance, the alternate blurring and sharpening (focusing and defocusing) of a picture, to call attention to key elements, or, perhaps, to carry viewers through phases of a dream sequence. *Slow motion* may be called for when an audience is asked to "watch what happens to the spring-action in these shoes when the basketball player jumps", while *fast motion* can emphasize a homemaker's hectic trips up and down stairs on housecleaning days.

STUDIO FACILITIES

Most television stations have several studios available to local advertisers, and each comes equipped with commercial production facilities. In addition, station personnel can provide copywriting and artistic services—sometimes "free," and sometimes for the cost of materials only.

SETS

A large studio may have several "general" sets, easily adapted to meet normal production demands, while a small studio, often specially designed for specific kinds of commercials, is apt to have a kitchen set, and maybe a living room/bedroom convertible. Common construction materials are "flats" which display various types of trim and backdrops; or, sometimes murals are used for background. If it's important to an automobile dealer, for example, that commercials appear against a variety of country scenes, artists can produce murals which correspond exactly to photographs taken of the selected spots. These devices often help achieve some of the visual variety called for in Chapter 8.

GRAPHICS

TV stations are usually equipped to prepare basic commercial artwork, and may be called on to design logos, address and sale-item cards, and photographic slides for local advertisers. Occasionally, more elaborate visuals are also required, and as long as their designs aren't intricate, they photograph quite well. TV cameras can't pick up minuscule details, and viewers have neither the time nor the inclination to study them in detail. Also, while dull, matte finishes reproduce beautifully, glossy, close-textured fabrics or pictures reflect light and cause difficulties. Finally, *motion* in visuals—or at least the suggestion of it—attracts and helps hold attention and interest.

When it comes to *lettering* on visuals, bold type faces are easier to read than light or frilly ones—as is true in the case of newspapers and magazines. Then, too, both the number of words per line and the number of lines per visual should be kept to a minimum. Granted, creative judgment must be exercised here, but it's important to remember the short amount of time each storyboard frame actually remains on camera.

LIGHTING

Lighting can also contribute to sales communication. Consider the following sequence: (1) two children in pajamas tiptoe downstairs late at night; (2) they proceed through a dark kitchen to the refrigerator; and (3) as they open the door and reach for a dish, they're "caught" by the flash of a camera. Obviously, the atmosphere intended is one of suspense—child-like intrigue—as the after-bedtime snackers undertake their mission. The proper choice of music may contribute much to the atmosphere desired, but lighting can also make or break the mood.

In a clearance sale commercial, a sweeping spotlight can transport viewers through a warehouse of values. Or, a row of blinking lights might lend theatrical fanfare to the opening of a new store. Our familiar word of caution, however, is again appropriate: *sales communication* first and foremost . . . and "entertainment" *only* if it's appropriate to the creative strategy.

FILM AND VIDEOTAPE

Both film and videotape equipment is growing increasingly more portable. Backpacks and hand-held gear permit on-the-spot recording in almost every imaginable locale. Likewise, a wide range of special effects (though not necessarily the same varieties) can be achieved in both film and videotape media. Still, the majority of nationally produced commercials today are filmed (at costs as high as $1,000 and more *per second* in the early 1980's), while the majority of local spots appear on videotape. (Note: since nearly all of TV program and promotional fare is on videotape, it's a common procedure for stations to transfer filmed commercials onto tape for convenience in airing them.)

Like their radio counterparts, TV station control rooms—and also mobile vans which record video material "on location"—have both reel-to-reel and cassette recorders available for use. (See Figure 9-6.) And, video production forms must be filled out and approved for every commercial. They are much more complex than the audio form presented earlier—especially in the case of film, where close to 200 check-list items may be involved. Figure 9-7 shows a videotape production estimate sheet, and Figure 9-8 shows one for film.

EDITING

As is true in the case of most TV programs, the majority of commercials are literally "made" in the editing laboratories, or at least on an editing console. Overly long scenes are trimmed to size, and unwanted words, gestures, and general stage "business" are deleted. Also "pieces" of a message can be joined or separated, and if several different "takes" of the same shot or scene were recorded, the editor might choose the one he or she deemed most appropriate: a 2-

FIGURE 9-6

Videotape Recorders in a Mobile Van in Salt Lake City

PHOTO COURTESY OF AMPEX CORPORATION

FIGURE 9-7

Videotaping Production Estimate

STUDIO VIDEO PRODUCTION	POST PRODUCTION
MAJOR PACKAGE	Editing
MINOR PACAGE	Minor production
ADDITIONAL EQUIPMENT	Recording studio
	Sound mixing
	Original music
	Library music
	Sound effects
ADDITIONAL CREW	Titles
PRODUCER	Mattes
CREATIVE/ART	Animation
	Opticals
MOBILE VIDEO PRODUCTION	Creative/art
	Artwork
MOBILE UNIT PACKAGE	Other _____
ADDITIONAL EQUIPMENT	
	DUBBING
	Video stock
	Video master
ADDITIONAL CREW	Video dub
PRODUCER	Cassette dub
CREATIVE/ART	
	SET & WARDROBE
LOCATION EXPENSES	Set design
	Set materials
Site rentals	Set construction
Gratuities	Props
Permits	Wardrobe (principals)
Police	Wardrobe (extras)
Firemen	Other _____
Transportation	
Petty cash	MISCELLANEOUS
Coffee, meals	Shipping
Other _____	Insurance
	Other _____
TALENT	
On-camera principals	
On-camera extras	
Narrator (V.O.)	SUBTOTAL
Stuntmen	
Living quarters	CONTINGENCY
Per diem	
Travel	SUBTOTAL
Other _____	
	AGENCY FEE
	SUBTOTAL
	TAX (4%)
	TOTAL

FIGURE 9-8

Film Production Estimate

CREW	Pre-Production/Wrap	Estimated	Actual	Shoot	Estimated	Actual	Weather
1. Producer:	days @			days @			
2. Asst. Director:							
3. Dir. Photography:							
4. Camera Operator:							
5. Asst. Camerman:							
6. Outside Props:							
7. Inside Props:							
8. Electricians:							
9. Grips:							
10. Mixer (or Playback:)							
11. Recordist:							
12. Boom man:							
13. Make-Up:							
14: Hair:							
15. Stylist:							
16. Wardrobe Attendant:							
17. Script Clerk:							
18. Home Economist:							
19. Scenics:							
20. VTR Man:							
21. EFX Man:							
22. Nurse:							
23. Telegr. & Operator:							
24. Generator Man:							
25. Still Man:							
26. Loc. Contact./Scout:							
27. P.A.							
28. 2nd A.D.							
29. Teamsters							
30.							
	SUB TOTAL A			SUB TOTAL B			

man days. . . . .   # man days. . . . .

PRE-PRODUCTION & WRAP/MATERIALS & EXPENSES	Estimated	Actual	
31. Auto Rentals (No. of Cars)			
32. Air Fares: No. of people ( ) x Amount per fare ( )			
33. Per Diems: No. of people ( ) x Amount per day ( )			
34. Still Camera Rental & Film			
35. Messengers			
36. Trucking			
37. Deliveries & Taxis			
38. Home Economist Supplies			
39. Telephone & Cable			
40. Art Work			
41. Casting (including equipment)			
42.			
SUB TOTAL C			

SET CONSTRUCTION (CREW FOR BUILD, STRIKE, PRELIGHT)	# MAN DAYS	Estimated	Actual	
43. Set Designer Name:				
44. Carpenters				
45. Grips				
46. Outside Props				
47. Inside Props				
48. Scenics				
49. Electricians				
50. Teamsters				
51. Men for Strike				
52.				
53.				
54.				
SUB TOTAL D				

man days. . . . .

SET CONSTRUCTION MATERIALS	Estimated	Actual	
55. Props (Not hand props)			
56. Lumber			
57. Paint			
58. Hardware			
59. Special Effects			
60. Special Outside Construction			
61. Trucking			
62. Messengers/Deliveries			
63.			
SUB TOTAL E			

STUDIO RENTAL & EXPENSES - STAGE:	Estimated	Actual	
64. Rental for Build Days			
65. Rental for Pre-Lite Days			
66. Rental for Shoot Days			
67. Rental for Shoot O.T.			
68. Rental for Build/Strike Days O.T.			
69. Total Power Charge & Bulbs			
70. Misc. Studio Charges & Service			
71. Meals (Lunches & Dinner for Crew and Talent)			
72.			
73.			
74.			
75.			
SUB TOTAL F			

LOCATION EXPENSES	Estimated	Actual	Weather
76. Location Fees			
77. Guards			
78. Car Rentals			
79. Bus Rentals			
80. Camper Dressing Room Vehicles			
81. Parking, Tolls, & Gas			
82. Trucking			
83. Other vehicles A/			
84. Other vehicles B			
85. Special crew equipt./clothing			
86. Air freight/Customs/Excess baggage			
87. Air fares: No. of people ( ) x cost per fare ( )			
88. Per Diems: Total No. man days ( ) x amt. per day ( )			
89. Breakfast: No. of man days ( ) x amt. per person ( )			
90. Lunch: No. of man days ( ) x amt. per person ( )			
91. Dinner: No. of man days ( ) x amt. per person ( )			
92. Gratuities, Tips and misc. outside labor			
93. Cabs and other passenger transportation			
94. Limousines (celebrity service)			
95.			
96.			
97.			
98.			
99.			
SUB TOTAL G			

EQUIPMENT RENTAL			
100. Camera rental			
101. Sound rental			
102. Lighting rental			
103. Grip rental			
104. Generator rental			
105. Crane/Cherry Picker rental			
106. VTR rental			
107. Production supplies			
108.			
109.			
SUB TOTAL H			

228

FILM RAW STOCK DEVELOP AND PRINT			
110. Purchase of raw stock: footage amount ( ) x per foot			
111. Developing and printing: footage amount ( ) x per foot			
112. Studio for transfer: No. of hours ( )			
113. 16mm or 35mm mag stock: No. of hours ( )			
114.			
115.			
SUB TOTAL I			

PROPS AND WARDROBE			
116. Prop rental/purchase			
117. Costume/Wardrobe rental/purchase			
118. Animals & Handlers			
119. Wigs & Mustaches			
120. Color Correction			
SUB TOTAL J			

DIRECTOR/CREATIVE FEES:	Estimated	Actual	Weather
121. Prep days			
122. Travel days			
123. Shoot days			
124. Post-production days			
125.			
SUB TOTAL K			

MISCELLANEOUS COSTS	Estimated	Actual	
126. Total payroll & P & W Taxes % of total of A,B,D, & K			
127. Air shipping/special carriers			
128. Phones and cables			
129. Misc. (Petty cash)			
130. Misc. trucking & messengers			
131.			
132.			
133.			
SUB TOTAL L			

EDITORIAL COMPLETION	Estimated	Actual	
134. Editing			
135. Asst. Editor			
136. Coding			
137. Projection			
138. Artwork for supers			
139. Shooting of artwork			
140. Stock footage			
141. Still photographs			
142. Opticals (incl. pre-optical)			
143. Animation			
144. Stock music			
145. Original music			
146. Sound effects			
147. Dubbing studio			
148. Studio for narration - including transfer to mag. No. of hours ( )			
149. Studio for mixing - including transfer to mag. No. of hours ( )			
150. Negative tracks			
151. Answer & corrected prints			
152. Contract items			
153. Film to tape transfer (incl. reprints & masters)			
154. Film to tape transfer - editorial fee			
155.			
156.			
157. Editorial Handling Fee:			
SUB TOTAL M			

TALENT NO.	Category and spot	Days	Tot. Hrs.	Fitting fee	Vers. fee	Ward. Allw.	Estimated	Actual	Weather
158.									
159.									
160.									
161.									
162.									
163. Audition fees									
164.									
						Handling fee			
					SUB TOTAL N				

TALENT EXPENSES

	Estimated	Actual	Weather
165. Per diem: No. of man days ( ) x amount per day ( )			
166. Air fare: No. of people ( ) x amount per fare ( )			
167. Cabs and other transportation			
168.			
169.			
170.			
SUB TOTAL O			

SUMMARY

		Estimated	Actual	Weather
171. Pre-Production costs; wrap costs	Totals A and C			
172. Shooting crew labor:	Total B			
173. Sets - Build/Shoot/Strike costs	Totals D, E, and F			
174. Location: Travel & Expenses	Total G			
175. Equipment costs:	Total H			
176. Film stock develop and print	Total I			
177. Props, Wardrobe, Animals	Total J			
178. Payroll taxes, P & W. and misc.	Total L			
179.	Sub-Total - Direct costs			
180. Director creative fees	Total K			
181. Insurance				
182. Mark-up (% of direct costs)				
183. Editorial and finishing	Total M			
184. Talent costs and expenses	Total N and O			
185.	Grand-Total			
186.				
187. Weather day				
188.	Handling cost			
189.	Total			
190.				
191.				
192.				
193.				
194.				

COMPLIMENTS OF ARTHUR BELLAIRE INC.

shot or a 3-shot; a high camera angle or a low one; a limbo effect or one with background.

Film editors work mainly by hand, utilizing various projection and viewing equipment, as well as cutting and splicing tools. In the case of videotape, however, manual labor has been largely replaced by electronic editing systems, which allow for automatic (keyboard) control of scene storage, indexing and retrieval, and edit point selection and preview.

ANIMATION AND SPECIAL EFFECTS

Fully animated spots are rare today, and even those with only partial animation are estimated at less than 5% of the total number of commercials on the air. Though highly appealing, this format is often considered too entertaining to sell; yet, *when called for* by a creative strategy, animation can lend otherwise impossible-to-show support to a reason-why message. For instance, it might take viewers: (1) underground, to explore a fresh-water source; (2) inside the sole of a shoe, to determine its strength; or (3) through the air on the back of a sound wave, to demonstrate the power of an amplifier.

Animation comes in several forms: full-fledged cartoons, stop-motion photography, and computerized images, including graphic transformations. Both of the first two involve single-frame camera exposure, and often require three months to produce. Individual drawings are photographed on individual frames of film, at the rate of 24 per second; thus, there are 770 of them in a 30-second commercial, and 1,440 in a minute.

Full cartoon animation takes viewers through fantasyland adventures (similar to those encountered in Walt Disney productions), while stop-motion is generally used to "bring products to life." Dollars may "march" to the bank, paint brushes become artists, and loaves of bread "breathe" with fresh-baked aroma. Kroger's "scissors" have been trimming away excess costs for several years, and Chuck Wagon's team of horses may still be seen parading across the kitchen floor.

The Pillsbury Doughboy, who made his debut in the mid-1960's, is a flexible rubber figure which is photographed in stop motion. Each picture taken shows the Poppin' Fresh character in a position about 1/32 of an inch removed from the previous one, so when the final film is run at normal speed, a smooth, life-like motion results.

A process known as *pixilation* records more substantial differences on each frame of film, so the resulting movement appears a little more "jerky." Such an effect produces an eye-catching "sketch" scene, as pictures or words (or both) "develop" hurriedly before the viewer. For instance, a recent McDonald's commercial appeared to create—almost "paint"—an entire line of breakfast entrees across the screen in a few seconds. In actuality, the completed scene was shot as an entity, and then electronically "erased," a portion at a time, until nothing was left. The entire film was then run *backwards*.

Computer-generated graphics utilize artist-prepared materials as input, and pass them through a central processing unit (which may include storage, logical, and arithmetic functions). The output is nothing short of exciting. "Flow" graphics give packages and logos distinct personalities—by allowing them to bloom and bounce, to shrink and swim, to crawl and climb. And the recently developed *telestrator* machine can create over 4,000 hues of color, and can place as many as ten special effects on top of each other for some incredibly intricate and complex designs.

Of course, not all effects need be so elaborate. A simple electronic device known as a "squeezoom" places any still or moving picture on the TV screen, and zooms it in or out, spins it around, splits it (or "doubles" it), and lets it "perform" in other ways which help convey a selling point or benefit. Also, an electronic "matting" procedure in videotape permits a performer to talk with his or her "identical twin" a short distance away (as Jonathan Winters has done in a variety of commercials). The actor or actress simply goes through *each* character's presentation separately, and the two scenes are shown simultaneously, while a black matte covers half the screen each time. The process is also feasible, but much more complicated, on film; in this case, "cut-outs" of images are inserted frame by frame.

A variation of this procedure permits talent to address viewers from "inside" products: dishwashers, tape recorders, even automobile engines. And finally, simple camera angles—and the positioning of objects close to and far away from the camera lens—can create "giant" and "miniature" effects. (Hence, a model railroad or airplane can appear life-size.)

Production companies specializing in animation and audio/video effects are located in Chicago, Detroit, and Atlanta, as well as Los Angeles and New York. Over 100 others, however, with local, regional, and national client rosters turn out high quality materials in Boston and Pittsburgh; in Cleveland, South Bend, and Minneapolis; and in Memphis, Dallas, Albuquerque, and Phoenix. Some deal exclusively in film or videotape, and some are experts in audio production, with staffs consisting of both composers and lyricists.

THE BUSINESS OF MONEY

TV commercial production costs increased 100% in the 1970's, and top-level directors now draw anywhere from $2-4,000 per shooting day. Some national (and especially regional) spots, however, still boast price tags under $10,000 (table-top demonstrations, frequently, and other commercials without on-camera talent). And, a number of very presentable live-action messages—slice-of-life and others—unfold for less than $20,000 (Note: *local* in-store and in-studio TV spots are still produced for $1,000 and less.)

Commercial talent fees are negotiable at nearly all levels, and producers endowed with persuasive ability often bring home enviable contracts. But all members of a creative team can help keep costs down—saving many thousands of dollars with a single, simple decision. They might ask themselves, for example, whether two or three singers could communicate a message just as well as five or six. Or, perhaps a solo instrument could lend a sense of enchantment not possible with a full orchestra, or even with a more "normal" dozen or so musicians.

In addition, while exterior, on-location filming is very realistic, it can prove unnecessarily expensive if existing interior sets would suffice. Figure 9-9 contains a property release form used by an advertising agency in Honolulu (where, because of ideal climatic conditions, much outdoor filming takes place).

Looking at the matter a little differently, if a commercial's emphasis is on package design and use, and the product stands ten inches high by five inches wide, there's rarely a need for a floor-to-ceiling studio set, complete with full decor and lighting effects.

Animation is usually more expensive than live action in terms of original production costs, although animated spots involve no residual fees (post-production payments made to talent, based on the number of times a commercial is aired). The vast majority of both acting talent and crew members are unionized, so in this business time is, literally, money. Advertisers planning to run a series of commercials with a similar theme and format often ask that extra footage be shot during a filming or taping session, so that several spots may be lifted therefrom; in fact, the resultant messages—frequently of varying lengths—were referred to as "lifts" in Chapter 8. (And a TV audio track may be lifted to form all or part of a radio commercial, too.) Also, on-camera *faces* cost a lot more than on-camera *hands* (without faces), and on-camera speakers carry a larger price tag than off-camera voices.

We wind up this chapter with a word of caution. Since this text doesn't get involved with media buying (either time or space), the costs of that activity haven't been considered. The reader should be aware, however, that a commercial costing $35-40,000 to produce may cost *four to five times as much* to air *once* on national prime-time television. Add the expense of repeating this buy over the course of a season, plus the residual fees noted above, and you can begin to appreciate the magnitude of this business.

FIGURE 9-9

Property Release Form

ADVERTISING RELEASE (PROPERTY)

DATE_____

Seigle Schiller Rolfs & Wood, Inc.

Advertising, Public Relations and Marketing Services

Financial Plaza of the Pacific, Honolulu, Hawaii 96813, Telephone (808)531-6211

(Client)_____

Dear Sirs:

In consideration of the sum of _____ now paid by you to me, the receipt of which is hereby acknowledged, and for other valuable consideration, I hereby irrevocably grant to you and to your respective officers, employees, nominees, customers, agents, licensees, successors and assigns (collectively called the "grantees"), the absolute, unrestricted and unlimited license, right, permission and consent to use and reuse, disseminate, copyright, print, reproduce, publish and republish, for any and all trade purposes or commercial or other advertising purposes, and in any and all media, my carport, garage or any other section of my residence located at

_____, Honolulu, Hawaii,

with such additions, deletions, alterations or changes therein as you in your discretion may make, with or without any advertising statements.

Very truly yours,

_____
(Name)

_____
(Address)

_____

COMPLIMENTS OF SEIGLE SCHILLER ROLFS & WOOD, INC.

The next chapter will take a look at different forms of *specialized* advertising media, and a unique retail campaign which utilized some of them.

STUDY QUESTIONS

1. What's the difference between physical scene changes and optical scene changes in a TV commercial?
2. What's the difference between a storyboard and a photoboard?
3. In television, is a "live" commercial the same thing as a "live action" commercial? Explain.
4. What kind of commercial production concerns are represented by TED?
5. Name and describe two different forms of animation used in TV commercials.

10

STRATEGY AND TACTICS IN SPECIALIZED MEDIA

A "fractionated advertising effort" is one that's broken down into pieces, or fractions. For instance, we might: (1) show one thing about a product or service in television, (2) deliver another message on radio, (3) illustrate and write something different in newspapers and magazines, (4) take another tack for in-store promotion, and (5) find a final approach for outdoor posters. What's wrong with that kind of advertising? It's of questionable value because repetition of a single idea helps make it memorable (and, in time, believable). Unless a sales story is astounding, it takes a number of exposures for it to sink in.

At this writing, one of your authors is trying to recall the name of a product positioned as the "smoker's toothpaste." He's seen one commercial for it . . . but if he doesn't see more, he might never get a chance to try the product. After a few exposures, however, he may learn how it works and be convinced to buy it. (By the time you read this, the product may be either a "best seller" or off the market completely.)

Fractionation is an economy trap because costs to advertise are going up. Ink, paper, postage, time, space, film, production, specialists' salaries, and nearly everything else is climbing. It's expensive enough for an advertiser to get one message across without trying to publish or broadcast four or five.

Fractionation is also confusing to consumers. Assume a person is interested in what a product can do—how it can solve his or her problem. In one medium the benefit described is A, in another it is B, and in a third it is C. Only the product name stays the same. A trilogy of attributes complicates a potential customer's ability to pick the product off a grocer's shelf or dealer's floor, or to select it from a catalog or display lot.

Thus, fractionation violates the principle of repetition, is economically unsound, and confuses prospective buyers. Yet, it's practiced frequently. Advertisers "know better," but the tactics often get out of hand. A great print idea simply doesn't seem photogenic enough for television, so we "do something else" for TV. Just as often, a superb television visual cannot be translated into print because "it needs motion, or mood." And for radio? Forget it, since there's no picture. But in a situation like this, do the agency and client accept a one-medium campaign? No, because that's a cop out.

The ideal of course, is a strategic and tactical approach that translates into all media: a coordinated, *single message* campaign. One idea, one picture (physical and/or mental), one specific attribute delivered to consumers from many different directions. And for how long? Until research shows that a large share of the target audience is aware of what the advertising is saying and showing. In Chapter 2 we identified this point as an element in the Advertising Objective. Following the formula, an established percentage of penetration or awareness should be achieved among an established number of people called the target market. And we have a much better chance of achieving a goal by communicating a single message than by reciting a litany of attributes. Not that a list can't be used to support an X-Y-Z appeal—but *one point* should stand out. The mark of professionalism is to make this appeal, based on a carefully planned strategy and highly adaptable tactics, perform in a variety of media.

Most major consumer campaigns use television and print, and radio and outdoor are probable. But that's only the beginning if a manufacturer, service company, or retailer intends to maximize impact, or, in trade jargon, to "produce a synergistic effect" with a campaign.

THE SPECIALIZED MEDIA

Technically, a "medium" is one of a specifically measured group; but there are many other persuasion vehicles that advertisers use. A strategic and tactical expression should be adaptable to most or all of them, since they're found almost everywhere: in public gathering places, in homes and offices, on streets and highways, and inside and outside of stores.[1]

In *gathering places*, such as fairs, trade shows, stadiums, or theaters, we find posters, programs, banners, literature and instructions, samples, specialty items, and more. In *homes and offices*, there is the telephone, along with direct mail, private delivery materials, special interest publications, and directories. *Street or highway* (and *transportation*) *media* feature posters that are limited by size and exposure time to short one-liners and single illustrations, while *stores* greet people with samples, displays, fliers, shopping bags, and public address systems.

Wherever the consumer is reached, and whatever communication vehicle does the reaching, the same message should be projected. That's the essence of coordinated advertising. So in developing the tactical part of a campaign there should always be the urgent question: how will it adapt? How will it carry over from television . . . into radio . . . into consumer magazines . . . into trade magazines . . . into newspapers . . . into outdoor . . . into direct mail . . . into packaging and inserts . . . into Yellow Pages . . . into posters . . . into trade literature . . . into sales meeting materials . . . into store displays . . . into shelf talkers . . . into . . .[2]

The list is endless and varies with the product and service. McDonald's, for example, shows its golden arches on everything from TV screens to sacks, and the latest slogan or theme line shows up in each restaurant in the chain. Go down the list of other fast food operations you know about, and check what they're saying and showing. The Colonel is everywhere for Kentucky Fried Chicken. His graphic sketch sits outside of his buildings, over the counters, and on buckets and boxes. He also gives his personal benediction to ravenous customers in practically every commercial. And, as we saw in Figure 1-3, on page 9, Taco Bell consistently features its adobe building and mission bell. Franchise companies such as these, along with Baskin-Robbins and Howard Johnson's, are particularly alert to the value of coordinated advertising and promotion.

THE PROCESS OF TRANSFERRAL

The best way we know to explain how strategies and tactics are "carried over" from medium to medium in specialized areas is to illustrate the procedure. Ideally, a lot of *planning* precedes the introduction of any product, because "pre-thinking" helps assure that total adaptation is possible. For example, the Campbell-Ewald advertising agency, in Warren, Michigan, took on what most practitioners would consider a tough challenge. Bil-Mar Foods, Inc., of Zeeland, Michigan, made hot dogs, ham, pastrami, bologna, and salami out of turkey meat. Most retailers who stocked any poultry-based meats at all considered them novelty items or diet foods; and under no circumstances did the stores carry more than one brand in this small category.

No major brand had surfaced, therefore, as a "name" with a customer following. Consumers were not very anxious to purchase turkey-based products, and less than 5% even knew they existed.

Fortunately, however, 90% of the people who did try the Bil-Mar brand liked it, and accepted it as a beef or pork counterpart. Advertising's job was then to inform the general public about this food category, convince them to try turkey-based cold meats, and persuade them to buy Bil-Mar.

From a marketing point of view the brand had to be positioned against conventional beef or pork competition as a nutritionally superior alternative or replacement for these products. Product quality and taste had to be stressed. With beef and pork prices at a high level, there was a natural cost advantage—but the turkey products were placed as top-of-the-line items in order to offset the impression that they were poor substitutes for the "real thing." A comfortable manufacturing-to-sale price spread made it practical to offer retailers introductory off-invoice allowances and discounts for featuring the products in their own advertising.

The creative strategy zeroed in on appetite appeal, primarily, with nutritional value as a secondary point. (In other words: "It tastes good, and is good for you.") As a matter of fact, the products were lower in fat and calories and higher in protein than their alternatives. Price was not to be mentioned because of the possible "second class" stigma. Comparative shoppers were certainly expected to notice the difference between turkey, beef, and pork costs, but the advertising didn't bring it to their attention.

Some marketers would automatically jump on low price as a key strategy to encourage consumer trial; and, granted, that leverage is often used in product introductions. But in this case the negative ruboff could have damaged the brand's image and distorted its perception in consumers' minds.

Up to this point, some research had been done and decisions had been made, but the product line still had no name. There were a number of ways to proceed, but since the main ingredient was turkey, that word seemed like a natural. What was needed next was a *benefit* word or phrase. How about "Good Taste Turkey" . . . "Top Taste Turkey" . . . or "Taste-T-Turkey"? Each would emphasize the "taste" part of the strategy. Other choices might be "Nutri-Turkey" or "Pro-Plus Turkey," to develop the nutritional, high protein values of the product. Or, a character-name like "Mr. Turkey" could fill the bill. Basically, that's how brands are named: by writing down every imaginable word combination on sheets of paper. Wild ones are discarded, and a few "possibles" are checked out to see if they've already been used or are standing by, perhaps, in the trademark register—waiting for products to adopt them.

Equally important, potential names are screened for their "versatility quotients." How comfortably do they move from one medium to another, say from television to matchbooks, through all of the specialized areas for communicating with consumers and the trade? As a potential copywriter or art director, we would hope you can see more promise in the name "Mr. Turkey" than in "Taste-T-

Turkey" or "Nutri-Turkey." However, the wishes of creative people are not always considered—and some product groups are saddled with "impossible" names.

"Mr. Turkey" had a high versatility quotient, as you will see. He was registered as a trademark and designed as a jaunty bird in a tuxedo for use in package identification. He was developed as spokesman for the product and was elected to star in television and radio commercials and in newspaper advertisements. He would appear on signs in the meat section of supermarkets, talk to buyers from the top of deal sheets, and chat with sales people through the Bil-Mar letterhead. His capabilities were endless. He could gobble from the side of a delivery truck, smile from a button, remind from a pen, ashtray, ruler, or calendar, and even walk around at a fair or ballgame.

To demonstrate Mr. Turkey's versatility, we'll examine actual pages from the Retail Kit used to introduce buyers to "reselling" the brand. The Kit was presented again and again as sales representatives fanned out across Michigan, Ohio, Wisconsin, Oklahoma, Indiana, and Minnesota. Then came Colorado, Kentucky, Tennessee, Pennsylvania, and New York. The Retail Kit's construction suggested a practical outline for presenting a coordinated campaign in basic media and specialized areas. Each page performed a specific task and, depending on the sales rep's knowledge of a prospect, could be collated in various ways. Some buyers wanted to know first about the company, while others wanted to get straight to the "deal." Still others were most interested in advertising support. Then, too, the salespeople told their stories differently, and the presentation was flexible enough to handle whatever page order worked best for each individual. Our particular preference is the following:

(1) *THE STORY*: This page talks about Bil-Mar Foods, Inc.—when it started and how it grew. It gives the impression of a quality company and Mr. Turkey is obviously the spokesperson (Figure 10-1).

(2) *THE PRODUCTS*: Here the product line is described and illustrated. Some consumer research is discussed, and taste and nutrition are highlighted. Notice the Mr. Turkey symbol on each package (Figure 10-2).

(3) *THE SEAL: Good Housekeeping*'s limited warranty may not be available for every product, but "if you've got it, flaunt it." For other products, a page of testimonials might be effective (Figure 10-3).

(4) *THE REACTION*: Statistics and comparative price advantages build a case for probable consumer acceptance. Buyers want to know that the time for new lines has come and that products will move (Figure 10-4).

(5) *THE PROMOTION*: Beginning with the always impressive "Your profit" phrase, this page starts to describe how the product will get its "pull" off the shelves. The Campbell-Ewald agency is given credit for its effort, and lots of excitement is promised: even a visit from Mr. Turkey himself (Figure 10-5)!

(6) *THE ADS*: This is a page of "slicks" for the retailer. Copy promises awareness, and advises that with Mr. Turkey, "you will have what your customers have been presold on and will come looking for." This section could be augmented with television storyboards and a cassette of radio commercials (Figure 10-6).

(7) *THE FORM*: The retailer can use an order blank at the bottom of this page to obtain point-of-purchase materials. We're particularly interested in their variety and in how the Mr. Turkey symbol is worked into these specialized area pieces. There is a leaflet on nutritional advantages of turkey which related to the secondary point in the creative strategy. In addition, there are shelf danglers, mobiles, shelf strips, and "special" price boards. What else might have been developed? Man-sized stand-ups of Mr. Turkey, giant posters for windows, Mr. Turkey audio tapes to use on the public address system, display case signs, and on and on. True, there is a problem of "over supply" when an abundance of material rolls into the stores; anything that's too complicated to set up, takes too much space, or is too unusual will *not* be used (Figure 10-7).

(8) *THE PROGRAM*: The bottom line question from every buyer is: "What will you do for me?"—in terms of price. Trade sources say supermarkets make only a 1% profit, so promotional allowances are critical. This page of the Kit tells the story (Figure 10-8).

(9) *THE PROFITS*: Here is the real bottom line—giving an example of what the retailer can expect from peg display and facings (Figure 10-9).

(10) *THE RESULT*: "So order now and stock up" is the clincher in any retail buying transaction (Figure 10-10).

Much more can be read from this presentation, from a selling point of view, but our interest is in the way Mr. Turkey is carried through it all, and how he appears in print advertisements and point-of-purchase materials. Figures 10-11 and 10-12 show a radio script and a TV photoboard from this same campaign, to give you an idea of the character's use in these media.

Voice auditions were conducted on both coasts and a Hollywood actor named George Brenlin was selected to become Mr. Turkey. For television, a three-foot Mr. Turkey puppet was built, so he could appear magically to families in eating situations and explain the advantages of his products. In radio, a jingle was used to introduce (1) jokes about turkeys, and (2) rapid-fire product information.

FIGURE 10-1

From Mr. Turkey's Retail Kit

Bil-Mar Foods was founded in 1938. Since then we have grown steadily in reputation and sales both with the trade and the consuming public.

Today we grow nearly two million turkeys annually. They are turkeys which have been raised on our own farms, fed our own special feed, processed with the most modern equipment and technology. For only by controlling the product from beginning to end can we assure ourselves of the kind of quality we want associated with our name.

We earned our reputation for quality many years ago with whole turkeys. Quality is still building our reputation with our very popular Mr. Turkey brand Turkey Franks, Turkey Ham, and Turkey Luncheon Meats. And, since success breeds imitation, don't disappoint your customers. Stock up on genuine Mr. Turkey brand products. The quality turkey meats from Bil-Mar.

THE STORY

242

FIGURE 10-2

From Mr. Turkey's Retail Kit

Ever since Mr. Turkey brand Turkey Franks, Turkey Ham, and Turkey Luncheon Meats were introduced to the public, they've been a big hit! And for good reason.

Mr. Turkey brand meats are all 100% turkey. No beef, no pork, no fillers. Just quality turkey seasoned the same way their beef and pork counterparts are. The result, delicious Mr. Turkey brand Turkey Franks, Turkey Ham, Turkey Bologna, Turkey Salami, and Turkey Pastrami.

In an independent taste test, a majority said the taste of Mr. Turkey brand products was the taste they expect in all-meat products. That is, they found little if any difference between the tastes of Mr. Turkey brand meats and the tastes of their beef and pork counterparts. And a majority also said they would consider buying Mr. Turkey products for their families.

All Mr. Turkey brand turkey meats—including Mr. Turkey brand sliced Turkey Breast and Smoked Turkey Breast—are protein-rich. With less fat and calories than the leading beef and pork hot dogs and luncheon meats. An important point with so many Americans calorie- and nutrition-conscious.

THE PRODUCTS

FIGURE 10-3

From Mr. Turkey's Retail Kit

For many years now, the Good Housekeeping Seal has been a signal of quality to the American consumer. It was established by <u>Good</u> <u>Housekeeping</u>, one of America's most highly respected magazines; and the right to use it is not easily come by. It is awarded only to those advertisers whose products and advertising claims meet the high standards of <u>Good</u> <u>Housekeeping</u>.

That is why we are so proud to have been given permission to display the Seal on Mr. Turkey's franks, turkey ham and turkey sausage products...and prouder still that ours are the only products of their kinds to be so honored.

Your customers know very well what the Good Housekeeping Seal means. More than that, a recent survey showed that almost 8 out of 10 women are influenced to buy a product when it has the Seal on it. Clearly, in these days, when shoppers are more careful than ever to make sure they're getting their money's worth, the Seal gives them one more reason to spend their money on Mr. Turkey products.

A LIMITED WARRANTY TO CONSUMERS
★
• Good Housekeeping •
PROMISES
REPLACEMENT OR REFUND IF DEFECTIVE

THE SEAL

FIGURE 10-4

From Mr. Turkey's Retail Kit

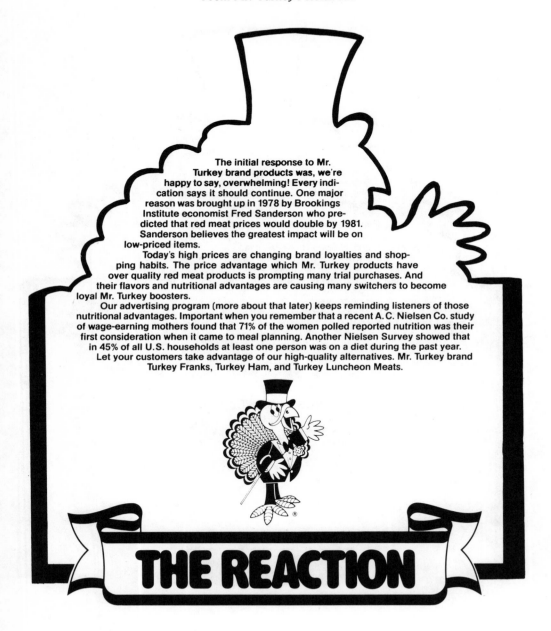

The initial response to Mr. Turkey brand products was, we're happy to say, overwhelming! Every indication says it should continue. One major reason was brought up in 1978 by Brookings Institute economist Fred Sanderson who predicted that red meat prices would double by 1981. Sanderson believes the greatest impact will be on low-priced items.

Today's high prices are changing brand loyalties and shopping habits. The price advantage which Mr. Turkey products have over quality red meat products is prompting many trial purchases. And their flavors and nutritional advantages are causing many switchers to become loyal Mr. Turkey boosters.

Our advertising program (more about that later) keeps reminding listeners of those nutritional advantages. Important when you remember that a recent A. C. Nielsen Co. study of wage-earning mothers found that 71% of the women polled reported nutrition was their first consideration when it came to meal planning. Another Nielsen Survey showed that in 45% of all U.S. households at least one person was on a diet during the past year.

Let your customers take advantage of our high-quality alternatives. Mr. Turkey brand Turkey Franks, Turkey Ham, and Turkey Luncheon Meats.

THE REACTION

FIGURE 10-5

From Mr. Turkey's Retail Kit

Your profit potential is greatly enhanced by the promotional programs that come from Mr. Turkey and yourself.

First, Mr. Turkey has teamed up with Campbell-Ewald—one of the world's largest advertising agencies (Chevrolet, Goodyear, AC-Delco)—and created some fine, effective television, radio, and print advertising. Together, we've placed our media standards high to ensure consumer reach and effectiveness is at a maximum.

We also make available to you some interesting point-of-purchase materials. There's an order form elsewhere in this folder.

To help you promote Mr. Turkey brand meats in your own store ads, we've also whipped up a little demonstration on ways to use our Mr. Turkey logo, Bil-Mar logo, package art, and nutritional claims to your best advantage. Also, don't forget our tie-in allowance. Your Bil-Mar sales rep will explain the details.

And, have some fun yourself! Create endless promotion ideas—from simple seasonal "Lunch Box Specials" and "Picnic Basket Specials"—to such "wild 'n crazy" things as a personal appearance by Mr. Turkey himself!

THE PROMOTION

FIGURE 10-6

From Mr. Turkey's Retail Kit

FIGURE 10-7

From Mr. Turkey's Retail Kit

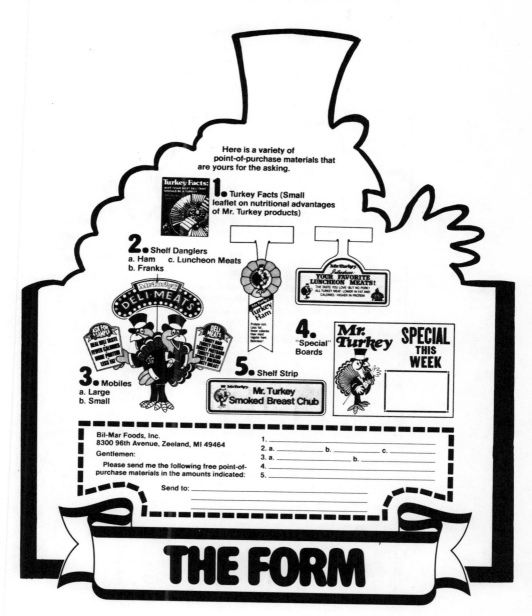

FIGURE 10-8

From Mr. Turkey's Retail Kit

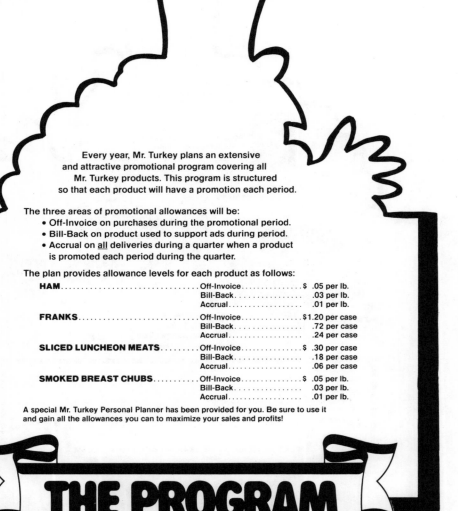

Every year, Mr. Turkey plans an extensive
and attractive promotional program covering all
Mr. Turkey products. This program is structured
so that each product will have a promotion each period.

The three areas of promotional allowances will be:
- Off-Invoice on purchases during the promotional period.
- Bill-Back on product used to support ads during period.
- Accrual on all deliveries during a quarter when a product
  is promoted each period during the quarter.

The plan provides allowance levels for each product as follows:

HAM . . . . Off-Invoice . . . . $ .05 per lb.
                                                        Bill-Back . . . . .03 per lb.
                                                        Accrual . . . . .01 per lb.

FRANKS . . . . Off-Invoice . . . . $1.20 per case
                                                        Bill-Back . . . . .72 per case
                                                        Accrual . . . . .24 per case

SLICED LUNCHEON MEATS . . . . Off-Invoice . . . . $ .30 per case
                                                        Bill-Back . . . . .18 per case
                                                        Accrual . . . . .06 per case

SMOKED BREAST CHUBS . . . . Off-Invoice . . . . $ .05 per lb.
                                                        Bill-Back . . . . .03 per lb.
                                                        Accrual . . . . .01 per lb.

A special Mr. Turkey Personal Planner has been provided for you. Be sure to use it
and gain all the allowances you can to maximize your sales and profits!

THE PROGRAM

COMPLIMENTS OF BIL-MAR FOODS, INC.

FIGURE 10-9

From Mr. Turkey's Retail Kit

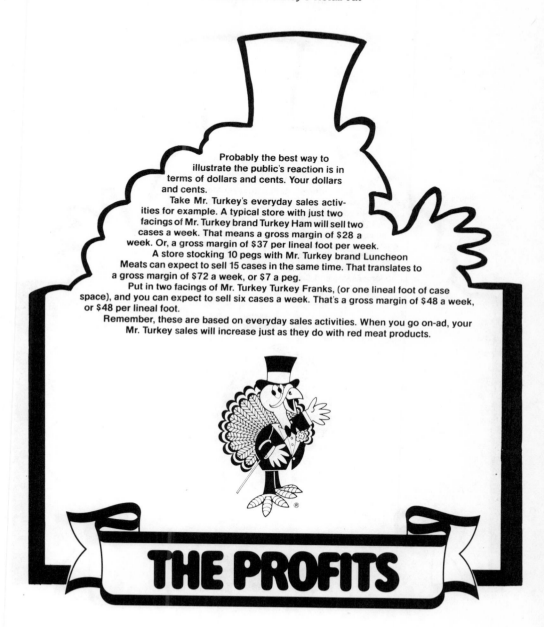

Probably the best way to illustrate the public's reaction is in terms of dollars and cents. Your dollars and cents.

Take Mr. Turkey's everyday sales activities for example. A typical store with just two facings of Mr. Turkey brand Turkey Ham will sell two cases a week. That means a gross margin of $28 a week. Or, a gross margin of $37 per lineal foot per week.

A store stocking 10 pegs with Mr. Turkey brand Luncheon Meats can expect to sell 15 cases in the same time. That translates to a gross margin of $72 a week, or $7 a peg.

Put in two facings of Mr. Turkey Turkey Franks, (or one lineal foot of case space), and you can expect to sell six cases a week. That's a gross margin of $48 a week, or $48 per lineal foot.

Remember, these are based on everyday sales activities. When you go on-ad, your Mr. Turkey sales will increase just as they do with red meat products.

THE PROFITS

FIGURE 10-10

From Mr. Turkey's Retail Kit

COMPLIMENTS OF BIL-MAR FOODS, INC.

FIGURE 10-11

Radio Commercial for Mr. Turkey

ANNCR:	And now, let's talk turkey.
MR. TURKEY:	(FLATLY) Gobble. Gobble.
ANNCR:	Thank you.
CHORUS:	*Oh, try a Mr. Turkey ham, Yes Sireee. A Mr. Turkey turkey ham. (WHISTLE) Tasty.*
MR. TURKEY:	Hi, Mr. Turkey here with three reasons to make your next ham a turkey ham.
WOMAN:	You're wearing a tuxedo.
MR. TURKEY:	I know.
CHORUS:	*Oh, try a Mr. Turkey ham, Yes Siree. It's the yummiest ham. (WHISTLE) Tasty.*
MR. TURKEY:	Reason number one. My ham is 100 percent turkey meat so there's more protein, less fat and fewer calories than regular ham.
CHORUS:	*Oh, try a Mr. Turkey ham. Yes Sireee.*
MR. TURKEY:	Reason two. It's all meat and no bone.
CHORUS:	*A Mr. Turkey turkey ham. (WHISTLE)*
MR. TURKEY:	Reason number three. Not only is there more protein. My turkey ham has a delectably smokey ham taste.
CHORUS:	*Tasty.*
MAN:	Juliet, Juliet, wherefore art thou my turkey.
WOMAN:	Oh, Romeo, you're such a ham.
MR. TURKEY:	Just look for me on the package.
MAN:	That tuxedo is dynamite.
MR. TURKEY:	Oh, thank you.
CHORUS:	*Oh, try a Mr. Turkey ham. Yes Siree. It's the yummiest ham. (WHISTLE) Tasty.*

Compliments of Bil-Mar Foods, Inc.

FIGURE 10-12

TV Photoboard for Mr. Turkey

BIL-MAR FARMS
"MR. TURKEY TALKS"

FRANKS

CODE NO.: BMFF 8013

LENGTH: 30 SECONDS

KIDS: Wowee, hot dogs!

MOTHER: The kids love your hot dogs.
WOMAN: They're turkey.

MOTHER: What? (SFX: BOING)
MR. TURKEY: Try my Mr. Turkey Turkey Franks.

KIDS: It's Mr. Turkey.
MOTHER: Hot dogs from turkey?

MR. TURKEY: Turkey makes the difference.

They're meatier, no filler, less fat and calories,

more protein than the leading all meat hot dogs.

MOTHER: But do they taste like regular hot dogs?

GROUP: You bet!
MOTHER: Delicious.

MR. TURKEY: And fewer calories.
MOTHER: Now that's a hot dog a mother can love.

MR. TURKEY: Try Mr. Turkey Turkey Franks. Turkey makes the difference.

GROUP: You bet!

Produced by Campbell-Ewald Co.

COMPLIMENTS OF BIL-MAR FOODS, INC.

And was it all worth it? Did the time and effort spent finding a tactical device that would carry over from measured media to specialized areas really pay off? Clearly, the meat industry is mammoth and the competition diverse. Swift, for example, has a market share of .06% and that company is a giant. Bil-Mar Foods had a .00013% share when it launched Mr. Turkey, but a year later was up to .0003%. The advertiser's sales more than doubled in 12 months, and the growth continues today.

SELECTING THE CARRY-OVER STRATEGY

Few creative executions begin in specialized areas and work back into the basic media. That is, a shelf-talker seldom works its way up the ladder to become the centerpiece of a TV commercial or a national campaign. Rumors do circulate—that the once famous "tiger in your tank" campaign for Esso (Exxon) came out of a poster design, and that the package design for L'eggs pantyhose, which looked like an egg, was the basis for the product name and the strongly unified campaign that followed. These stories have never been confirmed, but if they are true, they make a good case for beginning tactical work in specialized media.

An expert once said he would not approve any advertising campaign that wouldn't work on a billboard. The outdoor medium might not even be used in the campaign, but the key illustration and essential phrase would be there. And, one copywriter we know begins all of her campaign thinking by writing a sales letter to a consumer. Then, she rewrites that letter until it's absolutely convincing. Somewhere in it is the key positioning idea—the slogan, or at least its shadow—and all of the supporting benefits, the "reasons why," and the basis for consumer action. Even the illustration or demonstration may pop out. This writer approaches copy for a campaign as she would an enthusiastic note to a friend, talking about a new product she has found.

Finally, a very successful art director starts every project by quick-sketching the "essence" of the product. "Find its soul," he insists . . . and at day's end he has a drawing pad filled with 2 x 2 inch "essences" or symbols. They may represent caricatures of ingredients, problems a product can solve, portraits of consumer satisfaction, or the like—but they form a *mural* of the product from every conceivable angle. A few sketches are circled for further exploration, concepts are refined, and, finally, one or two emerge as strong campaign possibilities.

No matter how creative people work, each looks for a persuasive, memorable statement of a product that makes it different from the rest. If advertising tactics can then capitalize, or build, on this statement, they stand a good chance of producing results in every medium, general or specialized.

Think back now: tactics, or executions, grow from a formal strategy that an account team agrees is a good way to position a product. But if the strategy is vague, it will probably spawn anemic-looking tactics.

Assume the Prudential Insurance Company's strategy says: "The company is reliable and strong." Then the creative group has two words to work with. "Reliable" is hard to picture, but "strong" (or "strength") has excellent potential. Now let's "listen in" as the brainstorming process gets underway:

> "Strong as an ox!" "As iron." "As a lion." "As a *rock!*" "Rocks are solid." "People build with them." "Okay, strong as a rock. What rock?" "Granite." "The Alps, Himalayans, Rocky Mountains." "Rock of ages." "The Rock of Gibraltar." "Wait a minute—Prudential has the strength of Gibraltar!" DONE!

It's obviously not always that simple, but when creative juices start flowing, thoughts start moving . . . and they may set off a chain reaction that's truly amazing.

Ideally, every strategy contains what might be called a "workable word." Imagine what went on when a creative group was told that Pillsbury Frosting Supreme was soft, smooth, creamy, and very easy to spread:

> "How easy?" "Spread with what?" "Anybody got a knife?" "Use a piece of cardboard." "Hold it! So smooth and creamy, you can spread it with a paper knife."

Who knows exactly where the (ingenious) knife idea came from. What we do know is that a strategy statement someone wrote held the spark for the idea. "Spreadable" was the workable word. It provided an action basis for the visual demonstration, and the paper knife symbol could be worked into any medium.

Which strategies can be carried over into specialized areas? Those that contain a workable word—a distinctive idea which can be used to produce some kind of symbol. The symbol should project a product benefit and, with repetition, should be memorable. Let's look at some others.

VISUAL TECHNIQUES

The *logotype*, or signature, is probably the least complicated symbol, but it may also take the longest time to make an impression. For that reason, it usually is a long-term corporate investment rather than a short-term statement about a brand. Mobil Oil works with its name. In color, the letters are dark blue and the "o" is red. In black and white, the letters are black and the "o" is a gray tone. Visually, the "o" is used as a portal in television. The camera zooms in on it and moving pictures appear in the red frame.

Volkswagen has its "VW" in a circle in all magazine and TV advertising, on all literature, in front of every dealership and on every car, and in the Yellow Pages (which have their own "walking fingers"). Cluett capitalizes on the word "Arrow" with an arrow shot through it. Millions of shirts and thousands of advertisements have carried the symbol.

Major retailers have signatures that attract readers and viewers as effectively as merchandise in an advertisement. Women notice Saks Fifth Avenue, Bloomingdale's, or Neiman-Marcus *first*, and then look to see what the store is offering.

Kodak's "K" design in black or yellow is an attention peg as well as a signature. It appears on packages, in displays at photo stores, and on pamphlets and folders. And *numbers* also work well. Seagram's uses a red "7" with a crown on top, and the Phillips Petroleum Company has a shield with the number "66" on it.

All of these names in special type, letters, and numbers identify and unify their companies' advertising. And they are as practical in specialized areas as they are in general media.

Characters have tactical value, too. For example, Figure 10-13 shows Mr. Peanut with his top hat and monocle. And the Jolly Green Giant is the canopy over hundreds of separate canned and frozen foods. He stands silently on every package and in each advertisement and promotional piece, and then moves, and ho-ho-ho's on television. Incidently, he has gone through at least eight artistic modifications since his invention. He has gained a family of elves, who live in his own "valley," and a small, alter ego named Sprout. And they're all neighbors to the Keebler cookie and cracker elves who live in the big tree.

Then, too, all are related in spirit to Buster Brown and his dog, to Mr. Klean, to the historic midget, Johnny (of Phillip Morris fame), and to a host of other stars who stand up for cameras, shampoos, and cars.

Likewise, *animals* serve an identifying and unifying purpose. Greyhound still uses the dog on its vehicles and bus schedules, and Mack Truck's bulldog is a familiar sight at highway stops. Lincoln-Mercury cars are sold under the sign of the cat, and Buick's eagle hovers in all of its advertising. In fact, as noted in Chapter 5, automobile companies are particularly taken with animals in naming cars. There have been Cougars, Foxes, Hawks, Mustangs, Rabbits and many others. Each reflects a special personality that has tactical value.

Objects are not only valuable identifiers, but may express product benefits. The Rock of Gibraltar, as discussed, says the Prudential Insurance Company is "solid," while a red umbrella expresses

256

TV Commercial for Planters Peanuts

PLANTERS NUTS

"FUN"

Length: 30 Seconds

Comm'l No.: SBPN 6523

(MUSIC)

(MUSIC) SONG: Fun...

everyday can...

be fun fun 'cause...

'Cause it's fun...'

when you're munch, munch, munchin' Planters.

Fun, munchin' Planters...is fun, fun, fun.

Everyday can be fun, fun...'cause... 'cause it's always fun munch, munch, munchin' Planters.

(UNDER) Fun munchin' Planters is fun, fun, fun.
ANNCR: (VO) Add some fun to your day. Munch some Planters Nuts.

SONG: Munchin' Planters is fun.

Munchin' Planters is fun.

Munchin' Planters is fun.

MUNCHIN' PLANTERS IS FUN, FUN, FUN.

COMPLIMENTS OF STANDARD BRANDS, INC.

coverage and protection for Travelers Insurance. A sea shell clearly identifies the Shell Oil Company and appears in thousands of places, from service station signs, oil cans, and consumer advice booklets, to stockholders' reports. It's effective in any language all over the world. And what does the shell express? Perhaps a sense of symmetry, completeness, even naturalness, that is of value to the corporation.

Color can be used to create a campaign effect, set a mood, and suggest an attribute. At various times, for example, we've seen the Newport cigarette "blue" and the Kool cigarette "green." Both are cool, refreshing colors that are still used on the packages. Danskin tights make a virtue of white space in print advertising, and their pages are immediately identifiable.

When it comes to *illustrations*, the Marlboro Man in Marlboro Country is consistently rugged and outdoorsy. Even a border can be used as a unifying device. Scott Turf Builder shows grass growing in from all sides of a magazine page or a TV screen. The grass frame is also used on packages and in literature about the product.

Also, *packages* themselves are often used tactically to create campaign impressions. Mrs. Butterworth's syrup bottles talk to children at breakfast in the product's TV commercials, while an ivory white bottle with a three-masted schooner on it is tossed from man to man in exotic ports, to help sell Old Spice Cologne.

Gestures can create a homogeneous quality, too. "You're in good hands with Allstate" is a famous example . . . and there are green thumbs, thumbs up, "OK" signs, and handshakes.

AURAL TECHNIQUES

Phrases set to music add another campaign dimension. Names are sung: from the classic five-note "J-E-L-L-O" of years ago, to today's "Have a Coke and a smile," or "Weekends are made for Michelob." Advertisers ranging from fast food chains to financial institutions transfer printed slogans and theme lines to audio tracks for broadcast. Again, the point is to create a unified, non-fractionated advertising and marketing campaign.

In summary, advertising creative teams face the often awesome task of developing strategies and tactical executions that are effective in many different communication vehicles. A campaign's "big idea," centered around a solid X-Y-Z appeal, should attract as many of the five human senses as possible (and, ideally, reach people on that special "sixth sense" level of perception, too). The challenge is to create a memorable device that reflects campaign strategy and projects the primary consumer benefit.

Chapter 11 will examine methods used to determine the "payoffs" of successful creative strategy and tactics: action-inducing messages in all media. Advertising's intangible effects are often difficult to tap, but the measurement process is slowly gaining sophistication.

STUDY QUESTIONS

1. Name at least five different "pieces" of a fractionated advertising effort.
2. List three reasons why fractionation is not a recommended campaign practice.
3. What one specialized medium can be found on the streets, in stores, and at public gathering places?
4. What's one reason why a retailer might choose not to stress price in advertising messages?
5. Explain what is meant by the term "versatility quotient"—and why was it *high* for the Mr. Turkey name?
6. A retail sales kit may discuss a variety of different buyer concerns about a product line. Name and explain at least five.
7. What do we mean when we say every advertising strategy needs a "workable word"? (Give an example.)
8. Compare and contrast two visual and two aural symbols which may be used to help a strategy "carry over" from a measured medium to a specialized one.

ENDNOTES

1. J. Douglas Johnson, *Advertising Today*, Palo Alto: Science Research Associates, 1978, p. 129.
2. *Op. cit.*, pp. 229-246.

MEASURING CREATIVE EFFECTIVENESS

As noted throughout this text, while the ultimate goal of most advertising is to help increase sales, such results (even if measurable) are, at best, an incomplete criterion of advertising effectiveness. Suppose, for example, that you see a TV commercial tonight for Chevrolet, and that you've been thinking about buying a new car. Then, three months from now, you actually buy a Chevy—the same one you saw in the commercial. Can we say advertising "caused" you to buy that car? Of course not. Here are just a few of the other factors which may have influenced you:

(a) the price was right; (b) you liked the showroom dealers and trusted their judgment; (c) your family size changed, making this style of car appropriate; (d) with a new job, your need for a second car was suddenly acute, and your favorite dealer had this one available; (e) a friend or relative was excited over purchase of this car—or disappointed with a competitor's model; (f) you found promises of servicing, choice of colors and accessories, or a dealer-sponsored contest or giveaway appealing; (g) in your opinion, this car delivered better performance than others; or (h) you were impressed by news items concerning this car, reported in newspapers and magazines.

PROBLEMS IN TRACING ADVERTISING'S EFFECTS

The first obstacle to determining the effects of advertising on sales is, therefore, the interaction of other elements of the marketing mix, and of social forces acting in concert with those elements. How do we separate out the influence of advertising?

Second, while a TV commercial might spark your desire for a particular car, it can also raise doubts about it—in effect, turning you temporarily *away* from that car. Other advertisements in other media may then have both positive and negative effects on you . . . and we're faced with the problem of measuring the selling power of that *one* TV spot you saw first.

Third, any *element* of any advertisement may trigger a specific response, while other elements are ignored. A commercial's jingle may catch your attention and start a purchase-intent mechanism in motion—or, it might be an attractive model in a magazine advertisement or a local advertiser's "weekend special" headline in the newspaper.

In considering these three problem areas, research has found that advertising effects are often cumulative—long-term in their contributions to purchasing behavior—especially in the case of durable goods such as automobiles. If action is going to occur in the long run, however, *something* must happen in the short run, too; advertising research, therefore, concentrates on the measurement of attitudinal and motivational variables which *intervene* (in the short run) between consumers' exposure to advertisements and their ultimate actions in the market place. These variables, in fact, are the ones introduced in Chapter 3, and discussed as strategic principles thereafter.

SURVEY OR EXPERIMENT

Advertising research in creativity usually takes the form of either a survey or an experiment. Basically, a survey measures something *as it presently exists*: an attitude toward a headline, awareness of a brand name, or a state of confusion regarding claims for competing products. In effect, the survey sets out to answer the question: what's the current state of the matter we're interested in? And it proceeds by measuring this "state," being careful not to change or distort it in the process.

An experiment, on the other hand, involves a direct manipulation of elements. It seeks answers to a different question—namely, what *effect* will a specific operation have on an existing state? Now the experimenter actually exerts some pressure, imposes some restriction, or otherwise influences a pattern of events in a careful, deliberate, and scientific manner, and then measures the results. Copies of a newspaper advertisement might be shown to one group of readers in black-and-white, while a second group saw them in color; then, reactions could be compared. Or, two versions of a TV commercial might be involved—identical in every respect except that one had a male presenter and the other a female. Other manipulations might range from varieties of "distracting conditions" (measured for effects on comprehension of magazine advertisements) to different musical backgrounds in radio spots (measured for effects on interest levels and recall of selling points).

Surveys generally involve fairly large samples of respondents (often several hundred) which, if scientifically drawn, permit the projection of findings to even larger groups (such as regions of the country, or even the nation as a whole). Experiments are usually performed with small numbers of people (a few dozen or less), under tightly controlled circumstances, and while results can't be projected, they often shed light on the reasons why advertising messages succeed or fail as communication vehicles.

Sometimes findings from an experiment are important enough to warrant a survey. For example, if small groups of respondents in a test laboratory consistently indicate distrust of a new diet plan, following exposure to various advertising messages, it may be that dieting aids and plans in general are undergoing a credibility problem. If so, a large-scale attitudinal survey might save advertisers a lot of time and money otherwise invested in advertisements which miss their marks.

Sometimes, small group sessions, referred to as focus group interviews, are used to test the potential value of everything from concepts (theme ideas) to celebrity endorsers, illustrations, slogans, and jingles. Advertisements and commercials may appear in varying degrees of polish, and a group of 7-10 "likely prospects" for the product in question normally provide up to an hour of (rather "freewheeling") feedback.

Refer again to Figure 8-4b, on page 187. Creative guidance for the Blue Nun campaign came from focus group sessions. Respondents representing the target market heard commercials delivered by Joan Rivers, Louis Nye, Don Rickles, Shelley Berman, Mike Nichols and Elaine May, and Jerry Stiller and Anne Meara. This latter husband-and-wife team was selected as the most effective for delivery of Blue Nun's radio messages.[1]

STRUCTURED OR UNSTRUCTURED QUESTIONS

The questions asked of respondents in both surveys and experiments come in two basic forms: structured (or close-ended, or fixed-response), and unstructured (or open-ended, or free-response). Structured questions include, among others; (1) dichotomies (yes/no or agree/disagree types, for example); (2) multiple-choice items (perhaps a question asking which of four given advertisers makes a particular claim or utilizes the services of a particular spokesperson); and (3) scaled responses (calling for answers along a continuum which runs in five, seven, or more steps between two extremes, such as "interesting" and "dull"). In all of these cases, questions are worded in such a way that respondents must answer in terms of given alternatives; results are, thus, easy to tabulate and interpret. Such questions preclude, however, acquisition of much information on the motivations behind answers given.

Unstructured questions permit respondents to talk (or write) freely and at length about the subject at hand, and are especially useful in the following cases: (a) where the research team has limited knowledge of the kind of answers that questions might provoke; (b) where anticipations are for a great range of responses; (c) where there is interest in what respondents will volunteer on a subject before specific prompting; or (d) where an in-depth study of respondents' attitudes is desired. Of course, there is a price to pay for such advantages, since these open-ended responses are often time- and space-consuming, and can be difficult to analyze and compare.

CONTROLLING NON-ADVERTISING FACTORS

Now let's return to the problem of interacting marketing components and social forces. Generally, the best way to discover advertising's effect in a complex environment is to hold other elements constant while the content, number, size, frequency, or placement of specific advertisements is manipulated. A *market test* puts a selected marketing element into operation in a test city, where other elements can be controlled, to determine its probable effect in the total area served by a company's product. For example, the packaging, pricing, and general availability of a new brand of detergent might remain constant while advertising was varied. The number of advertisements might stay the same, but one month the only medium involved might be magazines; another month it might be newspapers, television, or radio.

Interviews with consumers in the chosen city could determine which medium resulted in the greatest: (1) awareness of the advertising messages; (2) interest in their claims; (3) believability; (4) ease of understanding; or (5) memorability. Or, only newspapers might be involved, while the basic message (or just the headline, illustration, or copy) was changed from week to week.

It's also possible to query customers at the point of purchase. Why did shopper A choose brand B instead of brand C? Was it because of price? Guarantees of service? Trade-in value? Or simply the desire to try something new? Probing here, by interviewers, sometimes results in a surprisingly accurate playback of advertisements and commercials on the part of consumers (particularly in the case of specially-advertised sales and bargains).

Another way to minimize the influence of non-advertising forces is to control advertising exposure. If a product or service is available only by mail—and only if ordered immediately upon receipt of an ad *through* the mail—sales results are not difficult to trace.

EXAMINING ADVERTISING FACTORS

Now recall the other concerns we have with advertising effectiveness studies: the influence of advertising messages in different media—and of specific elements within each message. The Advertising Research Foundation maintains that once media exposure has occurred, the creative components of advertisements go to work to produce advertising *perception* and *communication*. Perception involves receipt of the very least amount of content from a message—and is often measured through respondents' reports of basic awareness or "recognition" when shown or played a particular message.[2]

PERCEPTION

One of the leading research organizations involved in recognition research is Daniel Starch & Staff, whose Starch Message Report Service provides information on advertising readership. A respondent is shown selected advertisements and, on the basis of answers to appropriate questions, is classified in each case as one of the following: (a) a NON-READER (one who didn't remember seeing the advertisement in the medium being studied); (b) a NOTED READER (one who did remember seeing it); (c) an ASSOCIATED READER (one who noted the advertisement and saw or read some part of it which clearly identified the advertiser); and (d) a READ-MOST READER (one who read half or more of the copy).

Comparison is the keynote in using this form of readership data: one campaign against another; simultaneous campaigns or a new campaign against old ones; or, one client's advertisements against (1) those of competitors or (2) product group averages (cake mix X against cake mixes in general). Given Starch results, advertisers can then study their messages for themes and methods of treatment: product-in-use illustrations vs. results-of-use pictures; long copy vs. short; main idea in the headline vs. sheer attention-grabber.[3]

Starch has also done television research, providing information on *noted, associated*, and *mis-identified* commercials (the latter referring to incorrect brands matched with given commercials). Interviewing has been conducted both by telephone (with questions covering commercials viewed the same evening), and through personal interviews (with storyboards of commercials aired the previous day and evening).[4]

COMMUNICATON

Measurement of advertising communication involves playback of specific elements seen and heard in advertising messages.[5] Unfortunately, however, studies have shown that the recall and retention of material read, seen, and heard *may* be irrelevant to any kind of attitude or behavioral change. (Even though consumers may remember that Wheaties has been advertised for dozens of years as the "Breakfast of Champions," they may remain loyal purchasers of Kellogg's Corn Flakes.) Still, recall tests are easy to administer, provide tangible, quantifiable results of communication activity, and are widely used in advertising research.

Also, "learning" is considered so basic to our educational system that it's often believed necessary before purchasing behavior can occur.[6] After all, Kellogg's devotees can probably recall advertising for *their* cereal as well; and, having "learned" about Wheaties, they may influence others to buy it! So runs this and numerous other arguments, and, in the end (as Chapter 3 made clear), predispositions can't ever be observed directly. They're merely inferred—to account for behavioral activity.

MEASUREMENT TECHNIQUES

One simple recall technique is known as the Triple Associates Test. Respondents are asked: what kind of appliance manufacturer advertises that, 'The quality goes in before the name goes on'? The reply, 'Zenith,' associates a *product class* (appliances) with a *slogan* and a *brand name*. A variation of this method asks for *two* of the three associated items. To the question: who advertises, 'When you care enough to send the very best,' respondents must give the generic product (greeting cards), as well as the name Hallmark. (And if they don't know the correct answers, their "guesses" are often very revealing of the power of unrelated advertisements. For example, K Mart's slogan, "The Saving Place" may easily be associated with a bank.)

Gallup & Robinson, a highly experienced research organization which numbers among its clients many of the nation's leading advertisers and their agencies, conducts frequent television and magazine impact studies. Proven viewers and readers of selected TV programs and magazine issues are asked to recall specific commercials and advertisements seen within the 24-hour period preceding the interviews.

Reports supplied to advertiser-clients include detailed tables which show all of the specific copy points remembered and described, as well as respondents' attitudes toward buying the products advertised. Figure 11-1 is a page from one of Gallup & Robinson's TV commercial survey questionnaires, and Figure 11-2 is a similar page from a survey for magazine advertisements.

Both of these are examples of *aided* recall studies, in that respondents are *cued* as to what they're being asked to remember. It's also possible to conduct *unaided* recall research wherein respondents must identify and describe all advertisements they remember seeing in the last 24 hours. In this case, there is no "matching" of names with slogans, and no suggestion that a certain set of products might be involved. Each interviewee must probe his or her memory for information. (It should be noted, however, that *all* recall is "aided" to some extent—even if it's simply a mental trigger which gets respondents to think about *advertising*.)

RANKINGS VS. RATINGS

A fair amount of message testing deals with comparisons. After all, there are so many different creative approaches available, it's hard to be satisfied with evaluation of one isolated area. (Besides, most emotional reactions are relative anyway; layout A may look "good" next to layout B, but lose ground quickly next to layouts C and D.) Two basic types of information, rankings and ratings, may be obtained from comparisons.

Rankings

Ranking involves an ordering of advertisements (or parts thereof) according to the response desired by the advertiser (interest, credibility, persuasive value, or the like). Often, dummy layouts, storyboards, or tape recordings are used—unfinished messages at various stages of development. The *consumer jury test* involves a relatively small group of consumers (usually between 25 and 75) who represent potential buyers of the product or service involved. Each is asked to rank alternative messages or elements according to specific qualities or expected effects.[7]

Another ranking method is known as *paired comparisons*. In this case, respondents see advertisements in groups of two and are asked for preferences. Of course, consumers are rarely faced with a choice between just two brands; still, this method is simply and economically administered, has proven statistically reliable over time, and is often used in combination with other measurement techniques.[8]

The major drawback of ranking methods is the limited information they provide. Given four headlines: J, K, L, and M, ranked

FIGURE 11-1

Page from Gallup & Robinson IN-VIEW Questionnaire
(TV Commercials Study)

1. YOU MAY BE FAMILIAR WITH OTHER COMMERCIALS FOR

   _____,

   BUT THINKING <u>ONLY</u> OF LAST NIGHT'S COMMERCIAL, PLEASE TELL ME EVERYTHING YOU REMEMBER ABOUT IT.

   WHAT DID THEY SHOW AND TALK ABOUT?

   Suggested Probes:
   HOW DID THEY SHOW THAT?
   HOW DID THEY GET THAT ACROSS?
   WHAT ELSE DO YOU RECALL ABOUT THAT?

2. WHAT SALES POINTS OR ARGUMENTS FOR BUYING DID THEY SHOW OR TALK ABOUT LAST NIGHT?

   Suggested Probes::
   HOW DID THEY SHOW THAT?
   HOW DID THEY GET THAT ACROSS?
   WHAT ELSE DO YOU RECALL ABOUT THAT?

3. WHAT DID YOU LEARN ABOUT THE (product/service) FROM THIS COMMERCIAL?

4. WHAT WENT THROUGH YOUR MIND AS YOU WATCHED THIS COMMERCIAL?

5. THE ADVERTISER TRIED TO INCREASE YOUR INTEREST IN BUYING HIS (product/service). DID HE SUCCEED, OR NOT?

   ☐ Yes
   ☐ No
   ☐ DK

6. WHAT WAS IN THE COMMERCIAL THAT MAKES YOU SAY THAT?

7. WHAT BRAND OF THIS TYPE OF PRODUCT DID YOU BUY LAST?
   OR
   WHAT COMPANY'S SERVICE DID YOU USE LAST?

   ☐ Doesn't use

   ☐ Doesn't use

   Code Number   BRAND AND PRODUCT   *(Only one product to a page)*

COMPLIMENTS OF GALLUP & ROBINSON, INC.

FIGURE 11-2

Page From Gallup & Robinson RAPID AD MEASUREMENT
Questionnaire (Magazine Advertisements Study)

ASK FOR ALL ADS CODED "X" •

1. You may be familiar with other ads for but thinking only of this issue, please describe the ad as you remember it. What did the ad look like?

2. What did the ad say?

3. Just in your own words what did you learn about the (product/service) from this ad?

4. What went through your mind when you looked at this ad?

5. The advertiser tried to increase your interest in buying his (product/service). Did he succeed or not?

☐ Yes
☐ No
☐ DK

6. What was in the ad that makes you say that?

7. What brand of this type of product did you buy last?
OR
What company's service did you use last?

☐ Doesn't use

8. Had you ever seen this very same ad before you saw it in this issue?

☐ Yes
☐ No
☐ DK

• FOR ADS CODED "Y", USE SPECIAL "Y" PLAYBACK SHEET.

BRAND AND PRODUCT (Only one product to a page)

Code Number ☐ X ☐ Y

COMPLIMENTS OF GALLUP & ROBINSON, INC.

according to interest value, we may find that J is "more interesting" than M, which is more interesting than K and L. But we have no idea: (1) whether J is interesting enough to compel an audience to read further (in other words, *all four* headlines may be quite "uninteresting"); or (2) whether J and M are judged very nearly the *same* in interest value while there's a big gap between M and K.

Ratings

Rating procedures give us this kind of added detail, because they go one step beyond rankings. Actual numerical positions are assigned to advertisements along a scale extending between two poles. For instance, the *semantic differential* is a seven-point scale bounded by a set of polar (opposite) adjectives. Respondents might be asked to rate the interest value of a set of headlines on scales set up as follows:

(+3)	(+2)	(+1)	(0)	(−1)	(−2)	(−3)
Very Interesting	Interesting	Slightly Interesting	Neutral	Slightly Dull	Dull	Very Dull

(Note: Numerical values are not shown to respondents.)[9]

Returning to the example above, suppose headline J received +3, M received −1, K received −2, and L received −3. Now we have measures of both the direction (positive or negative) and the intensity (from "slightly" through "very") of feelings toward these headlines. We can see that J is clearly superior to the other three, while M, K, and L are all in trouble when it comes to interest—information which the ranking method didn't give us.

Sometimes, respondents may be asked to rate a particular store, as positioned through its advertising, on: cleanliness, economy, friendliness, variety of merchandise, and speed of service. The same procedure is then followed with advertisements for competing stores; and, finally, respondents are asked to rate an "ideal" store on the same characteristics. The resulting comparisons can prove eye-opening in terms of advertising communication.

A well-known five-point *Likert* scale ranges from "Strongly Agree," to "Agree," to "Neutral," to "Disagree," to "Strongly Disagree." Even nine-point scales have been used to rate the similarity of selected advertisements and claims (from "Highly Similar" to "Highly Dissimilar").

Rating devices eliminate stereotyped or ambiguous answers to research questions, and avoid problems respondents may otherwise have in articulating reactions. They're easily repeated over time and provide a reliable continuing measure of attitudes toward advertising messages and brand names.[10]

HOW TO BEGIN

The starting point in the evaluation of any advertisement is the basic statement of objectives in the overall marketing plan. John Keil, Creative Director of the Dancer-Fitzgerald-Sample advertising agency, advises research teams to make sure advertising messages *follow creative campaign strategy*. "Sounds simple and obvious," he says, "but I've found it's one of the greatest creative oversights."[11]

If the objective is to GAIN CONSUMER AWARENESS of a new cereal brand or slogan, research on the credibility of a headline claim is off base. (A recent study dealing with advertising slogans for banks found that slogan recognition wasn't even related to credibility.[12]) Rather, a popular measurement question here is: "When cold cereals are mentioned, what brands come to mind?" Or: "What advertising slogans for cold cereals can you think of?"

Then, again, if the objective is to COMMUNICATE A SPECIFIC PIECE OF INFORMATION (a new ingredient, perhaps, or a comparative test result), some type of recall question is clearly in order. When it comes to establishing and maintaining an image, however, or changing or reinforcing an attitude, ranking and rating questions are often employed, along with various multiple-choice, and adjective-matching techniques.

Professor Charles Frazer, at the University of Washington, has suggested some other important questions which advertising creativity research should answer, and they correspond to many of the creative principles we've discussed in earlier chapters.[13] First, is *one central selling idea* readily apparent and clearly communicated? A maxim at the McCann-Erickson agency proclaims that simplicity is the first and most important element of great advertising strategy, and specificity is the second.[14] So, research in this area must probe for both comprehension and recall of X-Y-Z appeals.

Second, does the advertisement *speak in prospects' language*— about their personal needs and desires? Here we're concerned not just with copy, but with visual and aural symbols, colors, sizes and shapes, music, talent, and the like. So, research queries often deal with perceptions of *values* of particular advertisements—their relevance to audience concerns and lifestyles.

Third, is the creative approach *tasteful* and *appropriate* to the advertiser involved—yet *distinctive*? In other words, is an advertisement's style (mood conveyed) and the treatment of it (technique employed) compatible with advertiser image, but original enough to position the product in a class by itself? Now research must ask: is an advertisement (or series of advertisements) successful in "breaking the boredom barrier" . . . in "finding the *exciting* way to tell a sales story" . . . in "saying things 'freshly' "?[15]

Fourth, do all parts of the advertisement *work together* to communicate the selling message: each making a *separate*, but not conflicting contribution? Now we're into (1) element testing: headline words or the opening lines of commercials, calls to action (hard sell vs. soft sell), and aural/visual effects; and (2) theme testing: the integration of all elements into a cohesive entity, and the continuity established between advertisements in a campaign.

Fifth, do all elements and overall advertisements capitalize on the *unique characteristics* of the medium or media in which they appear, and thereby emphasize key message claims—and the proof of those claims—in a *convincing* manner? John Caples, a veteran of 50 years in advertising, has noted that two forces are at work in the minds of advertisement readers, listeners, and viewers who are prospective buyers: skepticism, and the desire to believe. "Do prospects a favor," he advises, "by giving them evidence that what you say is true."[16]

WHEN TO DO COPY RESEARCH

It may be well at this point to ask just when all of this testing should occur. Three different opportunities present themselves: before the messages have been released to the media (at various stages in the planning process), during respondents' actual contact with the advertisements as they are run or aired, and sometime after the messages have been seen or heard.

THE PRETEST

By far the most important stage of testing, from the advertiser's point of view, is the pretest. If potential problems can be identified and corrected before advertisements reach the public at large, virtually millions of dollars in time and space costs (not to mention that priceless item called image) may be saved. Pretesting is also the most difficult kind of testing because it calls for evaluation in an artificial environment (since the advertisement is often in a semi-finished form, and respondents are usually asked to read, watch, or listen in unfamiliar surroundings, such as a test laboratory or theater). Increasingly, however, advertisers are recognizing the value of pretesting, and are using it for three general purposes:

(a) To develop insights into people's attitudinal make-ups and behavioral patterns which may suggest new advertising approaches worthy of research;
(b) To determine how well basic ideas and overall advertisements are likely to accomplish specified objectives;
(c) To discover reasons for strengths and weaknesses of creative ideas and techniques with the aim of making improvements.[17]

Both of the Gallup & Robinson tests represented in Figures 11-1 and 11-2, on pages 266 and 267, can be given as pretests. A "rough" version of a commercial is inserted into a regularly scheduled TV program on a UHF station in Philadelphia (through a special arrangement set up between the station and Gallup & Robinson). Likewise, a "planned" advertisement is placed in a "test magazine" which is personally delivered to selected homes by a Gallup & Robinson representative.

Audience Studies, Inc. (ASI), based in Los Angeles, provides four different pretest measurements of viewer reactions to proposed TV commercials: interest, involvement, communication, and effectiveness. Each involves a different kind of response, and may be considered representative of similar types of pretest research performed by other companies.

Interest. The interest measure consists of a "Profile Curve Score" presented electronically in the form of a graph. During commercial viewing in a theater, respondents turn dials, attached to their seats, according to their degrees of interest. Second-by-second reactions might find a viewer moving from a state of great interest to a rather bored position and back to one of moderate interest. The resulting graph would show respective rising, falling, and leveling periods. ASI then computes an "average" interest score which is compared with norms for the appropriate product or product class.

Similar electronic devices even pinpoint exact words or scenes which elicit a desirable or undesirable response. (For example, respondents may be asked to push buttons, pull levers, or otherwise manipulate gadgetry in order to indicate a credible spokesperson, a confusing claim, or an appealing vs. an unappealing slogan or jingle.)

Involvement. The involvement measure is an index of commercial image. After viewers have seen a commercial they're asked to examine a list of thirteen positive (favorable) adjectives, and to check the ones they feel apply to that particular message:

> appealing . . . clever . . . convincing . . . effective . . . entertaining . . . fast-moving . . . genuine . . . imaginative . . . informative . . . interesting . . . original . . . refreshing . . . unusual

After the percentage of respondents choosing each adjective is determined, all percentages are summed and divided by thirteen. The final average provides the "index" for the commercial.

Communication. The third measure, communication, involves both comprehension and recall and, again, takes place after commercial viewing. This time, respondents are asked to play back the brand name of the product advertised, then one selling point from the commercial, and finally, multiple selling points. Such feedback is presumed to indicate the extent to which the commercial communicated its message.

Effectiveness. Finally, we come to ASI's persuasive measure, called effectiveness. It's a "change" score, indicating the degree to which a commercial influences a respondent's desire for a product. The change takes place between the viewer's expressed interest in having a particular product—before and after he or she sees a commercial for that product. Prior to viewing, a questionnaire is administered. Respondents are advised that door prizes will be given away shortly and are asked to indicate which brands of a series of products they would like to receive if they win. After the commercials have run, each viewer rates them on five-point scales according to their effects on buying intentions: from "increasing it very much," to "decreasing it very much." The "score" is the number of respondents indicating an *increase* in the "desire to buy," shown as a percentage of all respondents participating.

THE COINCIDENTAL AND POSTTEST

Coincidental tests are frequently confused with posttests because in both cases the advertisements involved have been released to the media and are most probably still running. The difference lies in the time of measurement: coincidental tests take place *while respondents are in contact with the advertisements* (looking or listening). On the other hand, posttests ask respondents to *remember back* to an advertisement seen or heard in the past. Often, the time span is sufficient to require prompting, so the respondent is re-shown the message and asked for recognition, brand-name association, recall, or whatever. The Starch Service discussed previously is an example of a posttest, and both of the Gallup & Robinson tests mentioned can be given as posttests.

WHERE TO DO COPY RESEARCH

When research is conducted on a personal, face-to-face basis, the interviewer has the chance to explain and display materials for respondents, and to probe for detailed answers (and the reasons behind them). An experienced interviewer may spend as much as an hour or more with a respondent without causing fatigue or other discomfort. Such interviewers are expensive to hire (and train), however, and additional time and expense may be involved if they're asked to travel great distances to conduct their research.

TELEPHONE INTERVIEWING

In some instances, advertising effects can be measured over the telephone. It all depends on how "effects" are defined. Recall our previous discussion of the Triple Associates Test. If we're interested in the number of people who can associate a short advertising theme (such as: "We make it simple") with a specific name (Honda), we can probably find out as easily on the phone as we can in person. On the other hand, if research calls for credibility rankings of five magazine advertisements for household cleaners, we'd have a great deal of difficulty without visual exposure.

The questions used in telephone interviewing should be short, clear, easy to answer, and not in any way threatening or embarrassing to respondents. Also, it's usually a good idea to assure respondents of their anonymity in such surveys.

RESEARCH CONDUCTED THROUGH THE MAIL

Still another research medium involves the U.S. postal system. It's used by numerous advertisers whose basic research problems seem suited to this more impersonal, but still valuable, channel of communication. The response rate is often low (25% is common, although second and third mailings may help considerably). Also, the advertiser can never be sure just who it was that responded. Even if the questionnaire is addressed to the head of the household, any member of the family may provide answers.

Results of research conducted by mail are often slow in coming, even though some companies precede the mailing of a questionnaire with a telephone call to the intended recipient and/or offer rewards for speedy replies. Studies have shown, however, that two techniques are consistently effective in increasing response rates: (1) *follow-up* questionnaires, and (2) *monetary incentives* enclosed with the questionnaire.[18]

On the positive side respondents tend to reply quite candidly to mailed questionnaires. There is a fair amount of anonymity involved, compared to situations utilizing telephone and face-to-face interviews, and some respondents find it reassuring.

LABORATORY RESEARCH

Laboratory equipment is often used for experimental purposes—to compare creative approaches in advertisements for their abilities to register impressions and to gain nonverbal responses. For example, *eye-camera* studies, involving pictures taken of eye movements during exposure to advertisements, have found that gaze patterns are closely related to the presence of attention-gaining elements (including attractive models) in printed messages, and to on-screen action in the case of TV commercials.[19] People like to look at people, and seem to have a natural inclination to follow things which are in motion. When an X-Y-Z appeal can be displayed effectively with some kind of people-action, therefore, interest-holding properties may be built in.

The *tachistoscope* ("T-scope") is an instrument which mechanically controls the time of exposure to an advertising message. A respondent is permitted to see an advertisement for, say, a tenth of a second—and then asked for playback of message elements. Gradually, exposure time is lengthened until more of the message can be identified. Research teams liken this experience to that in which readers find themselves as they page through magazines or newspapers. Sometimes, advertisements are seen for only a fraction of a second; but if the brand name (at least) registers, some advertising communication has occurred. (Note: A recent T-scope study found that brand names which appeared in large, block letters, near the headlines in advertisements, had the best chance of registering.)[20]

Another device, called a *psychogalvanometer*, measures sweat gland activity during exposure to an advertisement or commercial. If a person becomes excited by a message stimulus, a "skin reaction" can be detected; responses are actually called "galvanic skin responses."

The major disadvantage of all of these measurement systems is the highly awkward position in which they place respondents. Eye camera operation generally requires that the participant's forehead be pressed tightly against a frame while his or her teeth are clamped around a dental "bite bar" (to prohibit any head movement during eye photography). In addition, a light must shine in the respondent's eye during the picture-taking procedure.

With the tachistoscope, subjects stare through a viewer into temporary "blackness." Then, the lighted message flashes abruptly before them (startling them considerably more than would an advertisement flipped over in a magazine or newspaper).

Finally, getting "wired up" to the psychogalvanometer resembles the prelude to a reading from an electrocardiograph in a hospital (or, possibly a lie detector test). And, of course, in all of these situations, the respondent is asked to "make believe you're seeing this at home—in your own living room." Still, such measurements can be useful in planning creative executions—if they're used in conjunction with other tests.

THE ROLE OF RESEARCH

Admittedly, we've barely scratched the surface in terms of copy testing procedures and organizations. But we've tried to highlight some of the research terms and techniques with which advertising creative personnel are likely to come in contact. Those interested in pursuing the subject are encouraged to consult the references listed at the end of this chapter.

Remember always that research in advertising creativity can assist copywriting, artistic, and production efforts, but can't necessarily define clear-cut paths down which creative teams should travel. Research results are guidelines to follow, not crutches to fall back on. Clarence Eldridge, who held top marketing positions at General Foods and Campbell Soup, noted that: "There is no single criterion by which the effectiveness of all kinds of advertising can be measured, precisely because advertising is not homogeneous with respect to its objectives, and the tasks that are assigned to it."[21]

True, in many cases (particularly at the retail level), there's neither the time nor the money for needed research; and, many "untested" advertisements and commercials prove highly successful—thanks to good judgment, coupled with past experience and intuition. Also, some "tested" messages fail miserably. But through continued improvements and refinements in techniques, research can help creative teams maximize their number of success stories.

Some people in advertising believe that ad-building is an art, and ad-measurement a science. But a little artistic input is valuable in copy research (especially in the design of questionnaires), while an appreciation for scientific techniques can be a tremendous help to copy, art, and production personnel in applying research findings to their own endeavors.

Another kind of research important to creative teams is the testing of *products*—to be sure that advertised claims are valid. A number of regulatory groups are vitally concerned with such tests, and they are the subject of our final chapter.

STUDY QUESTIONS

1. What are three basic problems faced by research teams in tracing advertising's effect on sales?
2. Differentiate between an advertising research survey and an experiment.
3. Give an example of a structured and an unstructured question that might be used in copy testing.
4. Using Advertising Research Foundation terminology, how do we measure advertising *perception* and *communication*?
5. Give an example of an aided recall question and an unaided recall question that might be used in copy testing.
6. Which procedure—rating or ranking—gives the advertising research team "more information" from respondents? Why?
7. What is the starting point in the evaluation of any advertisement or commercial?

8. Why is pretesting considered the most important stage of message testing?
9. Describe one pretest measurement provided by Audience Studies, Inc.
10. Name one piece of laboratory equipment used for experimental purposes in copy testing.

ENDNOTES

1. See J. Douglas Johnson, ed., *Campaign Report Newsletter*, January, 1979, American Association of Advertising Agencies, New York.
2. Advertising Research Foundation, *Toward Better Media Comparisons*, New York: Advertising Research Foundation, 1961, pp. 16-23.
3. "Starch Message Report: Scope, Method and Use," Mamaroneck, New York: Daniel Starch & Staff (Printed Material).
4. See *Media Decisions*, December, 1970.
5. Advertising Research Foundation, *op. cit.*, pp. 23-26.
6. Haskins, Jack B., "Factual Recall as a Measure of Advertising Effectiveness," *Journal of Advertising Research*, Vol. 4, No. 1, March, 1964, pp. 2-7.
7. Harper W. Boyd Jr., and Ralph Westfall, *Marketing Research: Text and Cases*, 4th Edition, Homewood, Illinois: Richard D. Irwin, 1977, pp. 617-618.
8. Blankenship, A. B., "Let's Bury Paired Comparisons," *Journal of Advertising Research*, Vol. 6, No. 1, March, 1966, pp. 13-17.
9. See Osgood, Charles E., George J. Suci, and Percy H. Tannenbaum, *The Measurement of Meaning*, Urbana, Illinois: University of Illinois Free Press, 1957.
10. Mindak, William A., "Fitting the Semantic Differential to the Marketing Problem," *Journal of Marketing*, Vol. 25, No. 4, April, 1961, pp. 28-33.
11. Keil, John M., "Can You Become a Creative Judge?" *Journal of Advertising*, Winter, 1975, p. 30.
12. Myron Glassman, "Recognition, Believability and Slogans," in *Challenge of Change to Advertising Education*, C. Dennis Schick, ed., American Academy of Advertising, Austin, Texas, 1976, p. 131.
13. Frazer, Charles, "Toward Some General Criteria for Evaluating Advertisements," in *Sharing for Understanding: Proceedings of the 1977 Conference of the American Academy of Advertising*, edited by Gordon E. Miracle, pp. 146-148.
14. See "A Point of View on Advertising Strategy," McCann-Erickson, Inc., *White Paper I*, October, 1972.
15. See Caples, John, "50 Things I have Learned in 50 Years in Advertising," *Advertising Age*, September 22, 1975, p. 47; Ralph Zeuthen, "Top-Notch Writing Offers Your Product or Idea a Better Chance," *Advertising Age*, April 21, 1975, p. 65; and William Bernbach, "Bill Bernbach Defines the Four Disciplines of Creativity," *Advertising Age*, July 5, 1971, p. 21.
16. Caples, John, *op. cit.*, p. 47.
17. National Industrial Conference Board, *Pretesting Advertising: Studies in Business Policy, No. 109*, New York: National Industrial Conference Board, 1963, p. 6.
18. David H. Furse, "Toward A Theory of Mail Questionnaire Response: A Fresh Look at Monetary Incentives and Follow-Up Mailings," in *Advances in Advertising Research and Management*, Steven E. Permut, ed., American Academy of Advertising, New Haven, Connecticut, 1979, p. 161.
19. See especially Nixon, H.K., "Attention Value and Interest in Advertising," *Archives of Psychology*, No. 72, 1924; James Spier Karslake, "The Purdue Eye-Camera: A Practical Apparatus for Studying the Attention Value of Advertisements," Unpublished Ph.D. dissertation, Purdue University, 1939; Sherilyn K. Zeigler, "Attention Factors in Televised Messages: Effects on Looking Behavior and Recall," Unpublished Ph.D. dissertation, Michigan State University, 1969.

20. E. W. Rhodes, N. B. Leferman, E. Cook, and D. Schwartz, "T-Scope Tests of Yellow Pages Advertising," *Journal of Advertising Research*, Vol. 19, No. 2, April, 1979, p. 51.
21. Eldridge, Clarence E., "Advertising Effectiveness—How Can It Be Measured," *Journal of Marketing*, Vol. 22, No. 3, January, 1958, p. 241.

RESTRICTIONS ON CREATIVE STRATEGIES AND TACTICS

Jokers in the advertising business claim that every creative team these days needs a lawyer: to keep the copywriter and art director from violating some rule, regulation, code or guideline intended to protect consumers. Practically all advertisements, particularly those for national media, are screened by one or more attorneys. They often request substantiation, suggest changes, and may kill campaigns before they're published or broadcast—or even presented to clients. Hence, some creative people, especially young writers and artists, claim their alternatives are blocked and ingenuity is stifled.

As consumers, they may be strong advocates of truth in advertising—for the public's sake and their own. However, when challenged to help sell goods, services, stores, or dealerships, they propose superlatives and questionable claims. They go for a strong hook, exaggerated claims, or puffery, and never mind the shaded truths. But with increased practical experience, they learn to keep their copy and visuals "inside the law" and realize they can develop persuasive messages without exaggeration.

THE LOCAL SCENE

In this chapter, we'll start with a local market, Minneapolis, Minnesota, and explain how advertising is controlled at the grass roots. Then we'll move on to show the national regulators who monitor major manufacturers and their agencies.

LOCAL ADVERTISER

Dayton's department store is more sophisticated than most marketers in the way it reviews advertising; strict rules are followed to avoid infractions. The company itself operates 16 stores in Minnesota, Wisconsin, North Dakota, and South Dakota—all part of the Dayton Hudson Corporation which consists of 588 stores in 44 states. Figure 12-1 shows the total number of units.

Each operating company is responsible for establishing its own guidelines similar to those illustrated in Figure 12-2. *Dayton's Advertising Policy* appears on the back of every copy of the *Dayton's Print Advertising Request* form, and signals the beginning of work on a newspaper advertisement, which may later be expanded to include commercials. The document starts with the buyer and is approved by the merchandise manager.

But how are legal problems avoided? Let's follow a piece of copy through the review screen at Dayton's. Young writers practically memorize the 17 Advertising Policy points, and become thoroughly familiar with a definitive set of regulations entitled: "Do's and Don'ts In Advertising Copy," published by the Council of Better Business Bureaus. In Dayton's advertising department each junior writer works with a senior writer who knows the rules from experience. Both are guided by information on the "Request" or fact sheet. All advertising messages go to the Copy Chief who is well acquainted with what can and cannot be said about products and services.

The next step is the Buyer, who specializes in a particular type of merchandise (so he or she is aware of prohibitions in that category, especially in terms of manufacturing and co-op arrangements). After these approvals, type is set and sent to the Proofreader who knows most forms of "legal-ese." And, when the material is in mechanical or proof form, the Advertising Director gives it the final okay.

Thus, in the screening process there are five probable reviewers: Senior Writer, Copy Chief, Buyer, Proofreader, and Advertising Director.

It is certainly "corporate-defeating" for a marketer with a quality reputation such as Dayton's to violate consumer protection regulations. If the stores do commit infractions, therefore, they're usually unintentional oversights. They slip through the review screen without being detected or properly understood.

FIGURE 12-1

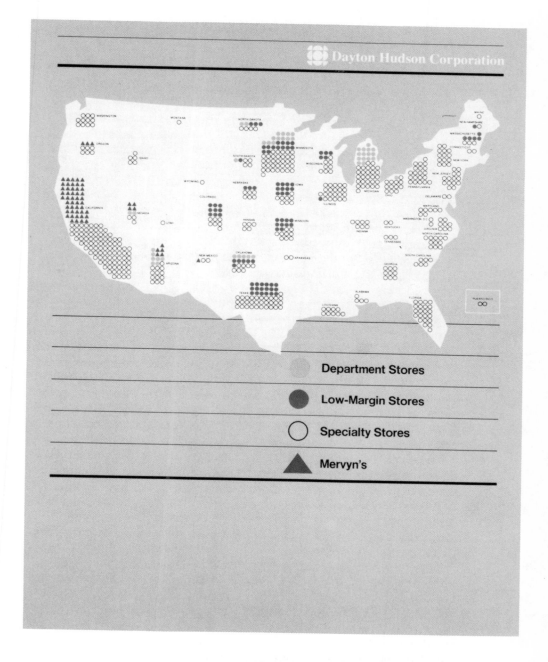

COMPLIMENTS OF DAYTON HUDSON CORPORATION

FIGURE 12-2

Dayton's Advertising Policy

DAYTON'S ADVERTISING POLICY

1. Scope of Dayton's Advertising Policies

Dayton's advertising policies apply to all forms of advertising, including the following media: newspaper, magazine, radio, television, direct mail, exterior signs and billboards, window display, interior display, signs, statement enclosures, tent cards and informative literature.

2. The Use of the Word "Sale"

a. "Sale" is an actual reduction from the regular price of merchandise from our stocks. A storewide "Sale." (Anniversary, Daisy, Jubilee) may include "Special Purchases" or "Irregulars" if identified as such in the ad.

b. Prices on items must be reduced a minimum of 10% to qualify as on "Sale" in departmental or divisional promotions and 15% during a storewide sale. Exceptions to this policy can be made in hardship cases if approved by the Executive Vice President, Merchandising or the General Merchandise Manager.

c. It is not permissible to bring merchandise into the store at a fictitious regular price that produces infrequent or isolated sales for the purpose of establishing an actual price.

d. At the end of the sale period, all sale merchandise must be returned to the pre-sale price or removed from the selling floor for a minimum period of one week, except when competition forces us to retain the sale price of merchandise as the regular competitive price.

e. Merchandise offered at "Sale" prices during storewide sales will not be displayed at a price as low as the sale price for a period of 30 days preceding or seven days following the sale event. Clearance merchandise signed as clearance during storewide sales may be reduced at any time during or following the sale.

f. The items offered must be at the outset complete in assortment.

g. Where there is a price range, i. e., $5 to $10, at least 10% of the merchandise must be at the lower price point.

h. Merchandise that is reduced by means of a markdown and which will return to the higher pre-sale price qualifies for use of the term "Sale." The mechanics of such offering may be either by a temporary markdown, or a permanent markdown with a subsequent after-sale markdown cancellation for the remainder.

i. It is not permissible to further reduce the price of Sale offerings during the event unless required by competition to further reduce price. Clearance merchandise identified as such may be reduced during the event.

j. If a department has permission to hand mark tickets, temporary markdowns must be marked in green pen.

National brand break date sales* and/or traditionally competitive sale* break dates that are run concurrently with one of our major storewide sales may be kept out on the floor during the sale. Headers, however, and in-store signing must not carry the major storewide sale header, but be signed with our year-around sale header.

*These sales must be pre-approved by the Executive Vice President, Merchandising.

Sale pricing of merchandising regularly stocked — see Policy 6-14-05, Merchandise Pricing.

3. The Use of the Word "Clearance"

A "Clearance" must represent at least a 10% saving to the customer from the price at which the merchandise last sold. The fact that assortments are incomplete need not be stated in the ad.

Merchandise that is reduced in price by use of a permanent markdown and which will not return to the higher pre-sale price is considered "Clearance." A "Sale" header must not be used in the offering of such merchandise. A "Clearance" header may be used, if desired. "Clearance headers" may not be used with merchandise which is being advertised as "Sale" merchandise.

Temporary markdowns (before and after counts) may not be used for clearance items.

If a department has permission to hand mark tickets, downward marking must be done in red pen.

4. Comparative Prices

Dayton's will allow the use of comparative prices in advertising or signing where the comparison is of a present price to a higher internal reference price for identical items of merchandise. The comparative may take the form of a direct comparison to a "regular" (which indicates the merchandise will return to the reference price at the conclusion of the event) or an "original" (which indicates the merchandise will be permanently marked-down) price. An implied comparison by means of percentage-off may be given, but only in conjunction with actual comparative prices. Dayton's will not allow comparisons with competitor's prices for identical items nor comparisons with other similar but not identical merchandise nor comparisons with manufacturer's suggested list prices. Form 1839 should be filled out and attached to Print Request Form 270.

5. Price Basis

The lowest competitive price shall be used as a basis for comparison in establishing a sale, special purchase or clearance price.

6. Range of Prices

We will never say "$5.95 and Up." We will use both limits when quoting a range of prices, e.g. $5.95 to $10.95.

7. Sub-standard Merchandise

a. If any advertised merchandise is not first quality, it must be stated in the heading or sub-heading of the advertisement. The abbreviation "IR" will not be used; we will use the terms "seconds" and "irregulars." These must be advertised as "special purchase," not "sale" (unless a reduction has been made from the price at which we first offered them at Dayton's).

b. Defective merchandise will be defined as "Seconds" or "Irregulars."

  1. "Seconds" — merchandise which has been repaired through mending.

  2. "Irregulars" — merchandise which contains irregularities in weave or knit, or defects in color or pattern.

8. The Use of the Firm Name

Dayton's is singular and takes a singular verb, e.g., "Dayton's is", not "Dayton's are."

9. Extended Payments

a. All advertisements made up mainly of home needs should carry a prominent announcement about extended payments.

b. Where extended payment is a strong stimulus to sales, it should be carried in other advertisements as well.

10. Fair Practice

Dayton's makes no reference whatever to competitiors or competitors' merchandise.

11. Superlatives

Superlatives may never be used in Dayton's advertising

12. Guarantee

The word "Guarantee" must never appear in Dayton's advertising. The guarantee of Dayton's, the Store, is behind every piece of merchandise we sell, not just certain items as the isolated use of the word "Guarantee" implies.

13. Restrictions on Customer Buying

Restrictions on customer buying, such as the use in the advertisement of phrases "No mail or telephone orders" and other restrictions on Deliveries, C.O.D.'s, "All Sales Final", etc., must have the approval of the Publicity Director, or General Merchandise Manager.

14. Vendor Paid Advertising

a. Vendor paid advertising (all media) must be in keeping with the character and tone of Dayton's advertising. It must always be first and foremost a Dayton's ad on vendor merchandise, not merely a vendor's ad run under the Dayton logo.

b. All copy for vendor paid advertising must be written by us or approved for use by the Advertising Manager.

c. All art supplied by the vendor must be approved by the Advertising Manager.

d. In no case will the name of the vendor be used larger than Dayton's name.

e. In advertising run by the vendor in his own name, either locally or nationally, it is permissable to list Dayton's as a dealer, with Dayton's name set in type (not our logo) provided that Dayton's is the only store listed for our shopping area. All such listings must have the prior approval of the Advertising Manager

15. Vendor Materials

a. Vendor distributive materials or handouts may be distributed in the departments subject to a routine check by the Advertising Manager. It is our policy to approve any of these pieces that are in reasonably good taste without regard to the strictly established rules for advertising or direct mail copy, except that they must in each case comply with our "comparative" policy.

b. Vendor distributive materials going through the mails must conform to all rules of policy and appearance that pertain to Dayton's advertising copy. They must be approved in all cases by the Advertising Manager.

16. Mail and Phone Order Considerations

The buyer's ad request should indicate mail and phone order selling whenever feasible. This form of selling is considered desirable, and it is up to the Advertising Manager to make a prominent appeal for mail and telephone orders in the ad.

17. Advertising of Special Offers

Special offers such as giveaways, free samples, trial offers, two items for one, and drawings for prizes, trips, etc., must adhere to Dayton's policy:

Two for One Free Samples — a. Offers providing two items for the price of one, or for 1¢ more, or bonus items may be advertised, provided copy states one price, e.g., "both for $5", or "sample size of (item) included with purchase of . . ."

Quantity Purchase — b. Quantity purchase (e.g. 1 pr. socks 75¢; 12 prs. $8.55, is permissible if the percent price reduction in the quantity purchase is 5% or greater.

Merchandise Giveaway in Competition with Other Departments — c. Offers combining unrelated items resulting in direct competition with other departments in the store, e.g., a set of dinnerware with the purchase of a dishwasher, may not be used by the Upstairs Store, but may be used by the Budget Store with the approval of the Publicity Director in each case.

Free Offer — d. Under no circumstances is it permitted to advertise merchandise as "free".

Trial Offer — e. In no instance may "trial" offers be sponsored by Dayton's. Dayton's may participate in vendor advertising of special offers provided copy is approved by the Advertising Manager, the store name is set in type and Dayton's is listed exclusively as the dealer in the area.

Special Offers Vendor Advertised — g. Drawings for prizes, trips, merchandise, etc., must be individually approved by the Publicity Director before they can be accepted, advertised or promoted in any way.

LOCAL ADVERTISING AGENCY

Grey Advertising, in Minneapolis, is a branch of a large firm headquartered in New York City, and Dayton's uses its services primarily for radio and television advertising. Creative teams and account people who work with Dayton's have retail experience and know the regulations. They receive fact sheets from their client, which often indicate certain traps to avoid.

One agency responsibility is to gather written documentation to support claims used in advertisements. This information may be requested by the media and/or public regulators. If there are problems, the agency lawyer gets involved and may contact the client's attorney. The point is to make sure that selling points and benefits are described and visualized properly.

LOCAL MEDIA

Media buying and selling policies may be found in the *Standard Rate and Data Service* for all major media. In the Contract and Copy Regulations sections, many of the items cover financial dealings between advertisers, agencies, and the publisher or broadcaster, but some explain why certain advertisements may be rejected. Also, many companies issue their own booklets with titles such as "Advertising Acceptance Guide" or "Continuity Acceptance Guide," and salespeople provide copies to customers and agencies. The basic rule is that all advertising matter is subject to approval of the publisher or general station manager.

Copy arrives in the advertising department from salespeople, or in the mail from advertisers and their agencies. Members of the sales staff review it for legal problems, and questions are resolved by the advertising manager. The print media also rely on proofreaders to point out problems. Broadcasters have continuity acceptance desks or departments where scripts, storyboards, or finished commercials must be approved before airing. (Radio and TV stations tend to be more strict than publications because they're licensed by the Federal Communications Commission and vulnerable to investigation if they don't operate "in the public interest.") All media retain attorneys with backgrounds in consumer protection law.

FIRST LOCAL SELF REGULATOR

The original Better Business Bureau operation began in 1911 as a "Vigilance Committee" of an Advertising Club in New York. But the Minneapolis BBB was also one of the country's first—and was established to eliminate fraud in advertising. Later, Bureau functions were broadened to monitor other marketing practices and the performance of business. The organization has expanded to cities throughout the country because business believes that *it* can best (1) correct abuses in the marketplace, and (2) provide the help necessary to aid consumers in getting satisfaction for their money.

Bureaus are non-profit corporations financed entirely by membership dues or subscriptions paid by firms in the community. Each agency is self-regulatory and works by obtaining the cooperation of businesses. Its functions include: (a) providing information requested about a company; (b) helping to resolve consumer complaints against a company; (c) providing consumer information to help buyers make intelligent purchasing decisions; and (d) offering consumer arbitration to resolve disputes between buyers and sellers.

In addition, the Bureau monitors advertising and selling, and alerts consumers to poor business practices; it distributes consumer information through printed literature to newspapers, broadcast stations, and buyers; it provides speakers for schools, civic groups, and business organizations; and it supplies the media with public information materials on consumer subjects and violations.

Better Business Bureaus are guided by two sets of rules. The short one is called *The Advertising Code of American Business* (See Figure 12-3). A much longer document, *The BBB Code of Advertising*, appears in Appendix III. Each member agrees to abide by both codes in the conduct of business.

Types of Complaints

Most consumer contacts with Bureaus are inquiries and not complaints. Wise consumers check with a Bureau *before* dealing with an unknown company, and this practice reduces the possibility of future problems. Information given to consumers is a summary of the actual performance record shown in files, and supplemented, if necessary, by special Bureau investigations. A local agency can draw on additional information compiled by the international BBB member network.

Some bureaus have a mechanism set up to handle business/consumer disputes. It acts as a mediator, bringing the complainant and company together to help resolve their problems. Arbitration usually proceeds quickly, without resort to costly court action, and is legally binding.

Each year the Bureaus have millions of contacts with consumers, and surveys indicate that the majority of complaints are handled to the satisfaction of both parties. A recent poll showed that Bureaus are the first choice of consumers in need of help; more consumers rely on them than on all government or other private groups combined.

The Minneapolis Better Business Bureau receives about 800 calls and letters every working day. Most of them are situations where people believe that they've been cheated in a trade deal, or that a guarantee or warranty has not been honored. Only about 12 percent of the complaints are related to advertising.

FIGURE 12-3

An Advertising Code

THE
ADVERTISING CODE
OF
AMERICAN BUSINESS

1 TRUTH . . . Advertising shall tell the truth, and shall reveal significant facts, the concealment of which would mislead the public.

2 RESPONSIBILITY . . . Advertising agencies and advertisers shall be willing to provide substantiation of claims made.

3 TASTE AND DECENCY . . . Advertising shall be free of statements, illustrations or implications which are offensive to good taste or public decency.

4 DISPARAGEMENT . . . Advertising shall offer merchandise or service on its merits, and refrain from attacking competitors unfairly or disparaging their products, services or methods of doing business.

5 BAIT ADVERTISING . . . Advertising shall offer only merchandise or services which are readily available for purchase at the advertised price.

6 GUARANTEES AND WARRANTIES . . . Advertising of guarantees and warranties shall be explicit. Advertising of any guarantee or warranty shall clearly and conspicuously disclose its nature and extent, the manner in which the guarantor or warrantor will perform and the identity of the guarantor or warrantor.

7 PRICE CLAIMS . . . Advertising shall avoid price or savings claims which are false or misleading, or which do not offer provable bargains or savings.

8 UNPROVABLE CLAIMS . . . Advertising shall avoid the use of exaggerated or unprovable claims.

9 TESTIMONIALS . . . Advertising containing testimonials shall be limited to those of competent witnesses who are reflecting a real and honest choice.

The Monitoring Process

The Minneapolis Better Business Bureau's staff reads newspapers daily and clips advertisements that look questionable. Radio and television are also checked, but it's impossible to hear and see every commercial, so most of the complaints about electronic media come from consumers or other businesses.

Once a violation of truth or accuracy is established or suspected, a form distributed by the national BBB, called "Advertising Double Check," is sent to the advertiser, questioning one or more objectionable claims, and asking for a reply. The advertiser then indicates: "Will not repeat," "Have revised," "Will revise by (date)," or "Unwilling to revise" (with an explanation). See Figure 12-4.

If the reply is not satisfactory, the staff discusses the problem further with the advertiser. When a company persists in its questionable advertising, the Better Business Bureau turns the file over to the Minnesota Advertising Review Board.

FIGURE 12-4

Advertising Double Check

BETTER BUSINESS BUREAU

A **BBB** *Service to Advertisers*

To:

THE PURPOSE OF THIS REPORT is to help you maintain and strengthen customer confidence in your advertising. The Bureau recommends that you double check the accuracy of the advertisement as indicated below, recognizing that the burden of proof lies with advertisers to substantiate their claims.

DATE OF ADVERTISEMENT:_____MEDIA:_____PAGE OR BROADCAST TIME:_____

ITEM:_____STATEMENT:_____

CAUSE(S) OF QUESTIONS:

☐ 1. Availability of Advertised Item ☐ 4. Description ☐ 7. Non-disclosure of Material Fact

☐ 2. Characteristics of Bait ☐ 5. Illustration or Layout ☐ 8. Underselling or Superlative Claim

☐ 3. Comparative Price Claim ☐ 6. Use of word Guarantee ☐ 9. Other _____

BASIS ON WHICH AD IS QUESTIONED:_____

BBB COMMENT:

☐ COPIES TO MEDIA DATE_____ By_____

TO THE ADVERTISER:

Retain original copy—return pink copy to the Better Business Bureau: Please record your disposition of this report so our files will reflect your comments and/or action.

☐ WILL NOT REPEAT ☐ HAVE REVISED ☐ WILL REVISE BY_____ ☐ UNWILLING TO REVISE
                                                        Date   (Explain Below)

COMMENTS:

DATE_____ By_____

FOR BUREAU SUMMARY ONLY:

COMMENTS_____ Processed by_____ ☐ Correction not required

_____ Forwarded_____ ☐ Corrected

_____ Adv. question area_____ ☐ Not Corrected

_____ Statistical classification_____ ☐ No Reply_____

FORM CBBB-R-100   Date

ADVERTISER'S COPY

SECOND LOCAL SELF-REGULATOR

This Board is the next highest private advertising review level in the state, and it consists of 32 members; half are chosen to represent consumers, while a quarter represent advertisers, and another quarter represent advertising agencies. Most of the complaints are about local and regional advertising which is specially developed for use in Minnesota cities and in the State; but members also consider national advertising which is published or broadcast all over the country in essentially the same form.

If a local advertiser refuses to provide substantiation for an advertising claim when it's requested by the BBB, the complaint is referred to the Review Board for action. The Chairman convenes a panel of four members: two consumers, one advertiser, and one advertising agency representative, to consider the complaint. If the claim is found to be valid, the objection is dropped. If it's still questioned, the advertiser is asked to withdraw or to change the advertising, after which the complaint is considered settled.

When an advertiser refuses to comply with the Review Board's decision, the company is given ten days before a story about the misleading advertisement and the advertiser's position is released to the media. If the Board believes local laws have been violated, the entire file is turned over to appropriate city or state government agencies.

Before we discuss local government agencies that may become involved in the case, however, let's examine some sample complaints and see how they were resolved.

SAMPLE CASE #1
Strategy: Lowest prices.
TV Commercial: "Talk about the lowest prices! We not only have the lowest prices but we guarantee them."
Complaint: Clipped by staff.
Position: Lowest price claims are impossible to prove and should not be used. Merchants cannot know all of the prices offered all of the time.
Disposition: Advertiser revised message.

SAMPLE CASE #2
Strategy: Testimonial endorsement.
Print: Statement in an advertisement, "Member, Better Business Bureau."
Complaint: Clipped by staff.
Position: Commercial use of the Better Business Bureau is forbidden by national policy. Such a claim is

misleading because it implies endorsement and the BBB does not recommend any company, product, or service.

Disposition: Advertiser agreed not to repeat the statement.

SAMPLE CASE #3
Strategy: Sale
Radio: "Giant liquidation sale! Everything must go!"
Complaint: Clipped by staff.
Position: Commercial did not disclose that the merchandise included (1) distressed items and discontinued models, not all of which were warranted, and (2) a "no cash refund" policy.
Disposition: Advertiser disregarded warning. Case referred to City regulatory authority. Better Business Bureau issued a "consumer alert" to be published or broadcast by media.

SAMPLE CASE #4
Strategy: Special price.
Newspaper Advertisement: "Shrimp Special only $5.95!"
Complaint: Customers wrote and claimed they were charged $7.50 for the special meal on Friday but no day was specified in the advertisement.
Position: No limitation was shown, so the customers were overcharged.
Disposition: Money refunded and advertisement was corrected to read, "Thursday's Special."

SAMPLE CASE #5
Strategy: Lowest prices
Print: "Will not be undersold!"
Complaint: Clipped by staff.
Position: Underselling claims are impossible to prove and should not be used.
Disposition: Advertiser agreed not to repeat the statement.

SAMPLE CASE #6
Strategy: Superlative claim
Print: "Largest selection of records and tape albums."
Complaint: Clipped by staff.
Position: Proof of superlative claim was requested.
Disposition: Claim was substantiated with submission of proof of claim.

SAMPLE CASE #7
Strategy: Saving

Radio: "Manufacturer's Suggested List Price $599; special price $486. Save $113!"

Complaint: Clipped by staff.

Position: List prices are not a valid basis for a savings claim unless these prices are the current selling prices of the items in the market.

Disposition: Dealer agreed not to repeat the commercial.

CITY REGULATOR

The Code of Ordinances for the city of Minneapolis established a "Consumer Affairs Division" to investigate and settle disputes in selling—especially in packaging, pricing, and advertising. "Tags," or $25.00 tickets, can be issued, and ordinance violators may be required to return "money, property, or other things" received from consumers.

While this agency handles about 5,000 complaints each year, those related to advertising amount to no more than five percent. The major problems are with auto sales firms and building rehabilitation companies. After a citation is issued, perhaps with media present to report the action, the violation may be marked for court action by the City Attorney. The agency Director may also suspend or revoke a retailer's vending license (that is, its right to trade with the public).

COUNTY REGULATOR

Hennepin County maintains an office of Citizen Protection/Economic Crime, headed by an Assistant County Attorney, with civil powers over consumer fraud and false advertising. The office can be reached 24 hours a day with the aid of an answering service. The complaint intake is handled by legal interns, some of whom are law students or college seniors interested in consumer protection. The law schools in the area provide credit for the work and some volunteers receive modest pay. Of the 800 inquiries handled each year, 500 may be investigated for litigation, 200 of them very thoroughly for possible trial. 150 are processed with criminal charges and two or three go to civil court.

In addition to consumer complaints, Citizens Protection/Economic Crime also receives "referral cases" from the Better Business Bureau, and City and State police, commerce, welfare, and revenue departments.

STATE REGULATOR

The office of the Attorney General of the State of Minnesota maintains a Consumer Protection Division under the direction of an Assistant Attorney General. This agency also resolves buyer/seller disputes, handles investigations, obtains restitutions, and, when necessary, prepares legislation to protect consumers. Certain types of businesses are singled out for what are considered deceptive practices. Examples are: (1) automobile companies (for odometer tampering); (2) health clubs (for not allowing members to cancel memberships); (3) employment agencies (for advertising jobs for which there are no job orders); (4) private trade schools (for advertising or using contracts that have not been reviewed by the Commissioner of Education); and (5) manufacturers and retailers (for producing and distributing toys containing certain defined "hazards").

Since many of the laws and violations just discussed relate directly to advertising, a company's reputation may be seriously impaired if infractions become public knowledge as they would in a court decision. In short, the city of Minneapolis, in the county of Hennepin, and the state of Minnesota, is a very unwise place for a business to get out of line. As we have seen, this market area has an "ideal" consumer protection operation.

THE NATIONAL SCENE

Now it's time to look at some of the companies, business organizations, media, and government departments with rules that affect advertising strategy and tactics at the national level.

NATIONAL ADVERTISER

Sears, Roebuck and Co., the country's largest retail merchant, has hundreds of stores and a formidable job of keeping its advertising above criticism. Practically every store prepares advertisements for its own market, and occasionally, through lack of knowledge or oversight, an infraction occurs. To help avoid these situations, the Merchandising Department distributes a continually updated book called the "Sears Advertising Policies Manual" which is designed to "perpetuate uniform adherence to Sears' own rigid standards of truthfulness and guaranteed satisfaction."

Another control the parent company has over employees who produce advertising in the field is its constant supply of "instant" advertisements. An artist is provided with illustrations, copy blocks, and layouts, to be cut and pasted for offset printing. There are also mats for the letterpress papers, plus sample scripts and television spots that can be ordered from a "library." And all of the words and illustrations in these materials have been previously reviewed by the legal department.

Many large stores have similar manuals to guide their employees, and the more sophisticated corporations have strategies and tactics, and even marketing plans, checked before prototype advertisements are created. New campaigns are thoroughly screened and, in some companies, every layout, storyboard, and radio script must be approved by the law department before it's produced.

NATIONAL ADVERTISING AGENCY

Account Service and Creative people who work with national media are well acquainted with regulations which apply to product categories. Nevertheless, agencies have legal departments, too. At McCann-Erickson Worldwide, Inc., the largest agency in the world, the legal staff is located at the headquarters office in New York. They are primarily broadcast experts because most national clients use electronic media; and, as noted earlier, TV and radio rules and regulations are very stringent.

The Interpublic Group of Companies, of which McCann-Erickson is a member, also has a law department. Attorneys at this parent company also review campaign strategies, tactics, copy, visuals, and prototypes for print. And, when appropriate, they discuss problems with client lawyers. Their goal is to avoid confrontations with consumers, the media, government, and other manufacturers.

At agencies with clients whose categories are highly restricted, such as toys, drugs, and personal products, attorneys are in constant touch with the networks, the Code Board of the National Association of Broadcasters, and the Federal Government departments and commissions who review advertising.

NATIONAL MEDIA

ABC, CBS, and NBC maintain staffs on both coasts to evaluate program content and commercials. One program practices department reviewed 42,000 spots in one year. Local stations affiliated with the networks count on them to approve or reject messages before broadcast; but each station has its own continuity acceptance person who has the final say about what leaves the transmitter. Once in a while, he or she will even reject a message the network has approved—if it's considered potentially upsetting to a local audience.

The "supreme court" in the broadcast clearance business is the National Association of Broadcasters Code Board, in New York, with a branch in Los Angeles. This staff handles what are called "sensitive subjects" and must give their approval before the networks will even review the material.

In the print area, each magazine has a copy acceptance staff or person. Regulations are not as strict as they are for broadcast because the advertisements are read by individuals, privately, not heard and seen by family or social groups who might be embarrassed by sensitive copy. They do make it a point to screen out advertising they consider misleading, fraudulent, or over-promising. *Good Housekeeping* magazine has, since 1902, made a point of testing claims in its laboratory. Products that check out may carry the magazine's "seal of approval"—a limited warranty that promises replacement or refund if defective.

Publishers also have trade organizations who play a role in restricting advertising. Newspaper Advertising Bureau and Magazine Advertising Bureau activities are similar to those of the trade organizations for electronic media: the Television Bureau of Advertising and the Radio Advertising Bureau. Their primary purpose is to promote the use of each respective medium, but if a copy problem arises, they do alert members and keep them informed.

NATIONAL SELF-REGULATOR

The Council of Better Business Bureaus has two missions: to be an effective self-regulatory force for business, and to indicate the active concern that business has for consumers. The executive office in New York maintains contact with major corporations, advertising agencies, and the media. It administers consumer information programs and handles self-regulatory matters related to national advertising. The Operations Office, in Washington, D.C., issues trade practice codes to some 150 local members, aids Bureaus across the country in handling consumer inquiries or complaints, and helps members standardize their operations.

The National Advertising Review Council (NARC) is a cooperative effort involving the Council of Better Business Bureaus, the Association of National Advertisers, the American Association of Advertising Agencies, and the American Advertising Federation. Its purpose is to enforce standards of truth and accuracy in advertising and it has become a very effective self-regulatory system. It works much like a judicial system in that complaints are entered in a lower "court," and, if not settled, can be forwarded to a higher one.

Here's a possible scenario: (1) a complaint about a national advertiser's copy is sent to the Better Business Bureau in Minneapolis; (2) an effort is made to contact the advertiser without success, so the paperwork goes to the Minnesota Advertising Review

Board; (3) the Board does not settle the case, so the material is sent to the National Advertising Division of the Council of Better Business Bureaus office in Washington; (4) the NAD investigates further, contacts the advertiser, and asks for claim substantiation. If the report is not satisfactory, the company is asked to modify the copy or stop running it.

(5) The advertiser who doesn't agree to this request may appeal to the "supreme court" in the system, the National Advertising Review Board (NARB); (6) then, five members, selected from a panel of 30 national advertisers, 10 agency executives, and 10 citizens who are not involved in advertising, will review the case. They may: (a) decide the complaint is not valid and throw out the case; or (b) modify the objection, or uphold it, and ask the advertiser to stop or change the advertising. (7) A refusal to comply means the file will be forwarded to an appropriate government agency for further action (and undoubtedly some unfavorable publicity). See Figure 12-5.

Most of the problems we've discussed to this point are handled by "agreement" before they arrive at any national or federal level. However, some advertising may catch the attention of a government agency who could start an inquiry at the same time a BBB is studying the situation.

FEDERAL GOVERNMENT REGULATORS

At least 40 Federal authorities, administrations, boards, bureaus, commissions, departments, offices, and programs can exert some control over advertising content and business practices. The following are a few of the most active:

I. *The Federal Trade Commission (FTC)* has under its control all advertising used to promote products sold in interstate commerce. It was established by the Clayton Act of 1914 to prevent restraint of trade and to keep competition free and fair. Over the years a number of amendments and acts have been passed by Congress to strengthen the Commission's powers:
   A. The Wheeler-Lea Act of 1939 gave the FTC broader jurisdiction over printed and broadcast advertising, especially for food, drugs, devices, and cosmetics;
   B. The Robinson-Patman Act of 1936 made it unlawful for companies involved in interstate commerce to discriminate in prices between different buyers of goods of the same quality, if the action lessens competition or creates a monopoly;
   C. The Wool Products Labeling Act of 1939, the Fur Products Labeling Act of 1952, and the Textile Fiber Pro-

294

FIGURE 12-5

Advertising Self-Regulatory Procedures

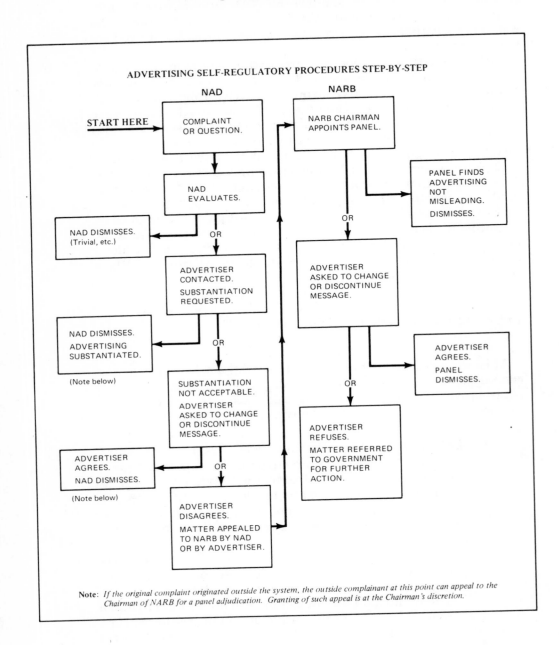

ADVERTISING SELF-REGULATORY PROCEDURES STEP-BY-STEP

Note: *If the original complaint originated outside the system, the outside complainant at this point can appeal to the Chairman of NARB for a panel adjudication. Granting of such appeal is at the Chairman's discretion.*

ducts Identification Act of 1960 protect the public from the mislabeling of these respective products;

D. The Truth in Lending Act of 1969/1970 insures that every consumer who needs credit receives meaningful information about the cost of borrowing;

E. The Magnuson-Moss Warranty/Federal Trade Commission Improvement Act of 1975 protects customers from deceptive written warranties.

II. *The Consumer Product Safety Commission* sets standards for potentially hazardous products, bans those that cannot be controlled by safety standards, and reduces unreasonable risk or injury to consumers.

III. *The Department of Health, Education, and Welfare (Food and Drug Administration)* protects the public against impure and unsafe foods, drugs, cosmetics, and other potential hazards. The FDA defends consumers against misrepresentation, including any written material about a product: advertising, instructions for use, and other copy that goes on the package.

The Library of Congress controls the Copyright Law of 1909, modified in 1978. Although not exactly a consumer protection activity, it does enter into advertising because it protects an "intellectual work" from being copied in its entirety. Ideas, themes, and concepts are *not* protectable, but "original" copy or illustrative material is. Not covered are slogans and familiar designs or symbols; but literature, music, and art can be copyrighted for the life of the author plus 50 years. Some advertisers copyright all of their messages, others protect selected pieces, and those who produce a great quantity of advertising do not bother to copyright anything.

IV. *The Department of Agriculture* cooperates with the FTC to enforce laws covering commercial poisons.

V. *The Department of Commerce* promotes economic development and technological advancement. The Patent and Trademark Office, one of its divisions, administers the Trademark Act of 1946, also called the Lanham Act. It protects brands and brand names, if they meet certain conditions, and are registered with the U.S. Patent Office. Protection is implemented by the use of an (R), "registered" or (TM), "trademark" symbol in advertisements and on packages. A company may complain to individuals and organizations who threaten the mark, and even go to court against violators to protect it.

VI. *The Office of Consumer Affairs* advises the Secretary of Housing, Education and Welfare, and the President, on consumer affairs matters.

VII. *The Department of the Treasury (Bureau of Alcohol, Tobacco, and Firearms of the Bureau of Internal Revenue)* is familiar to those who work on a liquor account, and they deal with similar organizations in practically every city, county, and state. The Bureau issues licenses for the manufacture and sale of alcoholic beverages, and revocation prohibits a company from producing its products. Part of the control process is a review of all advertising copy; it cannot be published until approved.

VIII. *The Post Office Department* is concerned with contests, offers, or guarantees that may use the mail to cheat or defraud the public, especially through the return of an entry blank or coupon. The majority of advertising cases concern medical cures, land development offerings, and get-rich-quick schemes. The Post Office can stop offenders by issuing a fraud order that cuts off their mail, and the most serious cases are referred to the Attorney General for prosecution. Publications are also under Post Office control because they're distributed by second-class mail. Statutes deal with obscene or otherwise offensive material, and stories that appear to be editorial but are really advertising must be marked 'advertisement.' Violations can lead to withdrawal of a newspaper's or magazine's mailing privileges.

IX. *The Federal Communications Commission* issues licenses to radio and television stations under regulations that insure they operate in the "public interest, convenience, and necessity" (in terms of both programming and advertising). If they do not, licenses can be revoked or the FCC can refuse to renew them.

Other Federal regulators and the businesses they influence include the Bureau of Animal Husbandry (meat grading); the Civil Aeronautics Board (airlines); the Federal Deposit Insurance Corporation (banks); the Federal Power Commission (public utilities); the Federal Savings and Loan Corporation (savings and loan associations); the Interstate Commerce Commission (railroads and trucks); the Securities and Exchange Commission (stocks and bonds); and the U. S. Public Health Service (medicinal preparations).

In summary, advertising messages are restricted all the way from their originating points through Federal government agencies. Infractions generally appear in the design of superlative styles of strategy and tactical executions of them. Often an advertiser fails to produce a meaningful (physical) difference in a product, so the advertising creative group is challenged to "find a benefit"—to make something special out of something that is not.

Your authors have noted a recent decrease in pressures against advertising. Consumer groups are not as critical as they were in the early 1970s, and Federal Trade Commission operations may be curtailed because of what some call "abuse of power." Also, there seem to be fewer complaints about advertising in the trade and public press.

Of course, this trend may be cyclical. We like to think, however, that there is now *less need* to supervise advertising. The public uproar made over indiscretions during the past decade may have been very effective. And, there may be an increasing inclination toward honesty, accuracy, and candidness. Let's hope so.

NOTE: For a definitive study of advertising regulation, see: *ADVERTISING AND GOVERNMENT REGULATION: A Panel Report from the American Academy of Advertising*, published by the Marketing Science Institute, Cambridge, Massachusetts, April 1979 (Report No. 79-106).

STUDY QUESTIONS

1. Name three organizations that may restrict advertising strategy or tactics: (a) at the local level, and (b) at the national level.
2. In terms of media reviews (screenings) of advertisements and commercials, prior to their release, why are radio and TV stations even more "strict" than newspapers and magazines?
3. What are three direct actions a Better Business Bureau may take to help consumers when legal problems arise in advertising?
4. What is the basic function of the National Advertising Review Board?
5. What's the difference between the "advertising concerns" of the Federal Communications Commission, and those of the Federal Trade Commission?

APPENDIX 1

MARKETING PLAN OUTLINE

SECTION I

ITEM

A. *FACTS ABOUT THE MARKET*
    1. Background of Market and its Development
        a. Types of products/services available in trade category   (1)
        b. Major changes and improvements in last five to ten years   (2)
        c. Factors affecting availability in the marketplace   (3)
    2. Trends in Market Volume
        a. Trend in total market
            1) In total and by product/service types (target market segments)   (4)
            2) Geographically   (5)
            3) By types of outlets   (6)
            4) Seasonally   (7)
            5) By price points   (8)
        b. Projected market volume (five to ten years)
            1) Total market   (9)
            2) By product/service types (target market segments)   (10)
            3) By price points   (11)
    3. Competition
        a. Brand names of leading competition   (12)
        b. Share of market breakdowns by brands
            1) Total market   (13)
            2) By product/service types (target market segments)   (14)
            3) By price points   (15)
    4. Industry Practices - competitive information
        a. Selling   (16)
        b. Pricing   (17)
        c. Distribution   (18)
        • d. Advertising   (19)
        e. Promotional   (20)
        f. Guarantees   (21)

B. *FACTS ABOUT THE CONSUMER*
    1. Interest in Purchase or Use of Product/Service
(22)   a. Total market
(23)   b. By product/service types (target market segmets)
(24)   2. Who Motivates the Purchase or Use/Who Makes the Purchase?
(25)   3. Brand Awareness and Importance in Purchase Decision
(26)   4. Frequency of Use/Purchase
    5. Usage of Client Product/Service vs. Other Brands
(27)   a. By age group
(28)   b. By income status
(29)   c. By sex
(30)   d. By family size
(31)   e. By presence of children
(32)   f. By educational level
(33)   g. By employment of homemaker
(34)   h. By type of dwelling
(35)   i. By geographic area
(36)   j. By population density
(37)   k. By occupation
(38)   l. By present ownership or use
    6. Product/Service Characteristics Liked/Not Liked By Consumer
(39)   a. Client vs. competition
    7. Product/Service Advantages and Disadvantages
(40)   a. Client vs. competition
    8. Consumer Preferences
(41)   a. Client vs. competition
(42)   b. By product/service types (target market segments)
    9. Design Considerations
(43)   a. Client vs. competition
C. *FACTS ABOUT THE CLIENT PRODUCT/SERVICE*
(44)   1. Usage/Acceptance
(45)   2. Strong vs. Weak Points
(46)   3. Client Quality vs. Competition
(47)   4. Pricing
(48)   5. Product/Service Development
D. *FACTS ABOUT MANUFACTURING OR SUPPLYING PRODUCT/SERVICE*
(49)   1. Ingredients or Elements
(50)   2. Source of Supply
(51)   3. Methods of Product Production or Service Supply
(52)   4. Quality Standards and Problems
(53)   5. Location of Plants Where Product is Produced or Outlets Where Service is Offered
(54)   6. Developments Which Might Affect Producing or Supplying Product/Service
(55)   7. Sizes or Units
(56)   8. Cost of Manufacturing Product or Providing Service
(57)   9. Research and Development in Process

SECTION II

PROBLEMS AND OPPORTUNITIES
    A. A review of the "Facts" developed in Section I to determine the specific problems with regard to:
(58)   1. Total market

(59)   2. Market segments
(60)   3. Trend developments
(61)   4. Competitive environment
           5. Consumer:
(62)   Awareness
(63)   Attitudes
(64)   Behavioral patterns
     B. A review of the "Facts" to determine special opportunities which might exist in:
(65)   1. Manufacturing costs or costs to supply
(66)   2. Pricing
(67)   3. Promotion/merchandising
(68)   ● 4. Creative strategy—positioning
(69)   ● 5. Media strategy
(70)   6. Present consumer usage/possible additional usage
(71)   7. Other special opportunities based on "Facts."
     C. Develop Client Product/Service "Market Potential" for a five-to-ten year period.
(72)   1. For total market penetration
(73)   2. For specific market segment penetration
           3. Develop estimate of market share
(74)   a. For total market
(75)   b. For each specific market segment
     D. Develop Payout Plan
(76)   1. Sales and Share objectives

SECTION III

MARKETING STRATEGY (LONG RANGE)

A statement of the long-range objectives (five to ten years) for the Product/Service with specific regards to total market and each specific market segment. Explain how the objectives will be accomplished.

(77)   1. Sales and market share/penetration goals
(78)   2. Promotion/merchandising
(79)   3. Pricing
     ● 4. Advertising
           a. Copy
(80)   1) Analysis of audience to whom copy should be directed
(81)   2) Review of consumer benefits the product/service offers
(82)   3) Statement of basic selling idea
(83)   4) Selection of most effective benefits to be featured in copy
(84)   5) Development of a copy strategy and copy plan
(85)   6) Art or visual treatment to be used
           b. Media
(86)   1) Review of types of consumers which constitute target audience(s)
(87)   2) Analyses of the ability and efficiency of various media to reach target audience(s)
(88)   3) Development of media strategy
(89)   4) Development of media plan
(90)   5) Media budget summary
(91)   c. Share of mind/penetration expected
(92)   d. Product/consumer research planned

(93)   e. Product design/quality
(94)   f. Manufacturing/production
(95)   g. Packaging
(96)   h. Consumer acceptance (usage)/awareness expected
(97)   i. Competition reaction anticipated
(98)   j. Distribution plan
(99)   k. Industry practice changes expected
(100) l. Gross profits anticipated

SECTION IV

MARKETING TACTICS (SHORT RANGE)

A statement of the short-range (12 months) actions that will be taken and goals for the Product/Service with regard to each market segment.

(101) A. When the Program will be brought to resale buyers and to outlets
(102) B. The Story that will be given to resale buyers and to outlets
(103) C. The promotional material to be made available
(104) •D. What the advertising will say specifically
(105) •E. Why the advertising will say what it does—Rationale
(106) •F. How the advertising message will be told and shown—Prototypes
(107) •G. Where the advertising message will be presented—Media
(108) H. How all the efforts will be coordinated and integrated
(109) I. How and on what basis the program will be evaluated
       J. Sales objectives or estimates for next 12 months
(110)   a. In total
(111)   b. By market segments
       K. Promotional/Merchandising objectives for next 12 months
(112)   a. By total market
(113)   b. By market segments
(114)   c. Costs
(115)   d. Possible sales point/price testing
(116)   e. Timing schedule
       •L. Advertising objectives for next 12 months
           a. Copy objectives
               1) Copy plan
(117)   a) Basic copy policy
(118)   b) Examples of basic copy idea
(119)   c) Copy themes directed to special groups or areas
(120)   d) Possible copy testing
           b. Media objectives
(121)   1) For total market and market segments
(122)   2) Schedule for each medium to be used
(123)   3) Costs
(124)   4) Possible media combinations and/or weights
       M. Possible product changes in next 12 months
(125)   a. Costs
(126)   b. Schedules of when changes may occur
       N. Possible changes in pricing in next 12 months
(127)   a. Costs
(128)   b. Schedules of when changes may occur
       O. Consumer or product/service research projects planned in next 12 months
(129)   a. Costs

(130)   b. Schedule of projects
(131)   P. Overall timetable chart for all activity in the next 12 months

SECTION V (OPTIONAL)

SINGLE TEST MARKET CONSIDERATIONS

(132)   1. Test market objectives
(133)   2. Test market plan
(134)   3. Test market selection
(135)   4. Test market schedules
(136)   5. Test market cost
(137)   6. Sales Department responsibilities with regard to testing.

CONTROLLED TEST MARKET CONSIDERATIONS

If a controlled sales test is to be used (with different advertising and merchandising to appear in combinations of markets)— how will the relative effectiveness of all or some of these points be measured?

(138)   1. Different media mixes
(139)   2. Different media spending levels
(140)   3. Different price points
(141)   4. Different product/service designs or forms
(142)   •   5. Different creative (art or copy) approaches
(143)   6. Different package designs or service presentations
(144)   7. Different forms of display
(145)   8. Different forms of direct marketing
(146)   9. Different product/service mix offerings
(147)   10. Different promotional programs or approaches
(148)   11. Different methods of sampling/couponing
(149)   12. Different color, style, size, deal offerings
(150)   13. Different market size or location results
(151)   14. Different consumer reactions or responses
(152)   •   a. advertising awareness
(153)   b. intent to purchase or use
(154)   c. actual purchase or use level
(155)   d. place where product purchased or service used
(156)   e. satisfaction under use conditions
(157)   f. intent to repurchase or use again
(158)   g. actual repurchase or use-again level

APPENDIX 2

TACTICAL CHECK CHART

PRINT MEDIA
ITEM

HOW USED
(Fill In For Each Project)

Headlines

____ Testimonial

____ Exclamation

____ Statement of Fact

____ Command

____ Question/Riddle

____ Invitation

____ Quotation

____ Play on Words

____ Benefit Orientation

____ News

____ OTHER

____ *Overlines*

____ *Subheadlines*

____ *Picture Captions*

Headline Ideas/Appeals

____ Role-Playing

____ How-To

____ Teaser/Curiosity

____ Humor

____ Grabber Words: Free, New, Sale, Win

____ OTHER

Body Copy

____ Product Tale: Success Story

____ Testimonial

____ Case History

____ Product Scene: Physical Features/

____ (Description) Benefits

____ Psychological Features/Benefits

____	Product Case:	Deductive
	(Explanation)	
____		Inductive
____		Rational
____		Emotional
____	Product Development	
____	Product Use	
____	After Use	
____	Product Extras	
____	Slogan-Messages	
____	Answers to Questions	
____	Adapted Cliches	
____	Convenience-Good Positioning	
____	Shopping-Good Positioning	
____	Specialty-Good Positioning	
____	Contrast Words	
____	Alliteration	
____	Rhyme	
____	Reinforcement Copy	
____	Attitude-Change Copy	
____	Brand-Image Copy	
____	Emphasis on Second Person	
____	News Emphasis	
____	Price Emphasis	
____	Positivism	
____	Comparativism	
____	Hard Sell	
____	Soft Sell	
____	OTHER	

Size of Advertisement

____ Less Than A Column _____
____ One Column _____
____ Multiple Columns _____
____ 300 Agate Lines _____
____ 600 Agate Lines _____
____ 1000 Agate Lines _____
____ 1/4 Page _____
____ 1/3 Page _____
____ 1/2 Page _____
____ 2/3 Page _____
____ 3/4 Page _____
____ Full Page _____
____ Two-Page Spread _____
____ OTHER _____

Design Principles
  Balance

____ Formal _____
____ Informal _____

  Contrast

____ Size _____
____ Shape _____
____ Color _____
____ Tone/Texture _____
____ Direction _____
____ OTHER _____

Motion

____ Left to Right
____ Top to Bottom
____ Large to Small
____ Greater Intensity to Lesser
____ Pointing Devices
____ OTHER

Proportion
  (fill in)

Unity

____ Borders
____ White Space
____ OTHER

Layout Formats

____ Conventional/Classic
____ All Type/Type Heavy
____ Poster/Picture Dominant
____ Mondrian
____ Multi-Panel
____ Omnibus
____ Circus
____ OTHER

Illustration

____ Package Dominant: Package As
                       Product
____   Package As
                       Functional
____   Package As
                       Logo
____ Black-and-White
____ Black and One
____ Black and Two
____ Black and Three
____ Natural Effect
____ Highlighted Effect
____ Original Artwork: Line Art
____   Toned Art
____ Shading: Airbrush
____   Silhouette
____   Screen
____   Halftone
____   Ben Day Tint
____ Photographs
____ Clip Art
____ Coupon
____ Pictorial Inserts
____ OTHER

Printing Processes

____ Letterpress
____ Gravure
____ Offset
____ Silk Screen

Paper

____ Book   _____

____ Newsprint   _____

Type Style

____ Roman: Old Style   _____

____   Modern   _____

____   Transitional   _____

____ Block/Contemporary   _____

____ Italic   _____

____ Script/Cursive   _____

____ Eccentric/Novelty   _____

Type Size
   (fill in)   _____

Use of Type

____ For Legibility/Reading Ease Only   _____

____ As Image/Theme Enhancer:

         Rugged   _____

____   Delicate   _____

____   Masculine   _____

____   Feminine   _____

____   Excited   _____

____   Calm   _____

____   Formal   _____

____   Casual   _____

____   Expensive   _____

____   Inexpensive   _____

____   Modern   _____

____   Old-Fashioned   _____

____   OTHER   _____

BROADCAST MEDIA ITEM

HOW USED
(Fill In For Each Project)

Radio/Audio

Vocal Image/Character

____ (fill in)   _____

Sound Effects

____ (fill in)   _____

____ Music: Original   _____

____   Adapted   _____

____   Stock   _____

____   Background   _____

____   Used As Logo   _____

____   Jingle   _____

____   Used As Doughnut   _____

____   Used As Sandwich   _____

Formats

____ Single Voice: Straight   _____

____   Carnival   _____

____   Personality   _____

____   Testimonial/
                   Endorsement   _____

____ Multiple Voice: Dialogue   _____

____   Interview   _____

____   Drama   _____

____   Humor   _____

Sales Approach

___ Hard Sell

___ Soft Sell

_____

_____

Special Effects

___ Crossfade

___ Segue

___ Stinger

___ OTHER

_____

_____

_____

_____

TV

___ Use of Animation (fill in)

___ Use of Real People

_____

_____

Formats

___ Focus On Individual: Celebrity

                                    Endorsement

___   Other

                                    Actor/Actress

___   Unknown

___   On-Camera

___   Off-Camera

___ Focus On Story: Playlet

                          Narrative

___ Focus On Product: Demonstration

                               Other

___ Focus On Technique (fill in)

_____

_____

_____

_____

_____

_____

_____

_____

_____

Sales Approach

___ Comparative

___ Non-Comparative

___ Use of Humor (fill in)

___ Singers: Solo

          Group

___ Dancers: Solo

          Group

_____

_____

_____

_____

_____

_____

Camera Shots

___ Long Shot (And Variations)

___ Medium Shot (And Variations)

___ Close-Up (And Variations)

___ Head Shot

___ Chest/Waist Shot

___ Knee Shot

___ 2 Shot

___ 3 Shot

___ Group Shot

___ Over-The-Shoulder Shot

___ OTHER

_____

_____

_____

_____

_____

_____

_____

_____

_____

_____

_____

Camera Movement

___ Pan/Tilt

___ Truck/Arc

___ Zoom

___ Dolly

_____

_____

_____

_____

Optical Movement

___ Cut/Take

___ Dissolve

___ Wipe (fill in)

_____

_____

_____

____ Fade

Special Optical Devices

____ Super

____ Split Screen

____ Freeze Frame

____ Matte Shot

____ OTHER

____ *Interior Set*

____ *Exterior Set*

____ *Graphics* (fill in)

____ *Lighting* (fill in)

Medium

____ Live

____ Tape

____ Film

____ Special Effects
(fill in)

APPENDIX 3

CODE OF ADVERTISING
(BETTER BUSINESS BUREAU)

Basic Principles

1. The primary responsibility for truthful and non-deceptive advertising rests with the advertiser. Advertisers must be prepared to substantiate any claims or offers made **before** publication and, upon request, present such substantiation promptly to the advertising medium or the Better Business Bureau.

2. Advertisements which are untrue, misleading, deceptive, fraudulent, untruthfully disparaging of competitors, or insincere offers to sell, shall not be used.

3. Advertisements should advise consumers of facts and qualities of a product that will allow a more intelligent choice.

4. An advertisement as a whole may be misleading although every sentence separately considered is literally true. Misrepresentation may result not only from direct statements but by omitting or obscuring a material fact.

I. Comparative Price and Savings Claims

An advertiser may offer a price reduction or saving by comparing his selling price with:
— his own former selling price;
— current price of identical merchandise sold by others;
— current price of comparable items sold by others.

In all cases, the advertising must make clear to which of the above the comparative price or savings claim relates.

A. *The advertiser's own former selling price*

When an advertiser offers a reduction from his own former selling price, the former price should be the actual price at which he has currently been offering the merchandise immediately preceding the sale, on a regular basis, and for a reasonably substantial period of time.

Descriptive terminology often used by advertisers includes: "regularly," "was," "you save $_____," and "originally" (If the word "originally" is used and the original price is not the last previous price, that fact should be disclosed by stating the last previous price.)

B. Current price of identical merchandise sold by others

Any comparison to the price at which identical merchandise is currently selling elsewhere in the market shall not exceed the price at which substantial sales of the article are made by representative principal retail outlets in the area. Such comparisons shall be substantiated by shoppings made by the advertiser prior to appearance of his advertising.

Descriptive terminology often used by advertisers includes "selling elsewhere at," "priced elsewhere at."

C. Current price of comparable merchandise sold by others

Any comparison to the price at which comparable merchandise is currently selling elsewhere shall not exceed the price at which substantial sales are being made by representative principal retail outlets in the area, and shall be substantiated by shoppings made by the advertiser **prior** to appearance of the advertising. In all cases the comparable merchandise must be of at least like grade and quality.

Descriptive terminology often used by advertisers includes: "comparable value," "compares with $_____ suits," "equal to $_____ dresses."

D. List prices

"List price," "manufacturer's list price," "suggested retail price" and similar terms have been used in the past deceptively to state or imply a savings which was not, in fact, the case. A list price may be advertised as a comparative to the advertised sale price only to the extent that it is the actual selling price by representative principal retailers in the market area.

E. "Imperfects," "Irregulars," "Seconds"

No comparative price should be used in connection with an imperfect, irregular or second article unless it is accompanied by a clear and conspicuous disclosure that such comparative price applies to the price of the article, if perfect. The comparative price advertised should be based on (1) the price currently charged by the advertiser for the article without defects, or (2) the price currently charged by representative principal retailers in the trade area for the article without defects, and the advertisement should disclose which basis of comparison is being used.

F. "Wholesale," "Factory to you," "Wholesale Prices"

Terms such as "factory to you," "wholesale," and "direct from maker" shall not be used unless all merchandise is actually manufactured by the advertiser. Terms such as "wholesale prices," "at cost," shall be used only when they are the current prices which retailers usually and customarily pay when they buy such merchandise for resale.

G. "Sales"

The unqualified term "sale" may be used in advertising only if there is a significant reduction from the advertiser's usual and customary price of the merchandise offered and may continue for a reasonable period of time not to exceed 30 days.

Time limit sales should be rigidly observed. For example, merchandise offered in a "one day sale," "three day sale," "Columbus Day sale," should be taken off "sale" and revert to the regular price immediately following expiration of the stated time.

Introductory sales must be limited to a stated time period and the selling price should be increased to the advertised regular price immediately following termination of the stated period.

Price predictions — Statements regarding savings based on predictions of an increase in price should not be used. However, an advertiser may currently advertise a future increase in his own price on a subsequent date provided that he does in fact increase the price to the stated amount on that date and maintains it for a reasonably substantial period of time thereafter.

H. "Emergency" or "Distress" Sales

Emergency or distress sales should not be advertised unless the stated or implied reason is a fact, shall be limited to a stated period of time, and shall offer only such merchandise as is affected by the emergency. When advertisers are located in communities having special laws governing distress sales, the advertiser shall conform with the requirements of such laws.

I. "Up to" Savings Claims

Savings or price reduction claims covering a group of items with a range of savings shall state both the minimum and maximum saving. Savings claims involving items comprising less than 10% of the total items offered in the sale should not be included in the price range.

J. Underselling Claims

Despite an advertiser's best efforts to ascertain competitive prices, the rapidity with which prices fluctuate and the difficulty of determining prices of all sellers at all times precludes an absolute knowledge of the truth of claims such as, "Our Prices are Guaranteed Lower Than Elsewhere," "Never Undersold," "We Guarantee to Sell for Less," "Highest Trade-In Allowances," "Lowest Prices."

Better Business Bureaus have always advocated that advertisers have proper substantiation for all claims prior to dissemination. Since underselling claims may be accurate at the time of the advertiser's investigation, but may not be accurate at the time of dissemination, such claims should be avoided.

II.   "Free," "Half-Priced," "Two-For-One," Etc.

"Free" in advertising may be used if:

A.   The product or service is an unconditional gift, or

B.   If a purchase is required, all the conditions, obligations, or other prerequisites to the receipt and retention of the "free," article of merchandise or service offered are clearly and conspicuously set forth in immediate conjunction with the first use of the word "free," leaving no reasonable probability that the terms of the offer will be misunderstood. A disclosure in the form of a footnote to which reference is made by use of an asterisk or other symbol placed next to the word "free" is not adequate.

In those cases where merchandise is required to be purchased in order to obtain a "free" article or service:

— the ordinary and usual price of such merchandise must not have been increased,

— the quality or quantity of such merchandise must not have been reduced,

— the "free" offer should be temporary. Otherwise, it would be a continuous combination offer, no part of which is free.

III.   "Cents-Off" Sales

It is recommended that the principles stated in the section dealing with "free" also apply to the advertising of "cents-off" sales. Advertisers should be aware that both the Food and Drug Administration and the Federal Trade Commission have issued comprehensive and detailed regulations governing "cents-off" representations for labeling.

IV.   Trade-In Allowances

Any advertised trade-in allowance shall be an amount deducted from the advertiser's current selling price *without* a trade-in. That selling price must be clearly disclosed in the advertisement. It is misleading to offer a fixed and arbitrary allowance regardless of the size, type, age, condition, or value of the article traded in, for the purpose of disguising the true retail price or creating the false impression that a reduced price or a special price is obtainable only by such trade-in.

V.   Credit

Whenever a specific credit term is advertised, it should be available to *all* respondents unless qualified as to respondents' credit acceptability. All credit terms must be clearly and conspicuously disclosed in the advertisement, as required by the Federal Truth in Lending Law and applicable state laws.

Advertisers should be aware of Regulation Z, issued by the Board of Governors of the Federal Reserve System, which contains comprehensive and detailed regulations for advertising of credit.

VI.   Extra Charges

Whenever a price is mentioned in advertising, any extra charges should also be disclosed in immediate conjunction with the price (e.g.—delivery, installation, assembly, excise tax, postage and handling).

VII.   "Rainchecks"

In all advertising of specific merchandise, the advertiser should be assured that his supply of the merchandise is adequate to fulfill the reasonably expected demand which such advertising may generate. In the event that a greater demand results, the advertiser should be prepared to deliver "rainchecks." The use of "rainchecks" is no justification for inadequate estimates of reasonably anticipated demand. Notwithstanding the above, an advertiser may advertise limited quantities by disclosing the number of items available.

VIII.   Bait Advertising and Selling

Bait advertising is an alluring but insincere offer to sell a product or service which the advertiser does not intend to sell. Its purpose is to switch consumers from buying the advertised merchandise, in order to sell something else, usually at a higher price or on a basis more advantageous to the advertiser. The primary aim of a bait advertisement is to obtain leads to persons interested in buying merchandise of the type advertised.

A.   No advertisement should be published unless it is a bona fide offer to sell the advertised article.

B.   The advertising should not create a false impression about the product being offered, laying the foundation for a later "switch" to other merchandise.

C.   Subsequent full disclosure by the advertiser of all other facts about the advertised article does not preclude the existence of a bait scheme.

D.   An advertiser should not use nor permit the use of the following bait scheme practices:

— a refusal to show or demonstrate the advertised article.

— disparagement of the advertised article, its guarantee, availability, services and parts, credit terms thereon, etc.

— selling the advertised article and thereafter "unselling" the customer to make a switch to other merchandise.

— refusal to take orders for the advertised article or to deliver it within a reasonable period of time.

— demonstration of a defective sample of the advertised article.

— a sales compensation plan designed to penalize salesmen who sell the advertised article.

E.   An advertiser should have on hand a sufficient quantity of advertised merchandise to meet reasonably anticipated demands, unless the advertisement discloses the number of items available. If items are available only at certain branches, their specific locations should be disclosed.

F.   Actual sales of the article as advertised may not preclude the existence of a bait scheme since this may be merely an attempt to create an aura of legitimacy. A key factor in determining whether or not the scheme is bait is a comparison of the number of times the article was advertised, as compared to the number of sales of that article.

IX. Guarantees

A.   The unqualified terms "guarantee" or "warranty" shall not be used in advertising.

B.   The advertising of guarantees and warranties shall clearly and conspicuously disclose the following:

— the nature and extent of the guarantee or warranty, including what products or parts are guaranteed or excluded from the guarantee, its duration, and what must be done by a claimant before the guarantor will fulfill his obligation, such as returning the product and paying service or labor charges.

— the manner in which the guarantor will perform. The advertisement must state exactly what the guarantor will do under the guarantee such as repair, replacement or refund. If either the guarantor or recipient of the guarantee has an option as to what may satisfy the guarantee, this should be clearly disclosed.

— the guarantor's identity shall be disclosed. Purchasers often are confused when it is not clear whether the manufacturer or the retailer is the guarantor.

C.   When guarantees are adjusted on a pro rata basis, the advertising should clearly disclose this fact and the basis on which they will be pro rated (e.g.—the time for which the product has been used and how the guarantor will perform). If adjustments are based on a price other than that paid by the purchaser, clear disclosure must be made of the amount.

D.   Claims such as "satisfaction or your money back" and "10-day money back" will be construed as a guarantee that full refund will be made at the purchaser's option. Any conditions or limitations on this guarantee shall be clearly disclosed. For example, if a vacuum cleaner is advertised "satisfaction or your money back," but refund will be made only if the vacuum cleaner is returned within one year of purchase, the advertisement must clearly disclose the "return" and "time" conditions.

E.   If "lifetime" or similar guarantees relate to any life other than that of the purchaser or original user, the life referred to must be clearly disclosed.

F.   The manner in which a guarantee is used frequently constitutes representations of material fact. In such cases, the guarantor not only undertakes to perform under the guarantee's terms, but also assumes responsibility for the truth of the claims made. Example: "guaranteed to grow hair or your money back" is a representation that the advertised item grows hair.

X. Layout and Illustration

The composition and layout of advertisements shall be such as to minimize the possibility of misunderstanding by the reader. For example, prices, illustrations, or descriptions shall not be so placed in an advertisement as to give the impression that the price or terms of featured merchandise apply to other merchandise in the advertisement when such is not the fact. An advertisement shall not be used which features merchandise at a price or terms boldly displayed, together with illustrations of higher-priced merchandise, so arranged as to give the impression that the lower price or more favorable terms apply to the other merchandise, when such is not the fact.

XI. Asterisks

An asterisk may be used to impart additional information about a word or term which is not in itself inherently deceptive. The asterisk or other reference symbol should not be used as a means of contradicting or substantially changing the meaning of any advertising statement.

XII. Abbreviations

Commonly known abbreviations may be used in advertising. However, abbreviations not generally known should be avoided.

For example, "deliv. extra" is understood to mean that there is an extra charge for delivery of the merchandise.

"New Battery, $25 W.T.," is not generally understood as requiring a trade-in.

XIII. Used, Rebuilt, Reconditioned, Etc.

Used, second hand, floor models, returned or repossessed merchandise should be clearly and prominently described as such.

The term "rebuilt" or "reconditioned" should be used only when the article has in fact been "rebuilt" or "reconditioned." "Rebuilt" means an article has been completely disassembled, reconstructed, repaired and refurbished, including replacement of parts. "Reconditioned" means an article has been only repaired, adjusted or refinished. When the word "reconditioned" or similar terms are used in advertising, connoting less than complete rebuilding, the advertising should describe exactly what has been done.

XIV. Second, Irregular, Imperfect

If merchandise is defective or rejected by the manufacturer because it falls below specifications, it should be advertised by terms such as "second," "irregular," or "imperfect."

XV. Comparisons—Disparagement

Advertising should be positive and should be built upon the performance and capabilities of the advertiser's own products or services. Truthful comparisons with factual information are helpful in making informed buying decisions.

Advertising which improperly or falsely disparages either a competitor or his products should not be used.

The following are directed toward the elimination of improper or false disparagement in advertising:

— the advertising must be analyzed on the basis of all the broadly applicable general rules and prohibitions against false and deceptive advertising.

— if a comparison of features or qualities is made with competitive products or services, implying over-all superiority, the comparison must not be based on a selected list of criteria in which the advertiser excels while ignoring those in which the competitors excel.

XVI.   Superlative Claims—Puffery

Superlative statements, like other advertising claims, may generally be classified as objective (factual) or subjective (puffery):

— objective claims are concerned with the tangible qualities and performance values of a product or service which can be measured against accepted standards or tests. As statements of fact, objective claims are susceptible to proof or disproof.

— subjective claims, on the other hand, constitute expressions of opinion or personal evaluation of the intangible qualities of a product or service, e.g.—taste, beauty, aroma, style. In general, they can be neither proved nor disproved.

Concern for the public's confidence in advertising generally has led many users and readers of advertising to condemn the use of any superlative. While superlative factual claims substantiated by the advertiser may be used, it is recommended that self-discipline be observed in their use. Similarly, subjective claims which may tend to mislead should be avoided.

XVII.   Testimonials and Endorsements

In general, advertising which uses testimonials or endorsements is likely to mislead or confuse if:

A.   It is not genuine and does not actually represent the current opinion of the endorser.

B.   It is not quoted in its entirety, thereby altering its overall meaning and impact.

C.   It contains representations or statements which would be misleading if otherwise used in advertising.

D.   While literally true, it creates deceptive implications.

E.   The endorser is not competent or sufficiently qualified to express an opinion concerning the quality of the product being advertised or the results likely to be achieved by its use.

F.   It is not clearly stated that the endorser, associated with some well known and highly regarded institution, is speaking only in his personal capacity, and not on behalf of such institution, if such be the fact.

G.   Broad claims are made as to endorsements or approval by indefinitely large or vague groups such as "the doctors of America."

H.   An endorser has a pecuniary interest in the company whose product or service he endorses, and this is not made known in the advertisement.

INDEX